1993

HELPING EXCEPTIONAL STUDENTS SUCCEED IN THE REGULAR CLASSROOM

Mary Elizabeth D'Zamko
and
William D. Hedges

PARKER PUBLISHING COMPANY, INC.
WEST NYACK, NEW YORK 10995

Library of Congress Cataloging in Publication Data

D'Zamko, Mary Elizabeth
  Helping exceptional students succeed in the
regular classroom.

  Bibliography: p.
  Includes index.
  1. Exceptional children—Education. 2. Mainstreaming
in education. 3. Remedial teaching. 4. Activity
programs in education. I. Hedges, William D. II. Title.
LC3965.D93 1985   371.9'046   84-26437

ISBN 0-13-386046-9

Printed in the United States of America

About the Authors

Mary Elizabeth D'Zamko holds a Bachelor of Science degree in Early Childhood, Elementary, and Science Education from Jacksonville University; a Master of Arts degree in Special Education from the University of North Florida; and a Doctor of Education degree in Curriculum and Instruction from the University of Florida.

Her professional experience includes 13 years as a teacher in public, private, and parochial schools, encompassing work in Project Headstart, grades 4 through 8, secondary science, and reading for handicapped pupils.

Dr. D'Zamko is an Associate Professor of Special Education at the University of North Florida, where she teaches courses in Special Education and Learning Disabilities, Special Methods, and Mainstreaming Skills for regular classroom teachers. Her duties at the university also include supervising interns placed in local schools. In addition, she serves as consultant to school districts that require mainstreaming skills for regular classroom teachers. Dr. D'Zamko has an extensive record of publications and presentations at national conferences.

William D. Hedges, Ph.D., has experience as a classroom teacher; an elementary, junior high, and high school principal; a curriculum coordinator; and a tenured professor at several universities.

Currently a professor at the University of Florida at Gainesville, Dr. Hedges teaches Curriculum Theory, Curriculum and Program Evaluation, and Microcomputer Programming and Applications of the Computer in the Classroom. In addition, he has served at the university as chairman of the department of Early Childhood and Elementary Education. Dr. Hedges was chairman of the Educational Research Division at the University of Virginia until 1965.

Author of more than 100 articles and 3 books, Dr. Hedges works extensively in the real world of the inservice classroom teacher through his affiliation with Florida's Teacher Education Centers.

Preface

The purpose of *Helping Exceptional Students Succeed in the Regular Classroom* is to give inservice and preservice teachers a practical reference to draw on in working with a diversity of pupils within the regular classroom. The book was written in recognition that to place the additional demands of mainstreaming on busy regular classroom teachers is to ask of them skills and insights which may not have been part of their preparation. Its intention is not to propose that teachers make major changes in what they are doing now, but to help them assist the pupils whose needs are different from those of the average pupils in the class.

The Classroom Teacher and Mainstreaming

Most regular classroom teachers are destined to have pupils in their classes who have been labeled exceptional. Current social forces such as legislation, the civil rights movement, and educational research have influenced the current trend towards retaining or returning exceptional pupils to the regular classroom, a practice generally referred to as mainstreaming.

However, the recent acceleration in mainstreaming appears to have been misunderstood by many educators. While recent legislation does mandate a free and appropriate education in the least restrictive environment for every handicapped pupil, the regular classroom may not be able to provide an appropriate educational environment for many handicapped individuals. The intent of the law is placement in a setting most suitable for developing the pupil's potential abilities.

Mainstreaming is based on the assumption that the educational and psychological needs of many pupils are best served in the regular classroom.

Exceptional pupils are those pupils who deviate from the average in mental, sensory, physical, behavioral, or communicative abilities to the extent that modification in the educational or physical environment are necessary for development to maximum potential. The success of the mainstreamed classroom is largely dependent on the teacher's attitude and ability to adjust classroom practice to meet the particular needs of these pupils. Regular classroom teachers' resistance to the mainstreaming movement often has resulted from teachers' lack of knowledge about these atypical pupils as well as lack of skill in techniques for teaching them. Regular classroom teachers have been expected to meet the diverse needs of these pupils when they feel their training has been inadequate.

How This Book Helps the Teacher

Helping Exceptional Students Succeed in the Regular Classroom will alleviate teachers' possible anxieties created by the mainstreaming movement by giving them the information and ideas they need to work effectively with all types of exceptional pupils in their classes. In easy-to-follow, nontechnical language, it provides: (1) a description of learning and behavioral characteristics of each major group of exceptional students, including the handicapped and gifted, (2) specific instructional strategies and curriculum adaptations for meeting the educational needs of each group of exceptional pupils in the regular classroom, and (3) suggestions to foster acceptance of exceptional pupils into the mainstream.

Chapters One, Two, and Three deal with the learning disabled, behaviorally disordered, and mentally retarded, respectively. Pupils with mild handicaps in these areas frequently receive most of their education in regular classrooms. These mildly handicapped pupils often exhibit common educational characteristics. Their daily instructional needs require similar techniques. Chapter Four focuses on gifted pupils. It appears that a common model for educating gifted pupils is placement in a regular class with part-time placement in a special class; hence, the regular classroom teacher shares the major responsibility for educating these gifted pupils. Difficulty in identifying culturally different and underachieving gifted students is addressed in this chapter

Speech and language disabilities are discussed in Chapter Five. The distinction between speech and language is clarified. More is being learned about the subtle manifestations of language disorders in the academic setting. Practical suggestions for handling these problems are included. Chapters Six and Seven concern the sensory disabilities of hearing and visual impairments. The impact of sensory deficits on learning and academic progress is explained. In Chapter Six, the subtle clues for identifying mild hearing loss are presented. Consideration is given to instructional techniques and the care of hearing aids in addition to environmental modifications that might be necessary. Ways to classify and define visual impairments are presented in Chapter Seven. The nature of this sensory impairment and its relationship to learning are followed by suggestions for the regular classroom teacher. Attention is given to specialized equipment and adapted materials and aids.

The organization of the first seven chapters follows a format that includes recognition characteristics, special teaching methods, curriculum considerations, selection of materials, and suggestions for fostering understanding and acceptance of atypical students. Chapter Eight addresses health and physical difficulties. The organization of this chapter is somewhat different from that of the previous chapters because of the diverse nature of these conditions. Chapter Nine focuses on ways to accomplish the education of regular and exceptional students in the classroom. Ways to organize classroom instruction to provide simultaneous individual and group work are suggested.

Appendix A contains a comprehensive model for preparing for successful mainstreaming. Although the model is specific to the physically handicapped, it can be modified for any type of exceptionality. Appendix B addresses questions frequently asked by teachers.

Mary Elizabeth D'Zamko, Ed.D.
William D. Hedges, Ph.D.

Acknowledgments

We acknowledge with deep gratitude the many professional educators who gave so generously of their time in reviewing the manuscript. To ensure both accuracy and practicality, the manuscript was submitted to an expert in each exceptionality area for suggestions and then to a classroom teacher to read it for clarity and feasibility. Special thanks are offered to Drs. Tom Serwatka, Lynne Raiser, John Venn, and Ted Hipple. Appreciation is also extended to Jo Rentch, Marion Birdsall, Kitty Doyle, Linda Ballard, Julie Kronquist, Michelle Cone, and Sherer Anderson. Our thanks to the many pupils who shared their experience with us.

Contents

Chapter 1
LEARNING DISABILITIES • 1

Chapter 2

BEHAVIORAL DISORDERS • 42

Chapter 3

MENTAL RETARDATION • 79

Chapter 4

GIFTEDNESS • 103

Chapter 5

SPEECH AND LANGUAGE IMPAIRMENT • 132

Chapter 6

HEARING IMPAIRMENT • 150

Chapter 7

VISUAL IMPAIRMENT • 177

Chapter 8

HEALTH IMPAIRED AND PHYSICALLY HANDICAPPED • 203

Chapter 9

ORGANIZING THE CLASSROOM FOR EFFECTIVE MAINSTREAMING • 223

Appendix A
PREPARATION FOR SUCCESSFUL MAINSTREAMING • 251

Appendix B
QUESTIONS TEACHERS MOST FREQUENTLY ASK • 256

CHAPTER ONE

Learning Disabilities

Difficulty in expressing one's thoughts, writing "deb" for "bed," reading "was" for "saw," difficulty with categorizing objects and ideas, being in perpetual motion, inability to concentrate because of background noise—any one or all of these behaviors could describe a learning disabled pupil. This heterogeneous group of pupils presents an enigma to parents and teachers. One moment they appear quite normal, and the next they appear to have severe learning problems.

Clues for recognizing learning disabilities, special teaching methods, curriculum considerations, and selection of materials will be presented in this chapter.

CLUES THAT MIGHT INDICATE LEARNING DISABILITIES

While there are numerous characteristics of learning disabilities, they can be categorized into several clusters.

Learning Potential

1. Near average, average, or above average in intellectual ability

Behavior

2. Disinhibition (impulsive talk and/or action)
3. Inattention (inability to focus on one activity)
4. Distractability (attention disturbed by noise, movement, visual stimuli, or one's thoughts)
5. Perseveration (inability to shift easily from one activity to another)
6. Quick mental fatigue for sustained performance on tasks
7. Social misperception (immature or inappropriate responses in social encounters)

Perceptual Disorders

Perceptual disorders involve distortion in organizing, interpreting, and/or expressing sensory messages.

8. Reversing, rotating, and/or transposing letters or words in reading and writing
9. Spatial difficulties (problems with orientation and directionality)
10. Difficulty in understanding and/or remembering oral messages
11. Difficulty in interpreting and/or remembering visual messages

Conceptual Disorders

Conceptual disorders involve poor ability to organize one's thoughts.

12. Language difficulties (problems with word-finding and word-organizing ability)
13. Confused or disorganized approach to task performance, employing an inefficient trial-and-error method
14. Thinking problems (difficulty with abstract organization of ideas)

Motor Performance

15. Generally poor fine motor coordination
16. Clumsiness
17. Hyperactivity (unusually high rate of purposeless motor activity)
18. Hypoactivity (unusually low amount and rate of motor activity)

A major distinguishing characteristic of learning disabled pupils is a *discrepancy between intellectual potential and academic achievement.* These are the pupils about whom teachers and parents often say, "I know (s)he could do better if (s)he would just try harder." One reason for these expectations is that learning disabled pupils have strengths and weaknesses. For instance, they may perform very well in mathematics but be disabled readers. This uneven achievement is a major discriminating characteristic between learning disabled and mentally retarded pupils. Learning disabled pupils have intellectual potential for normal achievement expectancy, but they do not learn by traditional methods.

Several specific behavioral characteristics are associated with learning disabilities. *Disinhibition* can be demonstrated verbally or motorically. Have you had a pupil who makes verbal statements or motor movements with no thought regarding the consequences? The pupil who has a penchant for making rapid, inappropriate verbal statements is exhibiting inhibition. These impulsive verbalisms often cause difficulty in social interactions. An example of motor disinhibition is the pupil who kicks his best friend for no reason. You might ask the pupil, "Why did you do that?" The honest response is, "I don't know." This behavior is quite perplexing to other pupils because one would think that the pupil "knows better," which he does, but he is incapable of controlling these impulsive actions.

Inattention is exhibited in the inability to focus on one activity for an expected period of time. Short attention span is closely associated with *distractability.* Many learning disabled pupils are distracted more than usual by noise, movement, and/or visual stimuli in the environment. They may also be unable to "disconnect" their mental thoughts. Most pupils can "tune out" these background and internal stimuli; however, some learning disabled pupils are overstimulated by these events.

An opposite behavior to those described above is *perseveration.* Some learning disabled pupils have great difficulty shifting their focus from one task to another. This is not the same as the pupil who does not want to stop an interesting task. Echolalia (repetitious verbalisms) is one example of perseveration. The pupil who is instructed to write one row of o's but who fills the paper and continues writing o's on the desk is another example. A ten year-old pupil named Emmett recently wrote "Emmetttttttttt" on his paper.

Another distinguishing characteristic of some learning disabled pupils is *quick mental fatigue.* These pupils perform well on the early part of a task, but this performance is not sustained until the task is completed. The pupil does not quit; however, there is deterioration in the quality of the work.

Social misperception is one of the greatest hindrances to the development of satisfactory interpersonal relationship and acceptance of these pupils into the mainstream. Responses in social interactions may be immature or inappropriate. For example, the pupil who persists in teasing another and thinks it is funny while the other pupil finds it extremely annoying is demonstrating social misperception. Another example is the pupil who overresponds to the situation. If there is a slightly humorous event, the learning disabled pupil may laugh longer and with more vigor than is normal. Dwelling on nonconsequential matters or trying to develop a conversation on "nothingness" also shows misperception. Some learning disabled pupils fail to derive the implications of facial expressions, postures, and other types of body language.

Perception has been described as organizing, interpreting, and/or expressing sensory messages. Certain brain cell groups analyze specific sensory information for features such as color, contour, and direction. These feature analyzers interact with other brain cell groups that respond to emotions, fatigue, and drugs. Disturbances in perception may result from the interaction of impulses from these two groups of cells.

Examples of faulty perception include such behaviors as writing "p" for "q" and reading "on" for "no." Some pupils exhibit spatial difficulties by writing letters of different sizes, on and off the line, as well as improper spacing. (See Figure 1-1.)

Some learning disabled pupils may have difficulty discriminating, understanding, or remembering auditory messages. One evidence of this problem is poor performance in phonics activities. Conversely, the pupil who has good auditory perceptual ability but poor visual perceptual function may spell "klif" for "cliff." This indicates that the pupil is relying on auditory processes to spell instead of perceiving visual aspects of the words. Pupils with visual perception difficulties may perform poorly in discriminating, understanding, or remembering visual stimuli.

Conceptualization difficulties may be exhibited in poor categorizing and organizing ability. These pupils frequently use a piecemeal approach in relating ideas. They may have difficulty when concepts are presented abstractly. Problem-solving ability may be inefficient, with a trial-and-error approach being employed.

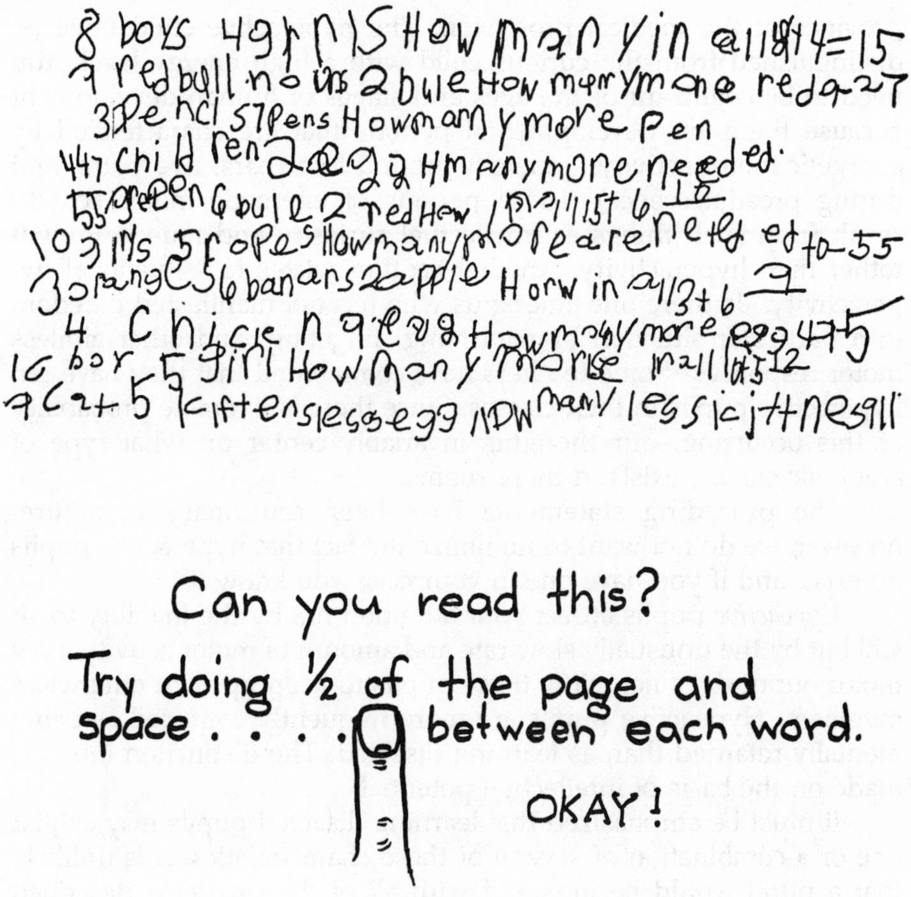

Figure 1-1 reads (child's handwriting):

8 boys 4 girls How many in all? 8+4=15
9 red ball no 3 blue How many more red? 27
3 pencil 5 7 pens How many more pen
4 47 children 2 2 22 How many more needed.
green 6 blue 2 red How ? 1+15+6 12
10 pins 5 ropes How many more are needed to 55
3 orange 5 6 banans 2 apple How w in all 3+6 9
4 chicken 9 egg How many more egg 475
16 boy 5 5 girl How many more in all 5 12
9 cat 5 kitten 5 legs egg How many legs in all thirteen 911

Can you read this?

Try doing ½ of the page and space . . . . between each word.

OKAY!

FIGURE 1-1

Poor *motor performance* can be characteristic of learning disabilities. Many pupils have fine motor problems that can be manifested in poor penmanship. This is not caused by poor instruction or lack of effort but results from ineffective fine muscle control. These pupils experience difficulty when attempting to manipulate small objects.

Clumsiness and uncoordinated gross motor movements can also be characteristic of some learning disabled pupils. This awkwardness shows up in playground and physical education activities.

Some learning disabled pupils are hyperactive. *Hyperactivity* has been defined as an unusually high rate of *purposeless* motor activity. Hyperactivity is an organic condition whose identification lies in the province of the medical profession. The hyperactive child must be distinguished from the curious child with a high energy level. You need to be cognizant of the ages and stages of human development because there are developmental periods that are characterized by energetic motor activity (generally around two years, five years, and during preadolescence). These periods of energetic motor activity result from such things as intellectual curiosity and muscle growth rather than hyperactivity. Another caution relates to "situational hyperactivity." Is there one among us who has not manifested boredom in a particular situation by squirming, fidgeting, and other aimless motor responses? Some teachers have commented that they have ten hyperactive pupils in their classes. Since there is a remote probability of this occurring, our thoughts invariably center on what type of academic climate exists in these rooms.

The preceding statements have been cautionary in nature; however, we do not want to minimize the fact that hyperactive pupils do exist, and if you have one in your class you know it.

Hypoactive pupils attract your attention not by the inability to sit still but by the unusually slow rate and amount of motor activity. Low motor ouput does not allow these pupils to keep up with other class members. Hypoactive pupils are more frequently confused as being mentally retarded than as learning disabled. The distinction must be made on the basis of intellectual potential.

It must be emphasized that learning disabled pupils may exhibit one or a combination of several of these characteristics. It is unlikely that a pupil would be impaired with all of the problems described above. Because characteristics of learning disabilities are numerous and diverse, this category of exceptional pupils forms an extremely heterogeneous group. Identification difficulty is compounded by the fact that the profile of one learning disabled pupil is very different from that of another. Some of these behaviors are characteristic of young children who are not learning disabled.

Age and degree of impairment are crucial factors to consider in identifying these pupils. Learning disability has been called developmental delay. Most of the caracteristics described above are common in young children. The benchmarks for concern are:

1. When the pupil is past the age at which one would expect the behavior to occur

2. If the degree of impairment intereferes with academic progress

SPECIAL TEACHING METHODS

Some learning disabled pupils will be more successful in the classroom if environmental controls are imposed. Extraneous noise should be limited. We often ask teachers to let a blank cassette tape run in their classroom and then listen to the tape to determine the noise level and types of noises. Invariably, the teachers are surprised at what is actually happening in their classrooms.

Occasionally pupils will function better in a study carrel. Most classrooms have limited space; a portable arrangement can be useful. We have seen a folding three-panel screen cut from a cardboard box. The panels are about 12 to 18 inches high when placed on a desk. This allows the teacher to observe the pupil while it limits visual distractions for the pupil. Letting the pupil decorate the outside panels can remove any punitive connotation that might result from the use of the carrel. In some classrooms teachers have made an adequate supply of the folding panels for each pupil to use during testing situations. This prevents the frequent complaint, "She's looking at my paper."

Another limitation that is helpful for many learning disabled pupils relates to the amount of print and the type of adornments on a page. We need to avoid "busy" pages because this often causes confusion.

Increasing the stimulus value of the material can improve attention and retention. Enlarging the size of the print, using color cues, underlining important words or ideas, using highlighting markers, and using configurations are examples of increasing the stimulus value. Auditory stimulation can be increased by calling attention to rhythms such as clapping for the number of syllables in a word, as well as by varying volume. We know of a teacher who used this technique. As he walked around the room lecturing or explaining material, he would shout key words. For example, "TRUMAN became president AFTER Roosevelt."

Understanding and remembering directions are frequent problems. Some hints that might be helpful include the following:

1. Use short, brief directions.
2. Use consistent language.
3. Write directions or steps on the chalkboard or a poster.
4. Alternate the use of colors for each step in a series of directions.

5. Record directions on a cassette tape.

6. Use diagrams or pictorial illustrations.

7. Provide a completed example.

Compensatory strategies are often required because of low reading performance. Readalong records and tapes, alternative texts and library materials on a lower reading level, repeated oral readings, and recorded word problems are among the strategies that might be used. Outlines and study guides are often helpful. The SQ3R technique has been found to be quite effective for learning content material. A brief summary of this well-known technique follows:

1. *Survey.* The pupil or class engages in a brief overview of the chapter by reading introductory sections, subheadings, picture captions, and summary sections.

2. *Question.* Speculations are generated about what questions may be addressed in the material.

3. *Read.* The material is read.

4. *Recite.* The recitation can be oral or written summaries or answers to questions.

5. *Review.* The content of the material is reviewed by any of a variety of methods.

Reviewing questions at the end of the chapter after step 2 has been a useful strategy for learning disabled pupils with whom we have worked. Oral completion of steps 1, 2, 3, and 5 will often result in satisfactory achievement by these pupils. Because they are intellectually capable, older pupils in particular will omit a complete reading of the material yet learn enough to do well when evaluated.

Ways to Provide Structure

As the characteristics of learning disabilities indicate, these pupils tend to be disorganized. This is reflected in such things as their approach to completing tasks and their use of time. They are unstructured lives who need a structured environment.

Routines in the classroom provide a sense of security for these pupils. They do not adjust easily to spontaneous changes in classroom routines. A daily schedule should be followed consistently. When assembly programs, field trips, and other unusual events occur, it is imperative that we prepare the learning disabled pupils.

Time management is a frequent problem area for these pupils. Indeed, time management is a prime consideration for all of us in a complex society; therefore, it is more essential for learning disabled pupils whose approach to life is disorganized.

The following procedures can help these pupils to develop preplanning skills:

1. Have the pupil keep a daily record of everything (s)he does with the amount of time engaged in the activities (Figure 1-2). It is best to give the pupil several completed examples that vary by including less frequent events such as dental appointments and

DAILY RECORD
Day of the week: _____ **Date:** _____
_____ Dressed for school.
_____ Breakfast.
_____ Traveled to school.
_____ School.
_____ Traveled home.
_____ Snack.
_____ Talked to Jane on the phone.
_____ Played baseball.
_____ "Goofed off."
_____ Helped with kitchen chores.
_____ Dinner.
_____ Talked to Sam on the phone.
_____ Studied.
_____ Watched TV.
_____ Prepared for bed.

FIGURE 1-2

parties, so that they understand that everything should be timed and recorded. This step is very important in clarifying the pupil's perception of the use of time. It is not unusual for the pupil to feel that study time has been disproportionately long.

2. Have the pupil list all future events that need to be scheduled. Provide a hypothetical list to suggest possible events.

- Shop for Tom's birthday gift.
- Study for history test.
- Mow grass.
- Go to library for books for science report.
- Practice cheerleading.
- Regular homework.
- Help Mr. Parker paint his garage.
- _____
- _____
- _____

3. After the pupil has an idea of how time is spent and future events that must be planned, it is time to develop a weekly schedule (Figure 1-3).

4. Once the weekly schedule is being planned and implemented successfully, the pupil can begin to keep a monthly schedule (Figure 1-4).

5. Pupils in the upper grades may find useful a schedule form that provides for specific subject matter assignments and various types of activities.

Some learning disabled pupils will need to be taught to recognize structure or organizational design in written work such as letter writing and paragraph development. A structured approach to solving mathematical problems may need attention. In summary, many learning disabled pupils function in a disorganized and unstructured manner; therefore, skill in these areas will need to be systematically developed.

Developing Thinking Skills

Forming and organizing mental images, reasoning logically, developing abstract concepts and generalizations, making inferences,

WEEKLY SCHEDULE							
	Sunday	Monday	Tuesday	Wednesday	Thursday	Friday	Saturday
6–7 A.M.							
7–8							
8–9							
9–10							
10–11							
11–12							
12–1 P.M.							
1–2							
2–3							
3–4							
4–5							
6–7							
7–8							
8–9							
9–10							

FIGURE 1-3

MONTHLY SCHEDULE					
Month:_____					
English					
Science					
Social Studies					
Math					
Club meetings					
Sports practice					
Social events					

FIGURE 1-4

and exercising judgment are types of thinking skills and abilities. Some learning disabled pupils are deficient in these areas, which is reflected in lowered academic performance. We can help these pupils develop and improve their thinking skills by continuously guiding them through the following sequence:

1. Have the student collect data by reading, listening, and observing.
2. Have the student discriminate differences and similarities in the data. Teacher questioning can be used to prod the pupil until the ability to make these discriminations improves.
3. Have the pupil categorize and classify the data. Labeling is important during this stage.
4. Have the pupil recategorize and classify the data in other ways. This continuous reorganization and restructuring is necessary to integrate new information and new experiences into the pupil's mental structures.
5. Have the pupil make predictions based on the data.
6. Have the pupil generate alternative predictions using the same data.
7. Have the pupil evaluate the alternative predictions by comparing and contrasting possible outcomes and their effects.

Questions and statements (written or oral) such as the following can be used to guide the pupils through this process:

"Where can we find...?"
"What do you notice about...?"
"Can you see ways to group...?"
"What would you call...?"
"Is there another way to group...?"
"What do you think about...?"
"Are there some different ideas about...?"
"What would happen if...?"

In addition to questioning techniques, constructing charts can help the pupil to see interrelationships. An example of a Social Studies chart is shown in Figure 1-5.

SOCIAL STUDIES CHART				
EVENT	WHEN	WHERE	WHO	RESULTS

FIGURE 1-5

After the data have been structured in chart form, the pupil can be guided by "suppose" and "what would have happened if" questions. It is important to challenge assumptions and predictions since many learning disabled pupils make literal interpretations. There appears to be rigidity within their thinking patterns.

Using Sensory–Motor Experience with Abstract Learning

Intelligence develops from early sensory–motor experience, according to developmental psychologists. The child learns temporal and spatial relationships, causality and' reversibility, object permanence, and the linking of events from sensory–motor experiences. These sensory–motor experiences are organized and interpreted by perceptual functions. Intact perceptual functions are necessary for concept formation. As language and thought processes develop, sensory–motor experiences remain important for learning. This is especially true for learning disabled pupils who, by definition, have a dysfunctional learning system, yet many remedial approaches concentrate on abstract cognitive learning and neglect the powerful influence of sensory–motor learning. By combining motor and abstract cognitive learning, the pupil becomes aware of space and time (he or she moves, feels, sees, and perhaps hears while engaged in the activity). Internal sensations emanating from within the body (proprioception) provide valuable input for learning. Associations are formed between motor and abstract cognitive learning.

For example, compare a dramatization of Abraham Lincoln delivering the Gettysburg Address with a reading of the address in a textbook. Preparing a set to replicate the location, having the approximate number and composition of the audience, and then presenting the speech with muted but passionate pleading as Lincoln might have done would develop a far more memorable image of this important event.

The point is that sensory–motor experience can facilitate abstract cognitive learning. Among the abilities that may be improved are the following:

- Temporal and spatial aspects of the environment
- Rhythm
- Attention to sound
- Imagery
- Associations
- Language
- Thought processes
- Self-concept and self-expression

Suggested activities for combining motor activities with cognitive tasks can be found in Chapter Three.

Improving Memory

Many learning disabled pupils have difficulty remembering things heard or seen. This creates frustration for pupils, teachers, and parents because the child is capable of learning but poor memory interferes with academic gains.

Recall of nonverbal messages such as the implications of facial expressions and body language, as well as environmental sounds such as street noises, is important to memories of past experiences. Types of memory that have been theorized include auditory and auditory sequential memory, visual and visual sequential memory, rote memory, short-term memory, and long-term memory.

Auditory memory involves retrieval of messages or experiences that have been heard. Auditory sequential memory is the ability to recall in a specific order items that have been heard.

Visual memory refers to the ability to retrieve messages or experiences that have been seen. Visual sequential memory involves recalling these messages or experiences in the order in which they were seen.

Rote memory results from mechanical repetition without emphasis on comprehension. For example, many preschool children learn to say the alphabet and to count but lack understanding of what these letters and numbers mean.

Short-term memory is the ability to hold a message or experience in one's mind for a relatively short time. The information learned by "cramming" for an examination but forgotten shortly after the examination exemplifies the use of short-term memory.

Long-term memory means being able to retrieve information that has been stored for a relatively long period of time. While compensatory measures can be helpful, academic progress is closely related to long-term memory. The pupil who cannot remember that short *e* says *ĕ* as in *bed* is continuously penalized in decoding words. Learning is built on combining bits and pieces of past experiences with new information.

A more complete discussion of factors that affect memory and strategies for "remembering to remember" is presented in Chapter Three. You are urged to review the suggestions made in that chapter.

A principle for compensation is to combine a strong ability as support with a weak ability. Help pupils with auditory or visual memory problems by using these modalities concurrently to reinforce each other. For example, the pupil who writes "hym" for "hymn" is depending on auditory input to spell the word. Emphasize the visual attributes of words with this pupil. Conversely, the pupil who writes "Packwood" for "Parkwood" has neglected an auditory component, and one should encourage this pupil to reauditorize words to remember (in the pupil's mind) how the words sound.

Readiness materials and special education materials are replete with activities for developing auditory and visual memory skills. The following suggestions are offered as a representative sample of these types of activities.

Auditory Memory Activities

1. Have pupils repeat telephone numbers and street addresses of emergency service facilities (police, fire, etc.).
2. Have pupils learn songs by listening to the words and tunes.
3. Play games in which the first pupil makes a statement, the next pupil repeats that and adds a statement, the third pupil repeats those statements and adds one, and so on.

4. Have pupils make up rhymes related to subject matter, such as, "In 1492 Columbus sailed the ocean blue."

5. Have pupils repeat oral directions.

Visual Memory Activities

1. Have pupils resequence cartoon strips (without words) that have been cut apart. This forces them to observe details in the pictures.

2. Have pupils describe configurations of words that are similar. By comparing *then* with *them*, pupils would be forced to discriminate that *them* is slightly longer than *then* because it has one more hump.

3. Have pupils repeat the sequence for a recipe that they have read.

4. Use tachistoscopic devices.

Inefficiency in copying from the chalkboard is a problem observed in many learning disabled pupils. These pupils are at a great disadvantage in the classrooom. This inefficiency appears to be related to poor visual memory. Usually the pupil's head is bobbing up and down as he or she looks from the paper to the chalkboard. When the other pupils have finished copying the exercise, the learning disabled pupil is significantly behind. The following suggestions may be helpful:

1. Have the pupil practice attending to larger units at one time. For instance, some try to copy one syllable at a time. Encourage the pupil to increase the length of the visual stimulus that she holds in her mind as she writes it down.

2. Help the pupil to practice internal auditorization as an adjunct to visual memory; that is, have the pupil say the letters or words to herself while she is translating the written information.

3. Write every other item on the chalkboard with a different color chalk. This helps the pupil to "find her place."

4. Allow the pupil to copy another pupil's work. Some of these pupils perform better with paper-to-paper copying than with chalkboard-to-paper copying.

Alternative Approaches to Reading

"Tell me what works!" Teachers make this request so often. One reason for the urgency of the request is the large percentage of the learning disabled population with reading problems.

This group of pupils has received attention from reading specialists and learning disability specialists. While there is overlap in the ways these specialists have viewed the reading problem, in general, reading specialists have focused on the development of specific reading skills while the learning disability specialists have focused on processing deficits. The current trend is a combination of these focuses; that is, emphasis on the processes by which the specific skills are taught.

It has become apparent that learning disabled pupils generally do not improve with the typical developmental approach to reading instruction. In an attempt to identify effective approaches, the stress has been on new methods, emphasis on parts of old methods, or combining elements of several reading approaches. Researchers have put various reading methods and programs to test. In virtually all instances, the experimental group has made significant progress. The implication is that teachers must be flexible in their approach to teaching reading. Because of the heterogeneous characteristics of learning disabled pupils, a diagnostic–prescriptive approach must be used. The pupil's strengths and weaknesses must be identified and an appropriate reading program matched to the pupil's needs and abilities. For example, a reading program with strong emphasis on phonics instruction would be inappropriate for a pupil with auditory perception difficulties.

Table 1-1 presents advantages and disadvantages of various reading approaches and programs for some learning disabled pupils.

While research into matching reading approach to the pupil's strongest learning modality appears to be inconclusive, some learning disabled pupils may benefit from this adjustment. Recognizing that the reading process employs both visual and auditory elements, some approaches to reading emphasize one of these elements more than the other. Table 1-2 may be useful in comparing approaches.

A few learning disabled pupils have made increased reading scores when the approach to reading was matched to the strongest learning channel. One caution you should be aware of is that reading instruction for these pupils should coordinate all reading programs that a particular pupil may be receiving. We have seen pupils being taught with a phonics program in the regular classroom, a sight-word approach in the Title I program, and a linguistic program in the special education resource room. How could progress be optimal under these conditions?

It is difficult to respond to teachers' requests for "what works." We need knowledge of many approaches to teaching reading and their

TABLE 1-1

Reading Approach	Advantages for Learning Disabled Pupils	Disadvantages for Learning Disabled Pupils
Basal	1. Comprehensive 2. Controlled vocabulary 3. Sequential introduction of skills 4. Reinforcement of skills 5. Diagnostic and evaluative material usually provided	1. Limited flexibility in teaching style 2. Individualized instruction not encouraged 3. Lack of depth of material necessary for skill mastery 4. Lack of provision for processing deficits 5. No choice of analytic or synthetic phonics instruction 6. Subject to repetition of the same stories and methods resulting from failure
Phonics	1. Effective decoding technique for pupils with good auditory abilities	1. Not effective for pupils with auditory deficits 2. May be taught in isolation 3. Comprehension neglected 4. Invariance in English language may cause confusion
Linguistic	1. Control for irregular spelling in initial stages 2. Gradual introduction of phonics 3. Extensive repetition	1. Little emphasis on comprehension in initial stages 2. Vocabulary controlled for regular elements and does not utilize spoken language of pupil
Language experience	1. Motivates with personal stories 2. Uses pupils' oral language 3. Can incorporate specific skill development 4. Can include language arts skills 5. Good for pupils with good visual–motor abilities	1. May be limited by pupils' language level 2. Lacks structured, systematic approach to skill development
Programmed	1. Small, sequential steps 2. Immediate feedback	1. Lacks direct instruction 2. May be confusing format 3. May be boring because of consistency

TABLE 1-1 (continued)

Reading Approach	Advantages for Learning Disabled Pupils	Disadvantages for Learning Disabled Pupils
Multisensory	1. Uses more than one sensory input to get messages to the brain 2. Can use an analystic approach (Fernald) or a synthetic approach (Gillingham–Stillman)	1. Lack of sequential skill development in some programs 2. Sensory overload experienced by some pupils
Rebus	1. Uses a rebus (picture) instead of a word to simplify initial stages of reading 2. Well-structured materials 3. Provides for transition to traditional print materials	1. Format appearing immature for older pupils

TABLE 1-2

Emphasized Learning Modality of Reading Approaches	
Auditory	Phonics
Visual	Sight
Visual–motor	Language experience
Auditory–visual	Linguistic

relationship to the pupil's best method of processing information as well as an intensive anaylsis of the pupil's reading problem.

Oral-reading miscues analysis is one assessment technique that provides a thorough understanding of how a pupil uses the reading process. The term *miscue* is used rather than *error* in order "to avoid the negative connotation of errors (all miscues are not bad) and to avoid the implication that good reading does not include miscues" (Goodman, 1969, p. 12). The theory is based on the belief that the pupil's miscues fall into distinct patterns. By recording and classifying oral-reading miscues, the teacher attempts to identify what strategies the pupil is using to read. The pupil's strengths and weaknesses form the basis for instructional methods. Because this approach holds promise and because of its complex nature, the reader is referred to Goodman (1969) and Hammill and Bartel (1982) for an extensive explanation of this procedure.

Because of the complexities of both the reading process and learning disabilities, it is difficult to make definitive summaries about the most effective teaching approach. Current research points to good pedagogy that employs knowledge of psycholinguistic processing and the relationship to various teaching approaches and the programs as they apply to the needs of a particular learning disabled pupil resulting in improved reading achievement. Kaluger and Kolson (1978) provide a comprehensive review of reading and learning disabilities with suggested remedial activities.

Suggestions for Teaching Arithmetic

Learning disabled pupils may have difficulty with arithmetic because of motor, spatial, temporal, visual perception, auditory perception, memory, and/or abstract reasoning deficits. These deficits may be manifested as described in Table 1-3.

Ashlock (1972), Bley and Thornton (1981), Hammill and Bartel (1982), and Reisman (1972) provide specific examples of the most common arithmetic errors. Suggested remedial procedures are included.

Applying several principles will be beneficial for these pupils:

1. Establish routines for arithmetic instruction.
2. Use consistent language until the process is mastered.
3. Provide numerous opportunities to apply new skills.
4. Ensure the meaningfulness of the material.
5. Employ concrete, manipulative learning materials.

Bley and Thornton (1981) state: "As mathematics becomes more symbolic, the concrete presentation of classification is generally deemphasized" (p. 19).

Suggested activities for learning disabled pupils who have trouble with arithmetic follow:

1. Use manipulatives such as buttons and chips. We observed a teacher who had the pupil drop chips into a clear plastic cup as he counted so that he could see how many chips represented the number, as well as getting auditory input to support this concept. Use Cuisenaire® rods and other comparative devices.
2. Use visuals. Materials for younger pupils usually have a generous

TABLE 1-3

SAMPLE ARITHMETIC PROBLEM AREA	
Deficit	**Possible Errors**
Motor	Forming numbers correctly Writing small enough for preprinted answer spaces
Spatial	Staying on the line Difficulty following directions: up–down, right–left, across Forming numbers of equal size Alignment of numbers Trouble with renaming
Temporal	Difficulty with time concepts
Visual perception	Discriminating numbers (3–8) Reversing numbers (6–9) Losing place (figure–ground) Filling in missing numbers (3 + = 5) Visualizing groups
Auditory perception	Understanding oral directions and explanations Discriminating numbers (15–50) Difficulty with counting patterns (5, 10, 15)
Memory	Retaining basic facts Remembering steps in arithmetic processes Copying sequence in story problems Retaining what appeared to be mastered from day to day
Abstract Reasoning	Word problems Place value Decimal concepts Temporal relationships Role of zero

display of visual illustrations. Materials for older pupils tend to rely more on abstract presentations. You may need to supplement your teaching by drawing and constructing visual representations.

3. Try providing verbal reinforcement with visual material. Activity 1 above illustrates this suggestion. Describing the computation process while working problems and clapping activities are other examples of verbal reinforcement.

4. Try using tactile presentations. These can be materials such as sandpaper numbers or strips of screen wire of various lengths

used to demonstrate concepts such as more–less. Another type of tactile presentation is to trace the number or problem on the back of the pupil's hand. We have had several teachers in training return from practicum experiences who were astonished at the success of this procedure (with some pupils).

5. Circle the number of the example in the assignment. Many pupils confuse the example number as part of the problem and include the number in computation.

6. Try using graph paper for alignment difficulties. There are various sizes of squares to accommodate pupils with fine motor or spatial deficits. The size of the squares can be decreased as the problem improves.

7. Use a visual structure such as the one in Figure 1-6.

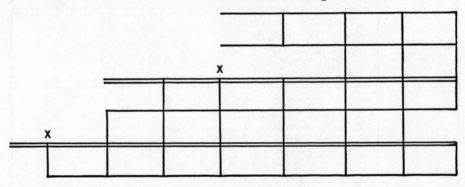

FIGURE 1-6

This type of structure can be particularly helpful in the initial stages of learning an algorithm.

8. Use time lines.

9. Use color cues. Colored chalk and marking pens can be used to indicate steps and direction of the process. Highlighters can be used to call attention to process signs (+, ×) and clue words ("more than," "times").

10. Vary the size of numbers to indicate the concept of comparative value (1 2 3 4). Graph paper can be used as a guide in getting this point across.

11. Provide a sample problem for each assignment. The referent problem can be particularly helpful for pupils with memory difficulties.

12. Relate class activities to increase temporal awareness to time. Using phrases such as "in five minutes," "earlier today," and "yesterday" will provide some basis for understanding time. Calendar work is useful, particularly in regard to special events and holidays.

13. Limit distractions on the work page. Some texts and duplicating sheets have extraneous material that makes the task more difficult for some learning disabled pupils.

14. Reduce the number of examples in the assignment. Some work pages are overwhelming to the pupil because of the sheer numbers of examples. They may also lose their place because of figure–ground deficits. These pupils are also slower in their rate of production.

15. Eliminate copying. It is quite painful for some pupils with motor problems to complete a long written assignment. Economy of time is another benefit for these slower pupils.

16. Use display charts. Charts that list the steps in an algorithm, explain process signs, and tell what key words indicate in word problems are examples of display charts that will help these pupils.

17. Play tallying games. Develop word problems based on game scores.

18. Have pupils use playing cards to develop games that require arithmetic computation. (There are several articles and books that provide playing card activities for teachers.)

19. Structure lessons around kitchen experiences. For example, have five pupils compute their equal share of a 42-ounce can of fruit juice, thereby gaining practice and insight into division with remainders.

20. Apply measurement in the classroom. Chart the growth of class members (a long-term project for certain ages), the growth of plants, and other measurements. Have pupils estimate distances, weights, and possible answers.

21. Have pupils use an abacus to facilitate their calculations.

22. Allow pupils with poor memory for facts to use a calculator.

23. Use a tape recorder or Language Master for pupils who do not read well or who benefit from auditory input.

Strategies for Teaching Spelling

Being close doesn't count in spelling. Lack of success in this complex skill may adversely affect one's educational and vocational progress.

Correct spelling requires many abilities. Among the most important are auditory discrimination and sequential memory, visual discrimination and sequential memory, and knowledge of rules for formation of derivatives. Table 1-4 provides some typical errors and possible causes.

The myth persists that repeated writing of the word to be learned is an effective practice. Research has shown that the following practices are effective:

1. Have pupils correct their tests under the supervision of the teacher.
2. The pretest–study–test method is best.
3. Words presented in single-column print are most effective.
4. Learning words by syllables is less effective than a synthetic word approach.

TABLE 1-4

Spelling Errors	Possible Cause
"fill" for "field" "were" for "where"	Auditory discrimination/memory (Does not hear sounds correctly.)
"aminal" for "animal" "psaghetti" for "spaghetti"	Auditory sequential memory (Does not remember the order in which sounds are produced)
"docter" for "doctor" "ladies" for "ladys"	Visual discrimination/memory (Confuses letters of similar configuration.) (Does not remember which letter of similar sound is used in a specific word.)
"pei" for "pie"	Visual sequential memory (Does not remember the correct letter order.)
"layed" for "laid" "partys" for "parties"	Lack of knowledge of rules for formation of derivatives

5. Proofreading skills improve spelling achievement.
6. Review and/or reteaching on a consistent basis improves retention.
7. A systematic technique to study unknown spelling words must be taught.

The following systematic word-study technique includes the major steps to be taught:

1. Look at the word carefully.
2. Say the word. (The pupil must be able to read the word.)
3. Cover the word or close your eyes and visualize (picture) the word.
4. Say the word.
5. Look at the word to see if your mental picture was correct.
6. Cover the word; then write the word.
7. Check your spelling.
8. Repeat steps 1 through 7 if necessary.

It is important for you and the pupil to analyze the consistent errors in order to identify the emphasis for remedial work. Have the pupil mark through the incorrect letter and write the correct letter above it. Have the pupil copy the corrected word beside the misspelled word.

Several remedial procedures may be helpful:

1. If pupils have difficulty discriminating or remembering the sequence of sounds, have them write the letter heard at the beginning of the words. Vary by listening for medial or final sounds, number of syllables, blends, and so on.
2. Have pupils draw the configuration of each word; then compare how the configurations are alike and different.
3. Some pupils benefit from a kinesthetic approach such as tracing the word in sand.
4. Have pupils write the word on the chalkboard and then trace it with their fingers until it disappears. The pupils receive internal feedback (the "feel" of the word) with this method.

147,207

5. Have pupils write the word with a small paintbrush and water on the chalkboard. The pupils should look at the word until it fades away. They may benefit from saying the word or letters while looking at the word.

6. Have pupils spell the word orally and clap softly for each vowel sound they hear. It may be helpful for the pupils to look at the word.

7. Use color cues; a different color for each vowel sound. We have used color to correct the omission of the middle syllable in words. The pupil consistently omitted the middle syllable ("Novber," "Octber"). By having him write the middle syllable in color, he was forced to attend to this part of the word.

8. Have pupils incorporate movement (hopping, etc.); one letter to a movement.

9. Have pupils type the word to be learned.

Proofreading can improve spelling performance. Some ways to improve proofreading skills include the following:

1. Have pupils select the correct spelling from several alternative spellings.

2. Prepare sentences with one misspelled word in each sentence. Have pupils circle the misspelled word.

3. Have pupils verify the suspected error with a dictionary.

Games such as spelling bingo, spelling baseball, and crossword puzzles can provide motivation for these pupils. Charting individual progress may stimulate some pupils to more effort. Allowing a point for each letter in the correct position can encourage those pupils who continuously experience failure.

Suggestions for Improving Handwriting

Poor handwriting has been attributed to numerous causes. Among these are poor fine motor control, poor visual discrimination and memory, and spatial difficulties. Disability in these areas is characteristic of learning disabilities.

Manipulative exercises can be used to strengthen muscles. Cutting activities, molding clay, and games that require clipping clothespins are typical manipulative exercises.

Chalkboard practice should precede pencil-and-paper writing. Large muscles of the shoulder, arm, and hand are used to make geometric shapes, lines, letters, and numbers. Dot-to-dot drawings on the chalkboard can be effective and fun.

Proper position for writing is an important habit to develop. The height of the table and the chair should allow for both forearms to be on the writing surface with feet flat on the floor.

Paper should not be placed at a slant for manuscript writing. For cursive writing the paper is slanted at 60 degrees to the left for right-handed pupils and reversed for left-handed pupils. A piece of tape can be placed on the desk as a guide. The nonwriting hand should be used to hold the top of the paper. Since many of these pupils are clumsy, it is helpful to attach the paper to the desk with tape. Some pupils will benefit from attaching the pencil or pen to the desk with a string.

The writing instrument is held between the thumb and the middle finger, with the index finger applying pressure. It should be grasped just above the sharpened point. Some pupils' writing performance is improved by using a large instrument such as a large crayon or primary-size pencil. Using a pencil grip or circling the pencil with a rubber band or tape is equally effective. This is especially helpful with older pupils because it looks more "grownup."

Special writing paper is available. Paper with raised lines can be used for the pupil who has difficulty with proper placement of letters. Paper with a variety of color-coded cues can be purchased. Graph paper is a valuable asset in teaching pupils with spatial difficulties.

The following suggestions may be helpful for pupils whose problems are resistant to improvement:

1. Tape alphabet forms to the floor. Have pupils walk or hop around the form. Have them reproduce the form with colored yarn.

2. Have pupils use a stick (broom handle) and their bodies to form the letters.

3. Write each letter in a paper plate with a red marker. Cover with cornmeal. Have pupils write the letter with their fingers. The red letter will provide feedback for correct formation.

4. Coat cooked spaghetti with vegetable oil. Have pupils form letters with the spaghetti. Colored letter forms can be used as a guide.

5. Spray shaving cream can be used to form large letters. Butcher paper provides a suitable surface.

6. Have pupils use a flashlight beam to trace letters on a chalkboard.
7. Have pupils form letters in wet fingerpaint.
8. Use colored directional cues such as green arrows and red dots.
9. Teach manuscript letter forms that are oval and slanted slightly. This will encourage left-to-right progression and will facilitate transition to cursive writing.
10. Teach pupils to start all lower-case cursive letters from the line.
11. Help pupils to form an association for a letter they have difficulty remembering. (A = Indian tepee. W = crown.)
12. Have pupils orally describe their movements as the letter is being written. This provides auditory reinforcement.

Teach pupils to monitor their own writing progress. Self-evaluation can be an effective technique for improvement. The pupils can compare their production to a model. Acceptable writing papers from other classmates can be used in addition to expected performance charts from commercial writing programs. Have pupils work on only one element of writing (slant, size) until progress is achieved. Pupils should keep a folder of their writing papers to compare improvement. This can be quite motivational.

There continues to be debate about the efficiency of teaching manuscript or cursive. The purported advantages of teaching manuscript include the following:

1. It more closely resembles book printing.
2. Handwriting movements are simplified, consisting of circles, lines, and diagonals.
3. Manuscript writing is acceptable for adults.

The purported advantages of teaching cursive are as follows:

1. Words are perceived as whole units.
2. Spatial judgments are minimized.
3. Left-to-right progression is emphasized.
4. There is a rhythmical flow, avoiding jerky stops.
5. Reversals are minimized.
6. Transition from one written form to another is minimized.

Successful writing has been achieved with both forms. The teacher must decide which system would be most appropriate for a particular pupil. A major problem develops when a pupil is being instructed in manuscript writing in the regular classroom and cursive writing in the special education resource room. It is imperative that teachers confer and agree on the best method to use so that writing instruction can be consistent.

Typewriting is often a solution to poor penmanship. Stress correct fingering and accuracy but not speed. The purpose is to provide the pupil with an alternative communication mode. It has been shown that typewriting has improved handwriting skills.

Working with Secondary Pupils

Learning disabled pupils pose a complex challenge for teachers at the secondary level. The impact of the learning disability interacting with the demands of the secondary curriculum may have a devastating effect on academic performance.

Because the academic "time clock" is running out for these pupils, consideration of several factors is imperative:

1. If the pupil has a school history that includes specialized remedial training and still has difficulty learning, further remedial work is not practical.

2. Remedial efforts for older pupils are less successful because of ingrained habits and less plasticity in the learning system.

3. These pupils are capable of learning, so if they can't learn the way we teach, we need to teach the way they can learn. This necessitates using compensatory methods to circumvent the learning disability.

4. Attention to the curriculum best suited to each pupil is necessary. Some pupils need more emphasis on functional life skills; some desire and can be successful (with compensatory methods) in a college prepatory program; some are best suited for a vocational preparation program.

5. Motivation is frequently a problem area. Often these pupils have experienced failure. Learning is more difficult for them; therefore, motivation suffers. Cooperative planning, goal setting, and evaluation standards are useful in enlisting the cooperation of pupils. Strategies to improve motivation are discussed elsewhere in this book.

Learning disabled adolescents may exhibit deficit skills in many areas. In *reading* they may have difficulty decoding words and understanding vocabulary and concepts. They may be penalized by a slow reading rate.

Language development may be primitive in linguistic production. Oral and written language may reveal deficient production of linguistic structures.

Writing deficits may include two distinctly different types of problems. Poor fine motor control can result in an unacceptable quality of penmanship. These pupils often experience frustration with long written assignments because it is tiring for them to write. Deficits in written expression may be revealed by poor sentence construction, difficulty in organizing ideas, and the mechanics of grammar (capitalization, punctuation, etc.).

Mathematics deficiencies may involve computation, conceptualization, and problem-solving difficulties. Some pupils need a practical approach to everyday arithmetic applications; however, many of these pupils can progress in higher mathematical skills if proper adjustments are made to accommodate their disability.

Study skills are often ineffective. Many pupils do not know how to analyze the textbook organization, how to outline material, how to take notes, or how to apply test-taking strategies.

Time management is an area that can result in frustration and poor academic performance. In addition to time demands for school-related tasks, social and employment endeavors take on added importance for adolescents.

Social misperception as a characteristic of learning disabilities has been discussed earlier in this chapter. Misperception and deficient communication abilities are critical for the adolescent. Success in this area has an impact on the overall functioning of these pupils.

In summary, teachers at the secondary level who have learning disabled pupils will probably need to modify curriculum, teaching, and evaluating strategies, in addition to providing alternative materials. With compensatory strategies, these pupils can experience success at the secondary level.

Refer to *Teaching the Learning Disabled Adolescent* (Mann, Goodman, and Wiederholt, 1978) and *Teaching the Learning Disabled Adolescent: Strategies and Methods* (Alley and Deshler, 1979) for a comprehensive description of educating learning disabled secondary pupils. Numerous strategies, methods, and materials are also suggested.

CURRICULUM CONSIDERATIONS

Learning disabled pupils in the regular classroom are expected to participate in the same curriculum as other pupils in the class. Nevertheless, there are a few considerations that may help these pupils to perform more satisfactorily. Among these considerations are:

1. Providing activities for remediating auditory perceptual difficulties
2. Providing activities for remediating visual perceptual difficulties
3. Providing activities for sensory–motor development
4. Teaching social skills

There is considerable controversy in the field of learning disabilities about the value of attempting to remediate perceptual processes. Many research studies have reported little or no improvement in reading following perceptual training programs. Responses to these findings have been that at the present time we do not understand how perception relates to the total learning process, and there is perhaps a missing link between perceptual training and academic progress of which we are unaware.

Another consideration relates to the age of the child. Remediation of learning processes is more successful with young children. As a child matures, the neurological system loses its plasticity of function and becomes more resistant to change. The following activities are, therefore, suggested for pupils below the ages of eight or nine years. Teaching compensatory skills is more effective for older pupils.

Because of the plethora of books, packets, and kits that are available in early childhood and learning disability materials, only representative activities are presented here.

Activities for Remediating Auditory Perception

1. Play guessing games by having pupils identify classmates by voice while they are blindfolded.
2. Present isolated speech sounds, having pupils signal when a particular sound is heard.
3. Present similar pairs of words, having pupils respond whether the words are the same or different.
4. Have pupils name objects that start with a particular sound.

5. Provide experience with nursery rhymes and poems that contain rhymes. Have pupils supply rhyming words.
6. Have pupils repeat directions that have been given orally.
7. Play games with cumulative responses, such as "I'm going on a trip and I will take..." Increase the number of items as auditory memory improves.

The following compensatory hints may help pupils with auditory perception problems to function more adequately in the classroom:

1. Use soundproofing equipment such as earphones and audio machines to eliminate distractions.
2. Combine simultaneous visual presentations with auditory presentations.
3. Give short, specific directions.

Activities for Remediating Visual Perception

1. Have pupils look at a geometric design and then select a matching design from several alternatives.
2. Provide a pattern to be replicated with needle and yarn.
3. Have pupils classify playing cards by pictures, numbers, or suits.
4. Have pupils match, sort, or group word cards.
5. Have pupils copy designs from the chalkboard. Start with simple designs, progressing to more complex patterns.
6. Demonstrate a story with action pictures. Scramble the pictures and have pupils arrange the story from memory.
7. Practice rapid recall of letters or words by using a tachistoscope.
8. Have pupils find a specific series of letters in words.

Some compensatory aids include the following:

1. Have pupils keep their desks or work areas clear of possible visual distractions.
2. Use simplified materials. For example, limit the number of arithmetic examples on a page.
3. Increase the stimulus value of visual materials by increasing the size of the print, using color, or projecting enlarged images (with an overhead projector).

Activities for Sensory–Motor Development

1. Have pupils manipulate objects to commands such as "across," "in front of," "in the middle," and so on.

2. Use dot-to-dot puzzles. Begin with designs on the chalkboard; then progress to worksheets.

3. Use beanbag and ball-throwing activities.

4. Have pupils reproduce block design patterns.

5. Design games in which the pupils are required to clip clothespins.

6. Have pupils carry and pour water in specified amounts. Colored water can be used.

7. Use tracing, lacing, and cutting activites.

8. Use visual tracking exercises. Pupils can follow a pinlight pattern or trace a pattern on paper.

Teaching Social Skills

Not all learning disabled pupils lack social skills. Some are able to use their social abilities to compensate for the deficits they experience in other areas. One such severely learning disabled high school pupil became an outstanding school leader because of his social aptitudes, although his disability resulted in exceedingly poor academic achievement.

Lack of awareness of interactional language sequences is one area in which some learning disabled pupils experience difficulty. In other words, some of these pupils are less skilled in initiating and maintaining a conversation or discussion.

Some deficit areas that might show up include the following:

- Failure to recognize that one interrupts at the pause or at the lowering of the voice

- Failure to recognize boredom or irritation with the topic

- Tendency to ask questions that result in constrained responses rather than producing extended responses

- Inability to interpret the nuances of facial expressions and body postures

- Introducing material too personal in nature

- Tendency to be followers rather than to dominate or lead a conversation

- Unawareness of language that is inappropriate for the specific situation
- Inability to remember the content of the conversation

There are several ways to improve these problems:

1. Use pictures to discuss clues that reveal emotions.
2. Use films to discuss the social implications of body language such as shrugging one's shoulders or tapping one's foot.
3. Use television to observe the salient features of social encounters.
4. Use movies to analyze effective and ineffective social interactions.
5. Use discussion to identify appropriate topics for conversations with peers, neighbors, strangers, and others.
6. Use role playing to demonstrate appropriate responses and to match expressions with the intent of various messages.
7. Use videotaping to practice organization of social encounters.
8. Use mental or verbal rehearsal to help remember key points of a conversation.
9. Use rap sessions to discuss personal experiences that have caused social difficulties.

Suggestions for a few specific problems follow:

1. Praise pupils (in private) when they smile and make eye contact while conversing with peers and teachers.
2. Do not reprimand pupils who tease. Instead, reward pupils who are teased if they do not respond to the teasing.
3. Ignore distracting noises. Praise pupils when they have discontinued the noise.
4. Have pupils generate ten alternative words to swearing.

Although there has been little or no attention to the effect of dress and grooming on social acceptance, some of these pupils become scapegoats because of odd appearance. Most school-aged children are very much aware of dress and grooming norms for their peers, particularly in the middle and upper grades. However, some learning disabled pupils with social problems appear not to perceive themselves as different and do not relate this to acceptance by their peers.

Perhaps some absurd outfits (which usually give the appearance of immaturity) are worn to attract attention, but they often generate negative responses instead of social acceptance. Counseling some of these pupils can result in positive changes in appearance, confidence, and social acceptance.

Other suggestions for teaching social skills are presented in Chapters Two and Three.

In summary, some learning disabled pupils experience social misperception, which is manifested in many different ways. Including a curriculum component on social skills has proven effective in improving these deficit areas.

SELECTING MATERIALS

Selection of teaching materials for learning disabled pupils deserves special consideration. Most classroom curriculum and instruction is textbook-based. Yet, because of the specific learning disability, the standard class textbook is often inappropriate. Reading level and format frequently cause difficulty. Modification and/or alternative materials may be necessary.

Fortunately, there are many sources of materials:

1. Extensive resource materials have been designed for learning disabled pupils. Two popular sources are:

   Developmental Learning Materials
   7440 North Natchez Avenue
   Niles, Illinois 60648

   Teaching Resources Corporation
   100 Boylston Street
   Boston, Massachusetts 02116

2. Remedial reading materials are often appropriate to meet the needs of some of these pupils.
3. Early childhood materials are good for remediation of perceptual deficits.
4. Materials designed for hearing impaired pupils are good for language deficits.
5. Materials designed for mildly mentally retarded pupils are good for basic skills and vocational training.

A few specific materials have been suggested in the subject area sections. You must analyze specific disabilities and attempt to find teaching materials that do not penalize the pupils.

Since reading level is often a problem, using materials from a lower grade may be indicated. You may secure lower, average, and higher level textbooks from the school depository, cut them apart, and prepare booklets with pupil-designed covers. Pupils are given booklets on their functional level. No two pupils have the same booklet design. Pupils are not "fooled" with devices such as these, but they do provide "facesaving" for pupils who are often subject to failure because of their learning deficits.

Recorded textbooks can also be useful. Readalong materials are similar.

Programmed materials can often be used successfully because of the small, sequential steps with immediate feedback of results.

Various machines such as the Language Master, calculators, and computers may be used to circumvent the learning problems. Manipulative materials are often appropriate.

In summary, if modifications and alternatives in instructional techniques and teaching materials are matched to pupils' specific needs, learning disabled pupils should make satisfactory progress in the regular classroom.

HELPING PUPILS UNDERSTAND LEARNING DISABILITIES

Learning disability is a perplexing condition for pupils, peers, parents, and teachers to understand. The discrepancy between potential and achievement and the decided strengths and weaknesses result in paradoxical behavior. Several types of activities can result in a clearer understanding of and a more accepting attitude toward learning disabled pupils.

Literature can be used to facilitate understanding. *The Tuned-in, Turned-on Book About Learning Problems* (Hayes, 1974) explains learning disabilities in addition to providing activities for groups to experience. Compensatory strategies are also provided. *Sue Ellen* (Hunter, 1969), *Kelly's Creek* (Smith, 1975), and *Left, Right, Left, Right* (Stanek, 1975) are representative of books that may be helpful. The use of literature can also be therapeutic for the learning disabled pupil. Biographies of famous people who were learning disabled can give encouragement to the handicapped pupil, as well as insight to his peers. Thomas Edison,

Woodrow Wilson, Albert Einstein, Nelson Rockefeller, and Bruce Jenner are among those who experienced learning problems.

Activities such as the following can provide novel experiences that help develop understanding. Have pupils read the stories in Figures 1-7 and 1-8.

It is important for pupils to realize that the learning disabled "see" the work in this manner. A "game" attitude toward these activities should be avoided. A discussion of how it would feel to experience the difficulties throughout the school day should result in a more emphathetic view of learning disabled pupils.

Learning disabled adults can serve as resource speakers for the class. Pupils tend to be intrigued with "how it was" stories.

Many learning disabled pupils can effectively explain what their school experience is like. A straightforward approach is often the best way to facilitate understanding.

Poor muscle control can be demonstrated by having pupils prepare a peanut butter and jelly sandwich with their nondominant hands. A variation would be to have pupils write a paragraph with their nondominant hands.

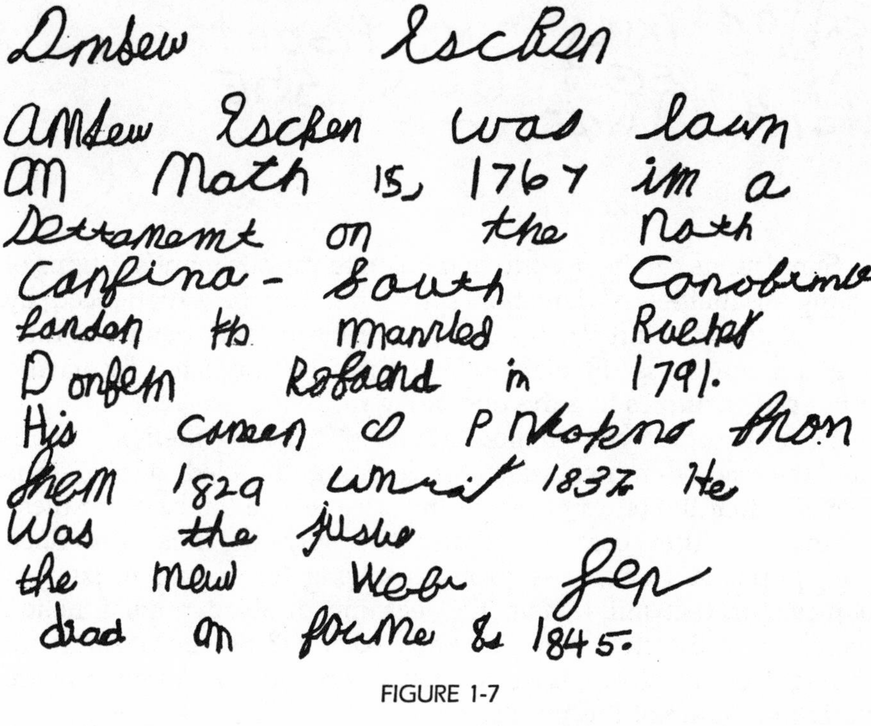
Dmbew Escken

aMbew Escken was lawn
an Math 15, 1767 im a
Settanamt on the Nath
Carfina - South Conobime
landen He manrled Raelat
Donfem Rofaand in 1791.
His canaen as P Nkokno fhon
frem 1829 unrit 1837 He
Was the fishe
the new wear fep
diad an foume 8 1845.

FIGURE 1-7

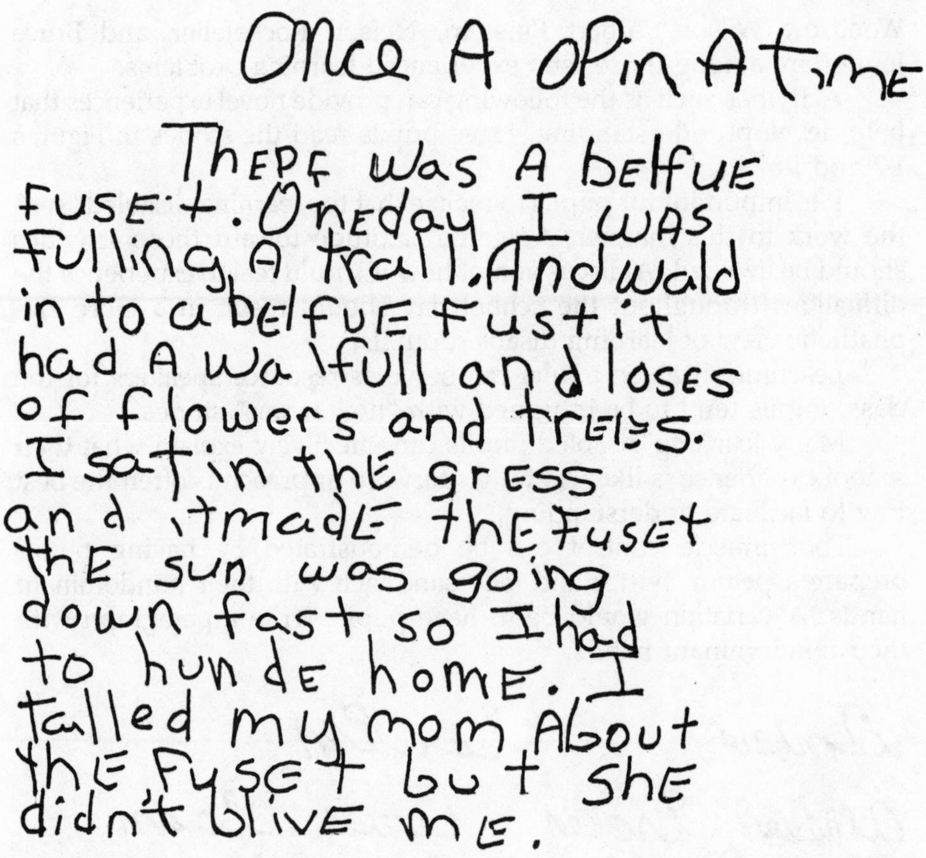

Once A OPin A time
Thepf was A belfue
fuse t. Oneday I was
fulling A trall. And wald
in to a belfue fust it
had A walfull and loses
of flowers and trees.
I sat in the gress
and itmade the fuset
the sun was going
down fast so I had
to hun de home. I
talled my mom About
the fuse t but she
didn't blive me.

FIGURE 1-8

Simulations can be used to demonstrate various manifestations of learning disabilities. Orientation difficulties can be experienced by having pupils hold index cards on their foreheads and then write their names on the cards. Spatial problems can be simulated by having pupils read examples like the one in Figure 1-9.

Because some type of modification of teaching methods or requirements is often necessary for learning disabled pupils, it is imperative that the other pupils in the class realize the basis for these adjustments. After completing activities such as those described above, pupils can often use problem-solving techniques to suggest modifications that might help the learning disabled pupil function more easily in the classroom. This approach will prevent resentment that might occur when classroom procedures and requirements are different for some of the pupils.

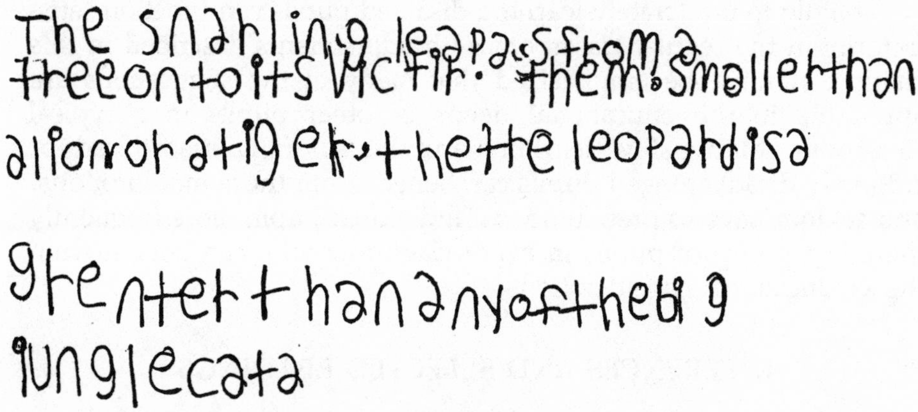

The snarling leapas from a
treeontoits victir: them smallerthan
alfonoratig ek,thette leopardisa

greaterthananyaftheth g
junglecata

FIGURE 1-9

SUMMING UP

The overview of learning disabilities points to the heterogeneous manifestations of this handicapping condition. Identification of mild to moderate learning disabilities often requires astute observation of pupils' behavioral and academic performance. Subtle clues can go undetected unless you look for a consistent pattern of behaviors that interfere with achievement. Distractability, perseveration, quick mental fatigue, social misperception, perceptual and conceptual disorders, and poor motor performance may all be symptomatic of learning disabilities.

The regular classroom curriculum may require little modification. However, some attention to remediation of perceptual disorders, sensory–motor development, and improving social skills may benefit some of these pupils.

The most frequent modifications made in the regular classroom to meet the needs of learning disabled pupils are in the area of teaching techniques. You need skill in a variety of approaches so that the pupils' strengths and weaknesses can be accommodated. "If they can't learn the way we teach, we need to teach the way they can learn" is an appropriate statement in regard to learning disabled pupils.

Alternative teaching materials may be needed for successful academic achievement by these pupils. In addition, materials specifically designed for learning disabilities and other disciplines provide a ready source of alternative teaching materials.

Mildly to moderately learning disabled pupils can function satisfactorily in the regular classroom with adjustments described in this chapter. It must be emphasized that many of the suggestions are applicable to the educational needs of other pupils in a typical classroom. Many slow learners and behaviorally disordered or culturally disadvantaged pupils can benefit from these modifications. You seldom have to prepare for an individual pupil; more frequently there is a group of pupils in every classroom who can benefit from these educational considerations.

REFERENCES AND SELECTED READINGS

Alley, G., and D. Deshler. *Teaching the Learning Disabled Adolescent: Strategies and Methods.* Denver: Love, 1979.

Ashlock, R. B. *Error Patterns in Computation: A Semiprogrammed Approach.* Columbus, Ohio: Charles E. Merrill, 1972.

Bley, N. C., and C. A. Thornton. *Teaching Mathematics to the Learning Disabled.* Rockville, Mass.: Aspen, 1981.

Cawley, J. F., and S. J. Vitello. "Model for Arithmetic Programming for Handicapped Children." *Exceptional Children* 39 (1972): 101–110.

Feldhusen, J. F., and D. J. Treffinger. *Teaching Creative Thinking and Problem Solving.* Dubuque, Iowa: Kendall/Hunt, 1977.

Frosting, M., and P. Maslow. *Learning Problems in the Classroom.* New York: Grune and Stratton, 1973.

Gearheart, B. R., and M. W. Weishahn. *The Handicapped Child in the Regular Classroom.* St. Louis: C. V. Mosley, 1976.

Goodman, K. S. "Analysis of Oral Reading Miscues: Applied Linguistics." *Reading Research Quarterly* 5 (1969): 5–30.

Hammill, D. D., and N. R. Bartel. *Teaching Children with Learning and Behavior Problems.* Boston: Allyn and Bacon, 1982.

Hayes, M. *The Tuned-in, Turned-on Book About Learning Problems.* San Rafael, Calif.: Academic Therapy, 1974.

Horowitz, R. S. "Teaching Mathematics to Students with Learning Disabilities." In J. I. Arena (ed.), *Building Number Skills in Dyslexic Children.* Novato, Calif.: Academic Therapy, 1972.

Hunter, E. *Sue Ellen.* Boston: Houghton-Mifflin, 1969.

Kaluger, G., and C. J. Kolson. *Reading and Learning Disabilities.* Columbus, Ohio: Charles E. Merrill, 1978.

Kirk, S. A., and J. J. Gallagher. *Educating Exceptional Children.* Boston: Houghton-Mifflin, 1979.

Kronick, D. *Social Development of Learning Disabled Persons.* San Francisco: Jossey-Bass, 1981.

La Greca, A. M., and G. B. Meisbov. "Social Skills Intervention with Learning Disabled Children." Paper presented at the annual meeting of the Midwestern Psychological Association, Chicago, May 1979.

Lerner, J. W. *Children with Learning Disabilities.* Boston: Houghton-Mifflin, 1981.

Mann, L., L. Goodman, and J. L. Wiederholt. *Teaching the Learning Disabled Adolescent.* Boston: Houghton-Mifflin, 1978.

Reisman, F. K. *A Guide to the Diagnostic Teaching of Arithmetic.* Columbus, Ohio: Charles E. Merrill, 1972.

Smith, D. B. *Kelly's Creek.* New York: Thomas Y. Crowell, 1975.

Spivak, G., J. J. Platt, and M. B. Shure. *The Problem-Solving Approach to Adjustment: A Guide to Research and Intervention.* San Francisco: Jossey-Bass, 1976.

Stanek, M. *Left, Right, Left, Right.* Chicago: Albert Whitman, 1975.

Stern, C. *Structural Arithmetic.* Boston: Houghton-Mifflin, 1965.

Stern, C., and M. B. Stern. *Children Discover Arithmetic.* New York: Harper and Row, 1971.

Turnbull, A. P., and J. B. Schultz. *Mainstreaming Handicapped Students: A Guide for the Classroom Teacher.* Boston: Allyn and Bacon, 1979.

CHAPTER TWO

Behavioral Disorders

Is there a teacher who has not experienced secret joy upon discovering that "Johnny is absent today"? Invariably, Johnny is a behavior problem in the classroom. Lucy, on the other hand, causes concern because she does not participate in activities or interact with other people in the classroom. Far from being a behavior problem, it is difficult to recognize that she is physically present. Pupils with behavioral disorders fall along this continuum, ranging from severely withdrawn to aggressive, acting-out behavior.

Several factors affect your notion of what behaviors constitute mild or moderate behavioral disorders. Your level of tolerance is an overriding consideration. The level of expectation varies greatly among teachers. Pupil responses to specific situations must also be taken into account.

The following personal illustration is offered for clarification. One of the authors served as a teacher in a junior high school setting where four teachers used a rotating schedule among four classes. Each teacher was responsible for teaching English, Mathematics, Science, or Social Studies to each of the four classes. One could stand in the hall centered in this cluster of classrooms and identify which teacher was in each classroom by listening to the pupils' responses. One classroom could be identified by the lack of noise. The teacher's low level of tolerance to pupil interaction was evidenced by hearing only the teacher's directions and explanations or the recitation of one pupil at a time. Sounds from the second classroom usually suggested that group discussion, small group activities, or individual projects were occurring. Occasionally, the teacher could be heard cautioning pupils about an unacceptable behavior, although most of the time behavior was acceptable to the teacher. The third classroom was similar to the second except that the noise level was somewhat lower and the teacher's voice was rarely heard. The fourth class left little doubt about the nature of the activity inside. There was the noise of pupils running around the room, children yelling from the classroom windows, books being thrown about, and uncontrolled talking; in other words, the class was totally out of control. The teacher's perception of what constitutes a behavior problem would be difficult to isolate from the situation.

The first teacher considered no pupil to be a behavior problem. The second teacher judged some behavior to be unacceptable. The third teacher identified no behavior problems. However, the fourth teacher felt that most of the pupils were trouble-makers.

The phenomenon was consistent throughout the school year. The teacher and subject area were the two most obvious variables in this situation. Since it is unlikely that four different classes would have a common reaction to one subject area, it appeared that the teacher was the most influential factor in determining pupil behavior. This illustration is not used to imply that teachers cause pupils to be behaviorally disordered but only to demonstrate the difficulty of classifying behavior as acceptable or unacceptable without considering all factors that affect the situation.

Some of the labels that have been associated with the group of pupils under discussion are behavior disorders, emotional disturbance, social maladjustment, neurotic behavior, autism, schizophrenia, and juvenile delinquency. For the pupose of this chapter, only mildly and moderately impaired pupils who are likely to be mainstreamed will be discussed. *Behavioral disorders* will be used in a generic sense.

The following definition of a behavior disorder by Kirk and Gallagher (1979, p. 389) provides a useful framework for identification:

a marked deviation from age-appropriate behavior that significantly interferes with (1) the child's own development, (2) the lives of others, or (3) both.

Identification clues, techniques for managing behavior, strategies for improving motivation, curriculum consideration, teaching materials, and fostering understanding of pupils with behavioral problems are presented in this chapter.

EIGHT CLUES THAT INDICATE BEHAVIORAL PROBLEMS

1. Excessively withdrawn behavior
2. Inappropriate types of behavior or feelings under normal circumstances
3. A general, pervasive mood of unhappiness, depression, or anxiety
4. Inability to build or maintain satisfactory interpersonal relationships
5. Aggressive or acting-out behavior
6. Tantrums
7. A tendency to develop physical symptoms, pains, or fears associated with school or personal problems
8. Immature behaviors such as playing with toys, pretending that objects are animate, excessive daydreaming, and being overly dependent

Quay (1969) has classified these behaviors into descriptive clusters, as follows:

1. Conduct disorders
2. Anxious, withdrawn behavior
3. Inadequate, immature behaviors

Quay also describes the socialized delinquent as displaying loyalty and behavior acceptable to a delinquent peer group but not respecting school and societal authority.

You need to exercise caution in expecting all pupils with behavioral disorders to have low academic achievement. Frequently, the behavior does not interfere with the pupils' schoolwork. Indeed, the average range of intellectual ability will include many behaviorally disordered pupils in the gifted category.

SPECIAL TECHNIQUES FOR MANAGING BEHAVIOR

Providing Structure

Many pupils with behavioral and emotional problems function more successfully in a structured environment. This does not mean total rigidity and inflexibility. In a structured environment, classroom design and organization, expectations, rules, and routines are clearly identifiable. It is important for pupils to understand the system and to participate responsibly in its operation. This structure provides the security needed by many of these pupils.

Physical layout of a classroom can define expectations. One classroom observed provides a good illustration. A fifth grade teacher of 33 regular students mainstreamed up to 6 exceptional pupils each class period. Classroom space was at a premium with 39 pupils each class period. Tables, shelves, and other furnishings were typical of those found in the average classroom. Individual, small group, and large group activities occurred simultaneously. For those pupils engaged in individual work, table dividers were used to make mini study carrels. The teacher used collapsible cardboard or Masonite dividers tied around the table legs with straps fastened with Velcro. (See Figure 2-1.)

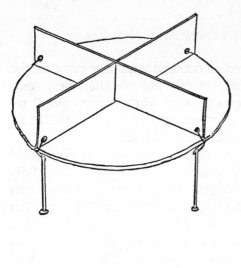
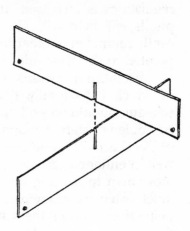

FIGURE 2-1

During small group activities, including peer tutoring, dividers were removed to indicate that interaction was permitted. Furniture was arranged to facilitate group discussion for large group activities. These furniture arrangements indicated expectations in a visible way.

There was also a quiet spot for the pupil who "lost control." A desk was placed in a small closet with the door removed, which provided an "office" for the pupil who needed to be removed from the group. This space was not used punitively, but rather it was described as a place "where others will not disturb you."

Another visible clue for behavior expectations in this classroom was the use of a traffic light. The teacher constructed a working model. The red light was turned on when the noise level was unacceptable. Amber light conditions allowed moderate noise and movement, with the green light condition removing most restrictions on noise and movement.

These examples show how explicit expectations can be indicated to pupils. They are not left to inferring subtleties.

There are four cardinal rules for effective use of rules:

1. Rules should be few in number.
2. Rules should be stated in positive and specific language.
3. Rules should be enforceable.
4. Rules should be cooperatively generated by the class.

If these guidelines are followed, successful implementation of the regulations is increased. If you consistently enforce the rules, soon pupils will help with the enforcement. One kindergarten pupil recently reminded another that "we don't use that word at school" as he pointed to the class rule regarding acceptable language.

Establishing classroom routines provides an orderly environment in which behaviorally disordered pupils function best. The daily schedule should be well thought out. Are all sedentary academic tasks scheduled straight through the morning, or are there opportunities for physical activities and less intense concentration? On occasion some well-intentioned teachers provide a brief period of rigorous dance or movement to rousing music and then try to move abruptly back to quiet, intensive academics. You need to plan transitional activities to help pupils reorient themselves. Changing the tempo of the dance and the music, a quiet oral reading by the teacher, or a brief filmstrip might be used as a transitional activity.

Classroom routines also need to be established for distributing and collecting papers, restroom privileges, and entering and exiting the classroom.

It is crucial to prepare pupils for unusual events such as assemblies, study trips, and guests who come to the school. Pupils need to know when, where, and what is expected.

Discipline

In discussing discipline, we must be clear about how the word is used. It has three fairly common meanings: (1) punishment, (2) good classroom management, and (3) the development of self-control in pupils. The second definition—good classroom management—is what we are using here. A number of practical techniques will be described.

First, let's discuss good classroom management, which has not been observed in any of the many discipline books. These comments about good classroom management derive from some 45 years of work between the authors in the public school classroom and in colleges of education.

First, the best classroom managers tend to possess the following characteristics: they are consistent, firm, and fair; they make no threats; they mean what they say; and they have immediate follow-through. They clearly respect all children and separate disapproval of a child's behavior from disapproval of that child. There are not many rules, but the ones that do exist are enforced. In contrast, poor managers are inconsistent, firm sometimes and vacillating other times, and unfair, if not capricious; they make lots of threats but don't mean what they say; and they may or may not follow through. With the latter types, pupils have a field day and teachers approach a nervous breakdown.

Rules should be few, but the ones that you have must invariably be acted upon; pupils quickly realize that this is the case, and the bulk of the problems disappear if the rules are not unreasonable. There are a few exceptions to this, of course, as with any rule.

Next in importance, you must understand and believe that just because you have a discipline problem, it is not necessarily your fault. For too long the teacher has been led to believe all problems are his or her fault. Some are, yes, but many derive from immature parenting skills. How can the classroom teacher be reasonably expected to resolve problems that have been developing in children over a period of years? In short, there will be times when you *must* exit a child from the classroom, and, if you are given sufficient provocation, you should not feel ashamed or guilty. This is important; too many teachers, being essentially altruistic and idealistic at heart, internalize the many problems encountered and blame themselves.

The final point has to do with the curriculum. A program that is relevant for pupils—work that is on their level, challenging but capable of being accomplished with reasonable effort—is, next to the behavioral traits indicated above, probably the most important preventive of behavioral problems.

However, even with all of the above, the fact remains that *all* teachers will have discipline problems. Not all discipline problems are capable of being resolved by the teacher; some are just too complex and of too long a standing in origin. In such instances, to maintain order (and all teachers must have order), there is probably no alternative but to remove the pupil from the classroom.

Nor should you hesitate to transfer pupils out of the class if it is deemed best for the pupil after careful investigation and conferences with parents, principal, and other adults important to the child's welfare, such as the school nurse or the school psychologist. Not all pupils and teachers "click." Unfortunately, many teachers in this situation are led to feel incompetent if a pupil is transferred.

On the other hand, some teachers actually generate discipline problems; these teachers need help themselves. They must be given expert guidance so that they will be able to realize how and why they are making problems for themselves and understand how to make the necessary changes in their own behavior. In a few instances teachers, should be removed from the classroom for the welfare of the children—again, only after careful investigation.

The following pages describe the kinds of things that you can do to improve the behavior of most of your charges most of the time—things that, assuming you are reasonably competent and of sound mental health, will help you.

Behavior Modification

One of the most powerful ideas in good discipline involves association. Briefly, this means that if an event immediately follows another event, there is, over time, a tendency for the second event to occur whenever the first one does, becoming associated with it. This leads to the practical ideas of reinforcement or reward. When the child does something good, if she is rewarded, the tendency to be "good," to behave properly, increases. This implies, for example, that it is important for children to learn to associate pleasure or fun with the act of reading, as this tends to increase their tendency to want to read.

One of the most feasible aids for teachers today comes from a field known as behavior modification. It derives from B. F. Skinner, who had a tremendous impact on the development of programmed instruction materials.

The basic principles underlying behavior modification and programmed instruction are essentially identical; each is designed to control and shape pupil behavior toward clearly defined, desirable ends. Another spinoff of behavior modification is performance contracting, which will be described later.

Just as animal trainers are able to produce seemingly amazing feats in animals, properly applied principles of behaviorism can likewise assist teachers in classroom management. We should emphasize that application of these principles is no miracle cure for problems. A bad home situation or an unfair or prejudiced teacher cannot hope to get very far, even when applying behavioristic principles.

Principle 1. The pupil must evidence the behavior before being reinforced. An example is the pupil who is continually out of his seat. The teacher, instead of frequently admonishing the pupil, tries to catch him in his seat and reward him verbally for sitting so nicely.

Some teachers do not have to resort deliberately to the above tactic. Somehow they seem to have established control early, and the pupils do not get out of their seats without permission. However, even teachers like these may encounter a "wiggleworm."

Assuming the wiggleworm is not afflicted with a version of hyperactivity—in which case there is little one can do but channel it and, at times, discover that medication is prescribed by the doctor—even the best of teachers will have difficulties from time to time.

Principle 2. It is important for the appropriate or good behavior to be rewarded immediately. This is a basic principle in animal training. The animal being trained or conditioned has to associate the reward with a desired action. To delay the reward, particularly for younger children, is to render it far less effective.

Principle 3. Initially, the behavior desired should be rewarded (reinforced) each time; later it does not need to be rewarded as often. Once the behavior has been acquired, only periodic approval or other reward (as token) is necessary. Slot machines exemplify this; the machines do not pay off every time, or even at regular intervals or in fixed amounts. If they did, we would probably all agree that soon few people would be playing them. In an analogous manner, the reward for the pupil can occur at irregular intervals, and the rewards may vary in degree or kind. We really have two principles operating here: both frequency and type of reward. This leads to the next principle.

Principle 4. Social rewards should always accompany tangible rewards. If juice, apples, peanuts, and so on, are given as rewards, the social reward—the smile or verbal approval—should always accompany the tangible reward. This is because the teacher will want to drop the tangible reward as soon as possible and keep only the social reward.

Walker and Shea (1976) suggest a number of tangible and social reinforcers, some of which are listed here.

Tangible food reinforcers recommended include apples, grapes, oranges, raisins, crackers, cookies, popcorn, peanuts, gumdrops, juice, and milk.

Social reinforcing activities to accompany the above include receiving verbal praise, having a picture posted on the bulletin board, being allowed to demonstrate a skill, getting a hug or a handshake or a pat on the back, sitting near the teacher at lunch, being allowed to sit with a good friend, being allowed free time, and having work displayed. Free time should really be free choice time; that is, the pupil is permitted to choose an activity such as an educational game. Unstructured free time may lead to additional behavior problems.

Token reinforcers include checks and points, happy faces and stars, behavior charts, rubber stamps in a notebook, trading stamps, good citizenship tags, and certificates.

Rewarding activities include games such as dot-to-dot, coloring books, blocks, bingo, word games, number games, and number puzzles. There are many classroom tasks that can be reinforcing too, such as erasing the blackboard, taking a note to the office, watering the plants, running the ditto machine, stapling papers together, feeding the fish, emptying the wastebasket, and many more, limited only by your imagination. Observing what pupils like to do will give you additional ideas for reinforcers.

From the multitude of possibilities, you can choose the ones you think most appropriate and try them. Some will work; some will not. Some will be most appropriate for young children; some will work only on older children.

When reinforcing the recalcitrant for good behavior, be careful not to neglect those who have been behaving. If you neglect these others, you run the risk of encouraging them to misbehave in order to be rewarded for good behavior.

Principle 5. After the pupil begins to behave satisfactorily, rewards should be irregular. This may seem strange, but it is true. As lotteries operate, the rewards are irregular in both frequency and size. In a similar vein, you can change the nature of the reward and its size or value. It seems that when children know they will be rewarded but are not exactly sure when and what it will be, this in itself is highly motivating.

Why It Works

Precisely why behavior can be shaped through techniques such as behavior modification is not known; what we do know is that it works. It is clear that the child comes to understand that when he or she behaves in a certain way, things that are desirable will occur from time to time.

Seldom will all children value the same reward; what one prizes highly another may care little for. Nor will rewards that work for most children at one age level work with much older or younger children. For example, the younger the child, the more concrete and immediate the reward must be. For older children, some rewards would be considered babyish or silly. Only by discussing the matter with pupils can you discover the kinds of rewards that are most suitable for a particular group during a particular period of time.

How to Implement Behavior Modification

As with any other complex set of skills, behavior modification techniques must be learned. We are all aware of the four basic steps in learning anything:

1. The desired objective must be understood. That is, we must be clear in our minds about what we are endeavoring to accomplish. In the case of behavior modification, one way to accomplish this is to read about it.

2. We must see it in action; we must observe it being used. Typically, in a school, there is at least one faculty member already good at behavior modification. There is no shame in going to observe—

with permission, of course. The teacher being observed will usually feel flattered.

3. The behavior must be practiced repeatedly. This is illustrated most graphically in the practice sessions of participants in all sports from football to ice skating.

4. We must have feedback on how we are doing. We must be able to perceive any discrepancies between the ultimate behavior for which we are striving and what we are actually doing. When we see the discrepancies, we get a lead on what we need to do in order to close the gap.

This process continues until mastery is reached. One of the best ways to acquire the skills of behavior modification is to contact a nearby college or university with a department of Special Education. Most such departments have courses in behavior modification and offer practical workshops for teachers.

In these workshops you can learn how to plot behavior to set a benchmark, to detect increases and decreases in its manifestation. One learns to break behavior down into a number of components, including frequency, duration, conditions under which it appears, type, intensity, and so on.

Practical Examples

One effective reinforcement technique is described by Dr. Paul George (1975):

> Pickle Jar Lottery. The teacher should acquire a large pickle jar, cardboard box, or the equivalent and make up some lottery tickets. Ask in cafeteria about a jar. Decorate the jar or box as colorfully as possible and place it in full view of the class, announcing the list of behaviors that will win lottery tickets. Remember to post the list of approved behaviors on the wall, in this and in all other strategies, and be certain to point out that pupils must be caught being good, and that they will not receive a ticket every time they do well. Then set about the process of randomly identifying good behavior.
>
> When a pupil has been caught being good, put his name on a ticket and drop it in the jar. Keep this up as frequently as you comfortably can. At some prearranged time or day known or unknown to the class (try both ways), conduct a drawing for one or more prizes. Begin with drawing relatively frequently and, as possible, gradually move to less and less frequent drawings.

Another technique is to set up a "Behavior Bank Account." A "Deposit Sheet" is maintained by each pupil. A specific list of ways to earn a deposit of a given amount is posted where all can see. Withdrawals are made for either listed bad behaviors or certain privileges the pupils can "buy" when they have a certain amount. To save time, deposits can be made in a number of ways. Teacher initials is one way of making a deposit. A better way is to have a few hundred precut squares or stamps, which are pasted in the book by each pupil, not unlike store trading stamps. Certain specified amounts entitle pupils to purchase clearly specified privileges. The trading stamp approach works well with many adults; it works no less effectively with pupils.

Difference Between Punishment and Elimination of Misbehavior

There is a strong tendency in our culture to administer punishment for misbehavior. While this will work at times, it is usually not the best approach. For one thing, punishment tends to suppress the misbehavior but does not always eliminate or extinguish it. Punishment also provides a model for aggressive behavior.

A good way to explain the difference between punishment and effective intervention through some form of behavior modification is given in Table 2-1.

OTHER APPROACHES TO DISCIPLINE

There are various schools of thought on effective discipline; frankly, all of the answers are not yet in. However, the tips given here on behavior modification fall into what can be called the Skinnerian or behaviorist camp. The other approach views people very differently; it stems more from existentialism and a phenomenological approach to

TABLE 2-1

Action	Nature of Reinforcement	
	Positive reinforcement	**Negative Reinforcement**
Add	Behavior increased	Behavior decreased
Remove	Behavior decreased	Behavior increased

human behavior. The latter is more of a point of view than a set of principles that you can use in the classroom. To become acquainted with it as such, you must immerse yourself deeply into the literature; there is no way to present a clear, succinct way of operating in the classroom.

There are important concepts to be grasped in both schools of thought; there is as yet no overarching theory that will encompass these two divergent approaches to working with human beings.

Remember that there is no short, easy recipe for effective classroom management. It requires planning, organization, consistency, fairness, firmness, compassion, understanding, empathy, and continual monitoring of your own behavior for the purpose of making it more congruent with what you desire.

Managing Surface Behavior

Long and Newman (1980, p. 236) offer 12 techniques designed to help you manage pupils who are approaching or experiencing a mild crisis situation. The procedures include planned ignoring, signal interference, proximity control, interest boosting, tension decontamination through humor, hurdle lessons, restructuring the classroom program, support from routine, direct appeal to value areas, removal of seductive objects, antiseptic bouncing, and physical restraint.

1. *Planned ignoring.* Ignore inappropriate behavior until it becomes acceptable. When pupils do not receive gratification from their actions, the behavior will diminish. Two facts to consider regarding planned ignoring are, first, that this technique cannot be used if the behavior is potentially dangerous to the pupil or others, and second, that inappropriate behavior will often increase initially before it is eliminated. You need to enlist other pupils in ignoring the behavior so that they do not provide reinforcement.

2. *Signal interference.* Many nonverbal signals can be used to communicate disapproval. Eye contact, facial expression, body postures, and finger snapping are examples. "The Look" can be used quite effectively as a control technique.

3. *Proximity control.* Standing near the pupil who is having problems provides a sense of protection and identification for the pupil. Some pupils respond well to touching, such as being patted on the shoulder.

4. *Interest boosting.* If a pupil is becoming restless, it may help to show interest in her work or to mention some personal interest of the pupil. Some activity related to the pupil's interest may be used to motivate her to complete the assignment.

5. *Tension decontamination through humor.* The use of humor in an anxiety-producing situation shows pupils that you are human. A camaraderie can develop between you and your pupils when humor is used to release tension during stressful times. One technique used effectively with junior high school pupils is to make up a song when a behavior problem is developing. The sight and sound of a dignified teacher spontaneously singing "I see a little boy who is very, very bad" to the tune of a nursery rhyme results in a hearty laugh by the class. It is beneficial to proceed immediately with the lesson to prevent a "silly session" from developing.

6. *Hurdle lessons.* Misbehavior can result when the pupil becomes frustrated with an assignment. If he has difficulty or breaks down during an academic process, providing personal help may prevent an undesirable episode from developing.

7. *Restructuring the classroom program.* It may be beneficial to restructure the classroom program or redirect a specific activity if tension or boredom is evident. All teachers have felt that they must press on to cover the planned curriculum. Most of us have experienced some difficulty with attentiveness and behavior because of this persistent effort. It would be wiser to terminate or restructure activities.

8. *Support from routine.* Many pupils perform better when they are given a daily schedule. This structure provides a sense of security. An outline of class or daily activities will help the pupils to know what to expect. Do you remember the feelings associated with the first days of junior and senior high school and college? As the routine of the term was established, the insecure feeling abated because you had established a routine.

9. *Direct appeal to value areas.* This is a way to involve the pupil and keep you from drastic attempts to control the situation. Long and Newman (1980, p. 239) present the following partial list of areas to which you can appeal:

(a) An appeal to the relationship of the teacher with the child, i.e., "You are treating me as if I did something bad to you." (b) An appeal to reality consequences, i.e., "If you continue to talk, we will not have time to plan our party," "If you continue with this behavior, these are the things that will probably happen." In other words, the teacher tries to underline cause and effect behavior. (c) An appeal to the child's group code and awareness of peer reaction, i.e., "What do you think the other boys and girls will think of that idea?" or "If you continue to spoil their fun, you can't expect the other boys and girls to like you." (d) An appeal to the teacher's power of authority. Tell the children that as a teacher you cannot allow this behavior to continue and still want to take care of them. The trick is to learn how to say "no" without becoming angry, or how to say "yes" without feeling guilty.

10. *Removal of seductive objects.* Objects that have particular appeal or are distracting to pupils should be put out of sight or removed from the classroom. Toys, money, pocket games, and noninstructional magazines are examples of objects that may compete for attention with academic activities.

11. *Antiseptic bouncing.* This refers to sending pupils on some mission out of the classroom when they appear unlikely to respond to verbal controls. The purpose of sending pupils out is not punitive but to help them get over negative feelings, uncontrollable laughter, and so on. Two teachers with adjoining classrooms can have a preplanned arrangement for each to accept a pupil from the other's classroom and to give him or her some job or message before returning to the original classroom. This provides an opportunity for the pupil to get his or her behavior under control.

12. *Physical restraint.* Occasionally, pupils may act in a way that is harmful to themselves and/or others. Physical restraint may be your only option. This is not intended in any way to be corporal punishment. You must be protective and not counteraggressive.

You should cross the pupil's arms in front of him while standing behind the pupil and holding his wrists. If may be necessary to hold the pupil on the floor in this position.

Long and Newman (1980, pp. 240–241) suggest four phases through which the pupil may go when being controlled:

1. *Phase 1.* The pupil fights being held and controlled. The pupil may swear and bite. You must not become counteraggressive during this phase. The pupil needs reassurance that he will be all right. "I

will let go when you calm down," or "When I feel you relax, I'll let go."

2. *Phase 2.* The pupil's defenses begin to come down, and inadequacy and immaturity become evident. Crying is not uncommon. Continue to reassure the pupil that he will feel better soon.

3. *Phase 3.* The pupil becomes quiet and asks to be released. Make the decision to release the pupil or not if you feel control has been restored and the cycle will not start over.

4. *Phase 4.* The pupil engages in some face-saving behavior such as making a sly remark. You may suggest that the pupil wash up at this point.

These techniques for managing surface behavior should be effective in the regular classroom. It is unlikely that many severely behaviorally disordered pupils will remain in the regular classroom.

Hints for Handling a Crisis Situation

The wisest technique for crisis situations is prevention. Often, the misbehavior can be controlled before it gets out of hand and the class gets involved in the incident. Reasonable consequences should be identified early in the school year. Be sure that the pupils understand exactly what is expected of them in your room. Most children easily learn what is expected in your classroom, but the behaviorally disordered child often does not. We need to help pupils to understand the consequences of inappropriate behaviors. ("If you do not come into the room quietly in the morning, you must spend ten minutes in the quiet corner.") Once you have established which behaviors are appropriate and which are inappropriate, be sure to follow through with the planned consequences. Watch and listen carefully as the pupils enter your room for hints of emotional upset. Is someone unusually aggressive, irritable, depressed, or agitated? By observing these mental states, you are preparing yourself for a possible crisis.

Remove pupils from seductive objects, activities, and people that can upset or distract them and lead to trouble. If you know that it is risky to let Billy and John sit together, then seat them far apart at all times. If you know that Susan can't resist the tempera paints and easel, keep the paint in a closed cabinet until art time.

A teacher with astute observational skills can see the problem developing. At this point it is best to take action with techniques for managing surface behavior. If a crisis situation does develop, try the following suggestions:

1. Do not get emotionally involved. Try very hard to stay calm. If a pupil is having a temper tantrum or is crying or fighting, this is not the time to scold. Don't "lose your cool." This is also not a time to argue. The "I won't"— "You will" syndrome is a no-win situation. You have clearly established classroom limits before the crisis, so the pupil knows what to expect as a consequence for inappropriate behavior.

2. Remove the pupil to a quiet place so that he can calm down. Ideally, this quiet place should be outside your room, but if that is not possible, have a designated place in your room for this. You might use a reading corner or study carrel for a "time out" area. Time out is not a punishment; it is a place for quiet, relaxation, and gaining control of emotions. It is also a place where pupils can request to go when they feel emotions overcoming them.

3. An alternative is to provide a supervised place for vigorous physical activity. Some pupils may find this a good way to release uncomfortable emotions.

4. During the crisis, do not accuse or embarrass the pupil. Do not compare his behavior unfavorably with that of others or insult him with comments such as "Grow up" or "You should know better than to act this way" or "You should be ashamed of yourself." He already knows he is doing the wrong thing. You can offer him the most support by being calm, firm, and in complete control of your own emotions. This is often hard for adults to do, but with practice it will get easier.

5. In an emergency situation, such as a fight that you cannot break up, have a plan ready. Choose two responsible pupils who can go for help, one to the office and one to a trusted colleague who will come to you immediately. Under no circumstances should you leave the scene. When emotions are very high, it often takes several adults to break up a fight.

6. When the pupil has paid the consequence for his misbehavior, forget it. Resist the temptation to say "I hope you have learned your lesson" or "Don't you think you owe someone an apology?" or "I'm glad to see you have yourself under control." Just drop it. This way the pupil knows that you will not nag him after he has gotten over the episode. The last thing he needs to hear is a

continued reminder that he is the master of inappropriate classroom behaviors. He already knows that. The crisis is over, and it is time to get on with the business of school. Include him back in the ongoing classroom activity as if nothing has happened. Do not allow continued discussion and accusations related to the incident.

7. Catch pupils when behavior is commendable, and give positive reinforcement. Why do we tell them when they are being bad and not when they are being good? If Jimmy's problem is calling out without raising his hand, be sure to compliment him when he does remember: "Thank you for remembering to raise your hand, Jimmy." These pupils know they are problems, and they are accustomed to being scolded; they are masters at turning out negative comments. Commenting on continued compliance with the class rules will get desired results much more quickly than a reprimand.

8. Group creative problem solving might be engaged in to generate alternative solutions to the conflict. Further discussion may be helpful if the conflict involves a long-standing feud between individuals or other factors that affect the whole class. This should not occur until all parties have had sufficient time to cool down. It is counterproductive to try to reason with emotionally upset people.

9. Provide enjoyable activities when the crisis is over. Do not punish pupils by removing them from school activities that are pleasurable or by giving them extra school work to do. Asking a pupil to write "I will not misbehave in class" 500 times will reinforce his hatred of written expression. Copying pages out of the dictionary will reinforce hatred of dictionary work. You are saying to the pupil, "I know how horrible writing is, so I am going to punish you by asking you to write." Head down on desk for ten minutes is better than copying a page out of the dictionary.

10. Send "glad notes" and "happygrams" to the pupil and to parents. It is also helpful to send positive messages to other teachers when the pupil rotates with departmental scheduling. One teacher drew a happy face on a card to send home each day. If the child failed to bring one home, the parents knew it had not been a good day and that there should have been a note to that effect. It's important for these pupils to know that the teacher and the parents communicate with each other about their progress. They will work harder to develop appropriate behaviors when they

know that the school and the home are working together to help them. Parents of behaviorally disordered children usually have experienced much negative communication from teachers. It is important for them to hear the good things as well. One teacher sent a good note home to compliment a fifth grader on her studious behavior, and the mother told the teacher, "That's the first time since Theresa went to school that anyone has ever said anything nice about her."

If you clearly establish your classroom rules, clearly explain the consequences and follow through with them every time, and stay calm and nonpunitive during a crisis, you will find fewer behavior problems in your class. The atmosphere in your classroom will be accepting but very firmly structured. The pupil with a behavior problem will feel more secure with you because there will be no doubt with him when he does lose control.

How to Use Pupil Contracts

A contract is a written or verbal agreement between individuals specifying the responsibilities of those individuals in regard to a particular activity or event. Contracts between teachers and pupils can be used as behavior management techniques. They can also be quite motivational to pupils. Contracting also prepares pupils for the "real world" if they are consistently enforced.

A major benefit of contracting is increased communication between teacher and pupil. Written contracts are better than verbal contracts for behaviorally disordered pupils. The teacher must clearly specify the objectives, either academic or social, and the rewards. If they sign the contract following discussion to be sure that everyone understands the agreement, the pupils cannot later blame anyone else for failure to achieve the objectives.

Usually, the teacher draws up the first several contracts with input from pupils concerning the reward. After the contracting model is working effectively, the pupils can assume more responsibility in developing the contracts.

A contract should have at least the following components: date of initiation, names of agreeing individuals, objectives, conditions, rewards, dates of termination, and signatures of agreeing individuals. If the contract is for an extended period of time, it is wise to include a date on which to review the contract. Figures 2-2 and 2-3 show typical contract forms.

```
┌─────────────────────────────────────────────────────────────┐
│                         CONTRACT                             │
│                                                              │
│                                    Date: _____   │
│  I, _____ agree to│
│  _____ │
│  _____ │
│  _____ │
│  _____ │
│  _____ │
│                                                              │
│  starting on _____ and finishing by│
│                         (date)                               │
│  _____. When I successfully com-│
│                   (date)                                     │
│  plete all of the above conditions, I may _____ │
│  _____ │
│  _____ │
│  _____ │
│                                                              │
│              Pupil: _____  │
│            Teacher: _____  │
│            Witness: _____  │
└─────────────────────────────────────────────────────────────┘
```

FIGURE 2-2

It's Positively Fun (Kaplan, Kohfeldt, and Sturla, 1974) contains contract forms and other materials for positive reinforcement.

The use of pictures or illustrations can add interest and visual attraction to the contract form. The pupils' interests or the subject of the contract can be focused upon.

Contracts can be used with groups of pupils, the whole class, and parents. Even three-way contracts with parents have been used successfully. In one case, a learning disabled adolescent was exceedingly unmotivated. The most motivational factor was a contract specify-

CONTRACT

What I plan to do: _____

_____

_____

_____

_____ .

I will start on _____ and finish by _____
                         (date)

Then I will be able to _____

_____

_____

_____

_____

_____

_____

_____   _____   _____
     (Student)   (Teacher)   (Date)

FIGURE 2-3

ing 90 percent achievement on each academic task, with the reward being an afternoon (three hours) of water skiing on Saturday with his father. The pupil, the father, and the teacher signed the contract, and it worked well. By the way, a week before the reward would be too long for a young child. Also, some behaviorally disordered adolescents will not respond to extended delay of gratification. As the pupils respond favorably to contracting, the payoff time can be increased.

If a contract does not work, it should be reviewed by the pupil and the teacher. Modifications may be necessary. This flexibility is necessary; however, contracting will not work unless it is consistently enforced. Do not allow negotiations to dissolve into manipulation.

With careful and cooperative planning of objectives and rewards, this strategy for improving academic and social performance is very effective.

Kounin's Group Management Categories

J. S. Kounin attempted to identify skills that have been used by teachers who were judged to be good managers of classroom behavior. The original studies were conducted in regular classroom settings and later replicated with emotionally disturbed pupils. The identified skills appeared to be effective with both groups.

Kounin's categories include (1) with-it-ness, (2) group alerting, (3) smoothness, (4) accountability, (5) overlapping-ness, and (6) seatwork variety challenge or valence and challenge arousal.

1. With-it-ness means that the teacher knows what is going on. As pupils might say, "She has eyes in the back of her head."
2. Group alerting means that the teacher tries to sustain pupil attention and keep all pupils involved. Several techniques are suggested for this category. Suspense can be created by asking a question and then pausing and looking around before selecting a pupil to answer. Avoid selecting responders in a predictable pattern. Alert pupils that they may be required to respond to the reciter's response. Circulate or look around during a pupil's response. Provide stimulating issues during group discussion.
3. Smoothness means that transitions between activities in the classroom flow in an orderly manner.
4. Accountability means that the teacher makes it clear that pupils are to demonstrate involvement in the learning activity.
5. Overlapping-ness means that the teacher can deal with two or more things at the same time. Answering individual questions about seatwork without disturbance while conducting a group lesson is an example.
6. Seatwork variety challenge means the teacher's ability to stimulate enthusiasm, involvement, and curiosity by avoiding boredom with more of the same types of activities.

Kounin's categories of skills provide a list by which each teacher might evaluate his or her teaching. For example, do you give each pupil an equal chance to recite, or are there pupils who are rarely called upon because you assume they don't know the answer? Over a period of time, they have no reason to prepare for recitation.

Magic Circle

Magic Circle is the popular name for the Human Development Program (1974) developed by Uvalde Palomaras, Harold Bessell, and Geraldine Ball. The intent of the program is preventive mental health emphasizing emotional and social development. Understanding of self, self-fulfillment, and effective interpersonal relationships are ultimate goals of the program. These goals are developed sequentially on the following levels:

1. *Awareness* of one's own feelings and those of others
2. *Mastery,* increasing one's self-confidence
3. *Social interaction,* improving one's interpersonal skills

Small or large group discussions can be held with the teacher or a peer as leader. It is important that peers assume leadership as their skills in the group interaction process improve. Meetings usually last from 20 to 30 minutes, although at the secondary level a 10-minute session can be effective. The circle formation allows for eye contact and other listening techniques to be employed easily. The leader selects a cue title on the level being dealt with during the circle session. After the session leader clarifies the cue title, each pupil is given a chance to share his or her experiences and feelings.

Basic ground rules for circle sessions are as follows:

1. Everyone gets a chance to participate.
2. Everyone must participate in active listening.
3. An atmosphere of acceptance must prevail.

Some examples of cue titles for each level are provided below.

Awareness
Something I like about myself
Misery is ...
A feeling I have sometimes that I don't understand

Mastery
How I helped someone do something they couldn't do
Something I just learned how to do
Something I resent help or interference with

Social Interaction
How something I did made someone else feel good
How someone got me to give them attention
How I had to resist others to do what had to be done

Numerous publications are available on the Magic Circle Human Development Program from:

Human Development Training Institute
7574 University Avenue
La Mesa, California 92041

Teacher Effectiveness Training

Teacher Effectiveness Training (TET) by Gordon and Burch (1974) provides specific techniques to improve communication between teacher and pupil. Active listening, I messages, and Method III problem solving are strategies that can be used as behavior management tools.

One of the most important aspects of TET is problem ownership. Ownership can be determined by asking, "Whom is the pupil's behavior bothering, the teacher or a pupil?" Joint ownership results when the problem causes emotional or physical pain to both pupil and teacher. After problem ownership is decided, the teacher chooses one of the techniques to resolve or alleviate the problem.

Bob complains that he is never chosen to be captain of the team; Sue didn't have time to finish the quiz; John lost his homework on the way to school. These problems cause distress for these individuals; therefore, ownership belongs to them. If pupils are to mature, they must be guided to find a solution without the teacher attempting to provide an answer.

Active listening is most helpful when the problem is one in which pupils tend to feel negatively about themselves. The teacher's responses indicate that he or she has time to listen and is interested in listening to the pupil-owned problem.

Active listening is modeled by the leader, and participants are expected to become active listeners themselves. For instance, the leader reflects back a student's thoughts by rephrasing what she said or by asking specific questions to clarify her statements, as in the following example:

Debbie: "I feel really scared when my parents go out and leave me alone."

Leader: "You are frightened to stay by yourself."

Debbie: "Yes, somebody could break in. I wish my parents wouldn't go out so much."

Leader: "You would like them to stay home more?"

Debbie: "I sure would. Seems like I never get a chance to be with my dad. He's always working or going somewhere without me."

Leader: "Thank you for sharing your feelings, Debbie. John, will you please review what Debbie has shared?"

John: "I think she said she's scared to be alone and wishes her parents would spend more time with her. I know what she means. My dad's in the Navy, and it seems like he's out to sea all the time."

By using active listening, the dialogue flows into areas of real concern without fear that the group will be judging or critical. All feelings are accepted.

Tanya continually interrupts the teacher when he is conducting a reading group; Joey sticks to the teacher like glue during recess. Teachers must claim ownership of these problems because they cause irritation and exasperation.

I messages are statements in which the teacher accepts responsibility for the feelings caused by the pupils' behavior. Tanya's continued interruptions might elicit a response such as, "I feel so upset when you continue to interrupt the lesson, because it will take so much time to finish the reading lesson that we will not have time for art." Most I messages follow the sentence structure, "I feel _____ when you ____ because ____." I messages allow teachers to express inner feelings without blaming the pupils.

Method III problem solving is a technique used when problem ownership is shared by pupil and teacher. There are six steps in the Method III problem-solving procedure (Gordon and Burch, 1974, p. 228):

1. Defining the problem
2. Generating possible solutions
3. Evaluating the solutions
4. Deciding which solution is best
5. Determining how to implement the decision
6. Assessing how well the solution solved the problem

I messages are often used in defining the problem. This clarifies personal feelings and needs. Solutions that have been brainstormed collectively by teacher and pupils are written on the chalkboard. Possible solutions are evaluated to determine if they really will solve the problem, if anyone will be hurt by the solution, and if everyone will be involved in the solution. A plan for initiation of the solution must be determined. After the solution has been implemented, its effectiveness in solving the problem should be assessed. If the problem has not been alleviated, returning to the beginning of the problem-solving process is indicated.

Reality Therapy

Reality therapy (Glasser, 1965) is based on the premise that all individuals (1) need to love and be loved and (2) need to feel worthwhile to others and to themselves. Unhappiness results when these needs are not fulfilled. The thrust of reality therapy is to help motivate pupils to learn responsible ways of responding to each problem situation.

The steps in the reality therapy process are as follows:

1. You must establish a personal relationship with the pupil. A personal relationship is indicated by the frequent use of the pupil's name, knowing the pupil's aspirations, and letting the pupil know that you care about him. Development of a personal relationship does not mean involvement in the pupil's private activities.

2. Deal with present behavior. What the pupils are actually doing is what causes the problem, not their feelings or attitudes. Pupils must be guided to focus on what they are doing that causes the problem.

3. Pupils need to make value judgments about the appropriateness of their behavior. Questions such as, "Is what you are doing helping you?" and "Is what you are doing helping anyone else?" help pupils to accept responsibility for their actions.

4. Have pupils develop a plan of action in which more responsible behaviors are chosen. The plan may need to be developed cooperatively by a pupil and the teacher. A plan should be specific and attainable and should replace negative behaviors with positive behaviors. The plan can be expressed in a written contract.

5. Have pupils make a commitment to implement the plan. Signatures on a written contract, verbal agreements, or handshakes are ways of indicating a commitment to planned change.

6. Accept no excuses if the planned outcomes are not achieved. Responsibility for failure is never shifted from the pupil to someone else or to a particular situation. No investigation of why the plan did not work is allowed. Another plan may need to be developed.

7. Do not administer punishment. Punishment can be used as an excuse to shift responsibility to the teacher. Pupils should experience the natural consequences of their behavior.

8. Do not give up when pupils have been unsuccessful in changing to more responsible behaviors. Pupils feel that there is hope for success if you continue to work with them. With persistence, pupil and teacher can start over and move toward a positive solution to the problem.

9. If the plan does not work, try to locate the failure points and then renegotiate a plan.

In using the reality therapy process, your role is one of support while helping pupils to plan and work toward more responsible behaviors to solve their problems.

Classroom Meetings

In *School Without Failure*, Glasser (1969) describes the use of classroom meetings for dicussing problems. Glasser describes problem-solving, open-ended, and educational–diagnostic meetings. Problem-solving classroom meetings provide a nonjudgmental way to discuss problem behaviors. The major rules for conducting classroom meetings include the following:

1. Any problem that concerns the class or any member of the class is eligible for discussion.

2. All discussion is focused on solutions to the problem.

3. The solutions should not include punishment or blame.

4. Meetings are conducted with teacher and pupils seated in a tight circle.

While the purpose of problem-solving classroom meetings is to find solutions to a problem that has meaning to the pupils, it also serves to teach problem-solving techniques for general use.

Transactional Analysis

Transactional analysis is a process that seeks to facilitate under-standing and communication by examining exchanges between an individual and others. The premise of transactional analysis is that by understanding human behavior one can learn to make rational deci-sions for oneself and to express one's personal feelings.

The personality is made up of three ego states, according to this theory. The ego states are the parent, the child, and the adult.

The *parent* ego state is the part of the personality that retains the messages learned in early childhood from parents or significant others. The remembered messages may be critical or kind. They have been referred to as "bossy" or "taking care of us."

The *child* ego state is the part of the personality that relates to the urges and instincts of childhood. The feelings of fear, guilt, happiness, and fun are examples of the child ego state.

The *adult* ego state is the part of the personality that gathers facts and organizes experiences and feelings for decision making. It is the part that makes sense and keeps the other two ego states out of trouble.

We know which ego state is active by the way we feel, the words we use, and how others react to what we are doing or saying. By understanding the ego states we can exert control over our interaction exchanges with others.

Transactional analysis can be effective with behaviorally disturbed pupils. It provides a structure for reeducation of self. Positive changes have been observed in the classrooms where the process has been implemented by skilled teachers.

There are numerous materials available for using the transactional analysis process. The *Transactional Analysis for Everybody Series* by Alvyn Freed (1976) is especially suitable for use in the school setting.

STRATEGIES FOR IMPROVING MOTIVATION

Utilizing Pupil Interests to Motivate Reluctant Learners

Utilizing pupil interests in the learning environment can provide strong motivation for learning. It is another way to indicate to pupils that they are known as individuals and that you care about what is important to them. Utilizing pupil interests also adds meaning and relevance to the learning situation.

Two ways to incorporate pupil interests are to use teaching materials that reflect pupil interests and to use reinforcement techniques that reflect pupil interests.

There are several ways to determine pupil interests. The *Van Nagel Diagnostic Series Packet* (Van Nagel, 1980) contains a typical informal interest inventory. Talking to parents is another method of determining pupil interests. Simply talking to each pupil is perhaps the most practical and least time-consuming way to discover pupil interests. Also helpful are observations of what pupils do when given choices.

The following example illustrates the use of pupil interests as reflected in teaching materials. A fourth grade pupil had learning problems. Susan's abiding interest focused on horses. To provide additional practice for reading skills, the teacher designed phonic, structural analysis, and comprehension exercises based on library materials related to horses. This provided motivation to complete the basal reading series work.

Susan had difficulty learning to subtract. Using her interest in horses, story problems such as the following were constructed:

> Mr. White had 9 Morgan horses and 4 Pinto horses on his farm. Ms. Fullard bought 2 of the Pinto horses. How many horses did Mr. White have left on his farm? (Mr. White and Ms. Fullard owned farms near Susan's home.)
>
> Susan had 15 horses in the corral. One day the gate was left open and 9 horses got out. How many horses did Susan have left in the corral?

This technique of using materials reflecting Susan's interest in horses lasted the entire school year. Faculty, other pupils, and her parents entered into the location of materials as well as contributing ideas for activities. The challenge to the teacher's skills became motivational. The greatest reward was Susan's academic progress.

Another application activity involves having each pupil list the name of his or her favorite food on the chalkboard. Then the words are classified into the appropriate syllabication generalizations. Response is more positive from this exercise than from constantly using textbook assignments.

Focusing on pupil interests is one way to provide positive reinforcement. Upon satisfactory completion of a lesson, pupils might be allowed to:

- Use a machine such as a tape recorder
- Rent the right to listen to a record

- Play a game
- Read a sports magazine
- Run the school track
- Receive a poster

They might participate in other types of activities depending on the particular pupil's interests. Notice that some of the suggestions above are applicable to older pupils. Many reinforcement materials can be obtained without cost to the teacher. Radio stations will often donate records. A supply of records can be maintained by renting the right to listen to the records rather than giving the records to pupils. I have acquired advertisement posters from motorcycle shops and sports car dealerships that proved to be effective motivation for secondary pupils.

Hints for Personalizing Instruction

Personalizing instruction refers to designing instructional activities around events in the immediate environment using the names of pupils, family members, teachers, and other school staff. Personalizing instruction is very motivational for pupils. It is a way to convey the message, "I recognize you as an individual. You are important. I know you and your world." Using the names of individuals in the immediate environment adds relevancy to learning activities. Pupils attend more readily to activities that are personalized.

Perhaps the most common example of personalized instruction in current use is the language experience approach to teaching reading. Stories are usually generated by pupils after they have shared some event. Kindergarten and primary grade teachers know how much the pupils enjoy reading their stories. It is unfortunate that this form of instruction is seldom used in other ways or with older pupils.

Phonics sounds can be taught readily using pupils' names. Prepare a brief story incorporating events that have meaning for the pupils, such as:

> Mr. Carson is our teacher's name. We went to a party at Mr. Carson's house. Connie brought cupcakes. Jody poured cola. Willie helped clean up after the party.

Have pupils circle all hard *c* sounds.

Using a mysterious theme in these personalized stories creates interest, resulting in attention and participation by pupils:

Henry and Helen went on a long journey. They crossed a high bridge. As they looked over the side of the bridge, a hand slowly came out of the water. ...

Various reading skills, such as sequencing events, can be taught with such passages.

Structural analysis skills can be taught through personalized sentences. For instance, the meaning of the prefix *un-* will become clear when presented in the following manner. Have pupils make up sentences with their names, including a word with the *un-* used as a prefix.

- Jody laughs uncontrollably.
- Sue's chair was uncomfortable.
- Sam said the weather was unpleasant at the picnic.

One college intern taught different levels of reading comprehension to reluctant readers using paragraphs that she wrote about the pupils. These paragraphs referred to events that had happened at school. This was a good idea, but it seemed time-consuming, and the teacher and the pupils might have become bored with repeated use of this technique. After three months, though, both she and those fourth grade pupils continued to enjoy the daily personalized stories.

Arithmetic instruction can be personalized very easily. Worksheets of examples like the following can be constructed, with space left blank for the names. This allows the worksheets to be used with different groups of pupils.

_____ had 10 baseball trading cards.

_____ has 17. How many did _____

and _____ have all together?

Mr. _____ lives 7½ miles from school. His motor-

cycle averages 86 miles per gallon of gasoline. How much gasoline

did Mr. _____ use coming to school this morning?

Personalized instruction can be applied to Social Studies as illustrated in the following example:

Jill, Billy, Tom, and Sharon were boating in the St. Johns River. The motor lost power, and the boat drifted to Hog Island. It soon became apparent that they would not be rescued. Describe how each person contributed to survival of the group.

Of course, teachers don't have time to personalize all learning activities in this manner. However, on those occasions when you find it necessary to prepare supplementary work, these types of activities can be developed. Your efforts will be rewarded by the enthusiasm pupils express in these learning situations. Over time, you will amass a fairly extensive collection of activities that can be personalized for different groups of pupils.

Personalization in the classroom can also be used to foster positive self-concept and to provide review. End-of-period or end-of-school-day reviews are very effective. As pupils are preparing to leave, recall contributions made by various pupils during the period or the day:

What are some of the things we learned today? Well, Jane told us that photosynthesis requires light. Sally showed us that fire requires air to burn by demonstrating with a candle in a jar. Joe ...

A sense of pride is developed as pupils hear their contributions. In order to be sure that all pupils are included, after the pupils leave, put a check on the class roster by the pupils' names you used. The next day, make an effort to identify and remember what other pupils contributed so that all pupils will be recognized.

This review also helps pupils to recall important ideas each day. A typical conversation in the American home every afternoon goes something like this:

"What did you learn at school today?" "Nothing."

The summary technique reinforces what took place at school and assists pupils in providing a somewhat more reassuring answer to "What did you learn today?"

CURRICULUM CONSIDERATIONS

Pupils with mild or moderate behavioral difficulties are expected to participate in the regular classroom curriculum. Because their behaviors may interfere with academic achievement, some of these pupils can be grouped with lower-achieving members of the class. However, some disturbed pupils achieve well and need the intellectual stimulation of an advanced group. One curriculum area that may warrant attention is the affective domain. A brief discussion follows. In addition, suggestions for teaching social skills are presented in the chapters on mental retardation and learning disabilities.

Developing Affective Awareness

Curriculum components to develop affective awareness generally focus on (1) understanding oneself as an individual and (2) understanding oneself as a member of a group and other aspects of group dynamics. Activity themes such as how one responds to stress, personal strengths, interests and limitations, personal goals, attitudes and values, and making responsible choices are among the topics usually included in units to develop understanding of self.

Activity themes for understanding group dynamics related to social influences such as appreciation and acceptance of differences, improving communication skills, drugs and alcohol or other social problems, parental conflict, interpersonal transactions, and respecting authority.

Types of activities used to develop affective awareness include group discussion based on pictures, short stories, or actual situations, role playing, and multimedia packages. The social studies curriculum can provide opportunities to apply analytic skills to problems faced by people. Creative language arts are excellent for enhancing expressive skills, particularly for passive, withdrawn students. Creative writing can be a very effective avenue for developing affective awareness. While teachers are not trained in the use of art, music, literature, and other therapies, they can use these creative subjects in therapeutic ways. Alternative avenues for communication can be provided.

Strategies and materials for developing affective awareness will be described later in this chapter.

SELECTING MATERIALS

Teaching materials for mildly or moderately behaviorally disordered pupils focus on three areas: (1) the use of relevant, everyday materials that reflect the pupils' interests, (2) materials for specialized management techniques, and (3) affective development materials. The use of relevant materials and materials for management was described earlier.

Representative materials for affective development are listed below:

Developing Understanding of Self and Others (DUSO)
American Guidance Service
Circle Pines, Minnesota 55014

Focus on Self-Development
Science Research Associates
259 East Erie Street
Chicago, Illinois 60611

The Coping With Series
American Guidance Service
Circle Pines, Minnesota 55014

FOSTERING UNDERSTANDING OF PUPILS WITH BEHAVIORAL PROBLEMS

Most pupils with behavioral disorders are ostracized or belittled by their peers. Excessively withdrawn pupils are frequently called "scaredy cats" or "dumbbells." "Bully" and "showoff" are terms commonly used with aggressive or acting-out pupils. How can the teacher help other pupils in the classroom to better understand why these pupils behave as they do?

Psychologists, psychiatrists, guidance counselors, special education teachers, and parents of behaviorally disordered children are among the resource persons who may come to the class. While these speakers will not focus their remarks on the behavior of specific pupils in the class, learning why people react differently to the same situation should provide insight into the deviant behaviors of others.

Values clarification may be helpful to promote understanding of atypical pupils. Hypothetical case studies can be constructed for pupils to react to. Magic Circle activities may also be used.

Class discussions and classroom meetings can be used effectively. Teachers will need to structure and guide these activities so that they do not deteriorate into gripe sessions about certain pupils in the class. The focus should be on problem solving.

Books may provide insight to older pupils. *Dibs* (Axline, 1965), and *I Never Promised You a Rose Garden* (Greenberg, 1977) are books with characters who are behaviorally disordered. Some of the Judy Blume books are appropriate for fostering understanding of these pupils.

Activities such as those just described also help behaviorally disordered pupils to better understand themselves. Frequently, these pupils know that they are a "problem" but fail to develop insight into the nature of the problem.

SUMMING UP

Definition of behavioral disorders is complicated by teacher expectations and tolerance level. Behaviors of concern range from being excessively withdrawn to being overly aggressive or acting out. Persistent depression, anxiety, or physical symptoms associated with a particular event are also clues. Immature behaviors in relation to age expectation, such as playing with toys or being overly dependent, can also be indicators.

The regular classroom curriculum should require little modification. Inclusion of an affective development component will usually be helpful.

Special consideration to providing structure and routine in the school environment is essential. Pupils must know explicitly what is expected of them, and these expectations must be consistent.

Many techniques for managing behavior have been discussed. Among these are suggestions for managing surface behaviors and crisis situations. Specialized behavioral programs such as Kounin's group management categories, Magic Circle, teacher effectiveness, reality therapy, and classroom meetings are representative of approaches that might be used.

Hints for increasing motivation of pupils include using pupils' interests in learning activities and for reinforcing desirable behavior. Ways to make learning relevant have also been suggested to influence pupils' motivation. Founded in theory, these practices are equally applicable for all pupils in the classroom.

Each behaviorally disordered pupil will have individual characteristics. You must identify the strengths in order to be successful in teaching the pupil. These pupils need good pedagogy as well as personal support in order to function satisfactorily in society.

REFERENCES AND SELECTED READINGS

Axline, V. *Dibs.* New York: Ballantine, 1965.

Frankel, J. R. *How to Teach About Values.* Englewood Cliffs, N.J.: Prentice-Hall, 1977.

Freed, A. *The Transactional Analysis for Everybody Series.* Sacramento, Calif.: Jalmar Press, 1976.

Gearheart, B. R., and M. W. Weishahn. *The Handicapped Child in the Regular Classroom.* St. Louis: C. V. Mosby, 1976.

George, P. *Better Discipline: Theory and Practice.* Florida Educational Research and Development Council, Vol. 9, No. 4. Gainesville, Fla.: Summer 1975.

Glass, R. M., J. Christiansen, and J. L. Christiansen. *Teaching Exceptional Students in the Regular Classroom.* Boston: Little, Brown, 1982.

Glasser, W. *Reality Therapy.* New York: Harper and Row, 1965.

Glasser, W. *Schools Without Failure.* New York: Harper and Row, 1969.

Gordon, T., and N. Burch. *Teacher Effectiveness Training.* New York: David McKay, 1974.

Greenberg, J. *I Never Promised You a Rose Garden.* New York: New American Library, 1977.

Hardman, M. L., M. W. Egan, and E. D. Landau. *What Will We Do in the Morning?* Dubuque, Iowa: William C. Brown, 1981.

Hewett, F. M., and F. D. Taylor. *The Emotionally Disturbed Child in the Classroom,* 2nd ed. Boston: Allyn and Bacon, 1980.

Kirk, S. A., and J. J. Gallagher. *Educating Exceptional Children,* 3rd ed. Boston: Houghton-Mifflin, 1979.

Kaplan, P., J. Kohfeldt, and K. Sturla. *It's Positively Fun.* Denver: Love, 1974.

Kounin, J. S. *Discipline and Group Management in Classrooms.* New York: Holt, Rinehart, and Winston, 1970.

Kounin, J. S., W. V. Friesen, and E. Norton. "Managing Emotionally Disturbed Children in Regular Classrooms." *Journal of Educational Psychology* 57 (1966): 1–13.

Kounin, J. S., and S. Obradvie. "Managing Emotionally Disturbed Children in Regular Classrooms: A Replication and Extension." *Journal of Special Education* 2 (1968): 129–135.

Long, N. J., and R. G. Newman. "Managing Surface Behavior of Children in School." In N. J. Long, W. C. Morse, and R. G. Newman (eds.), *Conflict in the Classroom*. Belmont, Calif.: Wadsworth, 1980.

Quay, H. C. "Dimensions of Problem Behavior and Educational Programming." In P. S. Gaurbard (ed.), *Children Against Schools*. Chicago: Follett, 1969.

Reinert, H. R. *Children in Conflict*, 2nd ed. St. Louis: C. V. Mosby, 1980.

Rhodes, W. C., and J. L. Paul. *Emotionally Disturbed Deviant Children*. Englewood Cliffs, N.J.: Prentice-Hall, 1978.

Turnbull, A. P., and J. B. Schulz. *Mainstreaming Handicapped Students: A Guide for the Classroom Teacher*. Boston: Allyn and Bacon, 1979.

Van Nagel, C. *Van Nagel Diagnostic Series Packet*. Jacksonville, Fla.: Super Systems, 1980.

Walker, J. E., and T. M. Shea. *Behavior Modification: A Practical Approach for Educators*. St. Louis: C. V. Mosby, 1976.

CHAPTER THREE

Mental Retardation

Mentally retarded, slow learner, cognitively disadvantaged—these are among the terms used to describe pupils who require a longer period of time and more repetitions to learn less material than average pupils in a regular classroom. These pupils experience difficulty in their schooling, with academic achievement below grade level.

Since mental retardation is associated with intellectual functioning as measured by intelligence tests, it would seem that identification would be easy. Mildly and moderately mentally retarded individuals generally score between 50 and 75 points on an intelligence test. However, adaptation to societal norms of appropriate behavior can be as important to performance in the classroom as an IQ test score. The following definition formulated by the American Association on Mental Deficiency incorporates these concepts:

> Mental retardation refers to significantly subaverage general intellectual functioning existing concurrently with deficits in adaptive behavior, and manifested during the developmental period.

Grossman (1977, p.11) states that deficits in adaptive behavior are determined by "the effectiveness or degree with which the individual meets the standards of personal independence and social responsibility expected of his age and cultural group."

The nonadaptability in preschool-aged children relates to slow development and maturation in skills such as walking, talking, toilet training, and interaction with other children. Ineffective adaptive behavior may inhibit success during the academic years. These children may exhibit limited incidental learning, difficulty in generalizing, and immature social behavior, and may be somewhat uncoordinated in physical activities. Social and/or economic inadequacy may be evidenced in mildly and moderately mentally retarded adults.

The interaction between intellectual functioning and adaptive behavior may result in one individual with an IQ score of 65 being classified as mentally retarded, while another individual with a similar IQ score might not be classified that way. Level of functioning or adequacy of adjustment is what counts.

This chapter will focus on identification characteristics, special techniques, curriculum, selecting materials, and fostering acceptance of mentally retarded pupils.

RECOGNIZING MILD MENTAL RETARDATION

Eight clues might indicate mild to moderate mental retardation:

1. General academic retardation (slow rate of learning, ineffective problem-solving skills)
2. Poor memory (especially short-term memory)
3. Difficulty with conceptualization (especially abstract concepts)
4. Deficient generalizing ability
5. Slow language development
6. Below-average imaginative and creative abilities
7. Short attention span and low tolerance for frustration
8. Play and social interests below those of peers

By definition, the mentally retarded will not function at the same rate or on the same level as "average" pupils. In fact, the primary characteristic of pupils who are mildly and moderately mentally handicapped is that they do not learn as quickly as average pupils, especially in academics. Memory, conceptualization, generalization, and language ability all have an impact on learning academic tasks. In many other areas, including physical appearance, such pupils are often indistinguishable from any other pupils. While they may have slow preschool development and some inadequacies in adult life, it is the academic environment that causes the most stress. Short attention span and low tolerance for frustration would seem to be natural consequences of this disadvantage in the school environment.

Play and social interests may appear immature for age expectancy. Mentally handicapped pupils may experience little success with games that have complex rules or require complex reasoning strategies. However, motor skills may be average to slightly below average. Some mentally handicapped pupils miss the subtleties of social interaction and therefore function at a less mature level socially.

We need to remember that each mentally retarded pupil will probably not exhibit all of the characteristics described above. Each pupil will have strengths that provide the classroom teacher with avenues for teaching.

An additional caution must be addressed. Some cultural and ethnic groups are more frequently identified as being mildly or moderately mentally retarded. Professional literature is replete with debates concerning the role of environmental deprivation in regard to this group of mentally retarded pupils. Certain intelligence test items are discriminatory against this population. It is highly likely that these pupils are not mentally retarded but lack developmental and readiness experiences for success in a typical academic setting.

USING SPECIAL TEACHING METHODS

Because the mentally retarded require more time and more repetition to learn less material, the following teaching principles should result in more effective learning:

- Use material that matches the developmental level of the pupil. Be sure that success is possible.
- Limit the length of the learning task to be commensurate with the pupil's attention span.
- Present the task in small, sequential steps.
- Introduce few elements of a concept in any period.
- Present concepts in a concrete manner.
- Provide repetition, especially distributed practice.

- Provide for transfer of learning by presenting the same concept in a variety of settings.
- Present learning tasks that are useful in real-life situations.
- Use creative repetition in presenting tasks by varying the presentation slightly to maintain student interest.
- Use the principle of overlearning to teach mastery and to ensure long-term memory of the material.

Keep in mind that the academic needs of the mentally retarded are as individually distinctive as for any other group of pupils.

Fostering Readiness for Learning

Because of the decelerated rate of development and learning, mentally retarded pupils will need a more extended period of readiness activities for academic preparation. These pupils are usually not ready to begin academic reading and mathematics at the same time as normal peers. They will need emphasis on one or more of the following areas:

- Reasoning ability
- Environmental experience
- Language abilities
- Attention span
- Visual discrimination
- Auditory discrimination

Reasoning ability is related to age and intelligence level. If cognitive development of mildly and moderately mentally retarded pupils is viewed from the perspective of Piaget's developmental stages, few progress to the formal operations stage. While it appears that mildly and moderately mentally retarded pupils progress more slowly through the sensorimotor, preoperational, and concrete operations stages, cognitive development usually truncates at this last stage. These pupils may not mentally develop abilities associated with the formal operations stage.

This means that during the primary grades these slower-learning pupils will need emphasis on activities to foster reasoning and thinking abilities that typically develop at these earlier stages. Sensorimotor activities basically refer to physically exploring the environment, which implies that primary teachers will provide activities that require manipulation of concrete objects.

During the preoperational stage of cognitive development (normally two to seven years of age) individuals use perceptual experience rather than logical reasoning to make decisions. This implies that pupils in this stage will act based on their experience instead of thinking about thinking or planning ahead. Conceptual thinking at this stage involves forming mental images that represent a specific event. These mental images are reflected in imitative play—for example, playing school or going to work. Remember that the cognitive development of the mentally retarded will be below chronological age. Varied experiences should be provided for these pupils to enhance the association of mental images of these events. Having pupils participate in simulations in primary and elementary grades will be helpful.

Another important characteristic of this stage is language development. During this stage labels are used first in a limited way; for example, all females are "mother." The concept of different classes develops gradually. In the early preoperations stage of development children generally consider a problem from only one aspect. They may not retain and apply several bits of information to the problem. Since the mentally retarded child will pass through this stage more slowly and at a later age, educational implications include providing extensive experience in conjunction with language development activities. New concepts to be learned may need to be presented in simpler terms than would be required for average pupils.

During the concrete operations stage of cognitive development (normally seven to eleven years of age) logical reasoning progresses less by trial and error and more by thinking out possible consequences in advance of action. However, this logical reasoning is based on what the child has experienced concretely. The mildly and moderately mentally retarded will usually not progress beyond this stage of cognitive development. Since these pupils will be functioning at this level during the late middle school and secondary school years, instruction must be designed to maximize learning. While it may not be possible to force a pupil to a higher level of reasoning ability, learning should not be severely hampered if the teacher presents the instruction on a level and in a manner that the pupil can comprehend. Material should be presented in a consistent, stable, and simple manner in which directions can be followed step by step.

The thrust of this discussion is for you to provide "learning by doing" activities. These slower-learning pupils will benefit from practical, concrete experiences throughout their school years.

Although the overall goals of academic, social, and vocational competence are the same for mentally retarded pupils as for average pupils, the goals must be adjusted to a basic level because of the slow rate of learning, the need for more repetition, and the mastery of less material.

Many school districts have identified basic minimum skills for each subject at each grade level. This usually becomes the curriculum for slow-learning pupils. The curriculum should focus on those skills and concepts that have practical application for everyday living. As each unit of work is prepared for the class, select those objectives that will be most useful in preparing the mentally retarded for independence in later life. For example, learning about proper nutrition has far more practical value than learning atomic structure.

The *environmental experience* of many of these pupils may be characterized by a lack of the types of stimulation that prepare them for success in school. Limitation to academic progress may be imposed by such factors as different sociocultural mores and language differences. The following are among the activities that can be used to provide experiences that will prepare these pupils to be more successful with academic work:

- Field trips
- Films
- Role-playing social situations
- Sensory-motor activities (cutting with scissors, climbing)
- Walks in the immediate environment to notice the world around them
- Opportunities to talk about family members

Language ability will usually be below age expectation in mildly and moderately mentally retarded pupils. However, verbal language used in daily life may not be different from that of average pupils. Many of these pupils come from environmental backgrounds that have not been conducive to development of language skills. These factors indicate a need for an intensive readiness program of language activities. For sample activities and suggested books, refer to Chapters Five and Six. Numerous language development kits are available. Among the most popular are the *Peabody Language Development Kits*, available from American Guidance Services, and *Distar Language I* and *II*, available from Science Research Associates.

Attention span will need to be commensurate with academic expectations. While the length of the task may require some modification, positive reinforcement techniques may be used to increase attention span. Some helpful techniques follow:

1. Start with moderately short tasks.

2. Allow pupils to cut and color, listen to a record, receive a star or sticker, or play an academic game if the task is finished to acceptable criteria. Slowly increase the task requirements and shorten the time required to complete the task.

3. Chart the minutes that pupils remain on task. Encourage pupils to "beat their own record." Be sure they are aware that it is important to stay on task.

4. Give pupils praise or points to be exchanged for a reward if they work on task until a timer rings. Start by setting the timer for a short time and gradually expand the task and shorten time requirements.

5. Teach on a concrete rather than an abstract level.

6. Give assignments that pupils are capable of achieving.

7. Allow pupils to move to a different desk or table between segments of a task. For example, when they complete one row of arithmetic problems, they may complete the next row in a different location.

8. Make assignments that are relevant to real life.

9. Combine a motor activity with cognitive tasks such as role playing a reading story or social studies concept.

Visual discrimination relates to recognizing and remembering shapes of symbols such as letters and numbers. You need to emphasize relevant cues in your teaching as less intelligent pupils tend to be attracted to all cues observed. Some types of visual discrimination activities follow:

1. Place cardboard footprints in a pattern on the floor. Have pupils repeat the pattern by matching their left and right feet to the correct footprints.

2. Play command games using prepositional phrases such as "through the door," "above the table," and "to the left side of."

3. Give pupils a page of newspaper advertisements. Have them circle all of the different formations of the letter *a*.

4. Have pupils match lower- and upper-case letters.
5. Have pupils find hidden objects in pictures.
6. Have pupils reproduce block design patterns.
7. Use sewing yarn or weaving activities.
8. Have pupils locate names in a telephone directory.
9. Have pupils draw configurations around words and symbols.

Auditory discrimination refers to differentiating and remembering sounds such as letters and words. Auditory discrimination may be improved by the following types of activities:

1. Record the voices of class members for pupils to identify.
2. As you read a list of words, have pupils raise their hands every time they hear a particular sound such as "*b*each, cat, *b*ean, *b*utter, rope."
3. Randomly alternate two sounds such as p and f. Have pupils signal each time they hear the p sound.
4. Have pupils identify the rhyming words after hearing a poem or nursery rhyme.

More extensive lists of auditory discrimination activities can be found in the chapters on hearing impairment and speech and language impairment. An additional source of activities can be found in reading readiness materials, as well as the phonics exercises that accompany basal reading materials.

Using Multisensory Teaching Techniques

Multisensory teaching techniques include presenting information to pupils through two or more learning modalities. For example, using a filmstrip with a sound track presents information through the visual and auditory senses. Tactile (touch) sensation is often combined with kinesthetic (motor) sensation. This combination is frequently referred to as the *haptic modality*. When you have pupils trace a sandpaper letter while saying the name of the letter, visual, auditory, tactile, and kinesthetic information is being presented.

Poor information processing is among the manifestations of mental retardation. Multisensory teaching techniques have been recommended as an attempt to improve the information-processing abilities of these pupils. Combined sensory stimulation should strengthen the information signals or stimuli passing through the central nervous system. Exercise caution, however, because some pupils become overstimulated.

Some examples of multisensory teaching follow:

1. Using the Language Master or similar devices
2. Using motion pictures
3. Using filmstrips with sound
4. Using books with follow-along records
5. Using talking calculators
6. Tracing letters or words on textural surfaces while saying the sounds
7. Tracing letters or words on the backs of pupils' hands while saying them
8. Walking on tape letter while saying the name or sound
9. Using dramatizations

It should be noted that multisensory techniques involve pupils in active learning.

Combining Motor Activities and Cognitive Tasks

There has been much debate about the efficacy of perceptual–motor training resulting in improved academic achievement. The consensus is that perceptual–motor training may improve the neurological learning system, but if you want academic advances, direct teaching is needed. However, correlations have been shown between certain types of perceptual–motor activities and academic achievement. Piaget and other developmental psychologists emphasize the importance of motor activity in the earlier developmental periods, the lack of which is characteristic of school–aged retarded pupils.

The point to be made here is that a human being is an integrated entity; therefore, it makes sense to combine motor activities and cognitive tasks.

Perhaps Bryant Cratty (1969b) has most lucidly summarized the major relationships and advantages in combining motor activities and cognitive tasks. The major points follow:

1. One must be able to develop accuracy in movement to reflect the intellect. As Bannatyne and Bannatyne (1973, p. 10) state, "the

only way 'out of' our bodies for expressive or communicative purpose is through motor activity."

2. Appropriate levels of arousal or alertness can be facilitated through motor movements. It appears that muscle tension from moderate activity will result in activation of optimum levels of arousal to perform cognitive tasks.

3. Participation in active games is motivational in learning cognitive concepts. Given the choice of completing a phonics workbook page or building a phonics ladder, there is little doubt about which activity is more motivational.

4. Attention span can be increased by lengthening the time of the motor activity. Pupils must focus on the task for a longer period of time.

5. Self-concept can be improved as the quality of motor movements gets better. It has been shown that perceptual–motor abilities of some mentally retarded pupils decline during the early teens. Repeated failure in games and similar activities has been suggested as a possible cause. Attention to improving the quality of motor movements would probably result in higher esteem for these pupils.

6. The kinesthetic learning modality has long been advocated as an effective teaching method for certain pupils including the mentally retarded. Using motor activities as a learning channel is a common practice among early childhood educators. Typically, this important learning channel is neglected as pupils progress upward through the grades.

7. Problem solving can be applied to decisions about motor movements. Pupils can devise alternative strategies for accomplishing specified motor tasks.

These points indicate that you should at least try combining motor activities with cognitive tasks. It appears that the probability for successful learning will be enhanced. The following are examples of activities that combine motor movements with cognitive tasks:

1. Place vocabulary or math facts to be learned in the squares while playing hopscotch.

2. Have pupils write spelling words on small cards or strips of paper; then cut the words into syllables. Scramble the pieces and reconstruct the words.

3. Distribute cards (some with arithmetic problems and some with answers) randomly among pupils in the class. Have pupils move from their desks to another place in the room and read the problems on their cards. Then let the pupils with the correct answers carry their cards to the person with the problem.

4. Have pupils walk a tape ladder on the floor while listening to a musical scale to learn about musical pitch.

5. To demonstrate the concept of compound words, have two pupils hold a word card with the individual words; then physically move the individual word cards together and apart.

6. Have pupils choose the correct letters you name from a scrambled assortment of magnetic letters.

7. Demonstrate the concept of cooperation by conducting a three-legged race.

8. Have pupils form two lines of unequal length to illustrate the concepts of *longer* and *shorter.*

9. To develop comprehension of sequence, give several pupils sentence strips, each containing a historical fact or event in the story. Have the pupils physically arrange themselves in the order in which the events occurred.

10. Use manipulative arithmetic aids.

Teaching for Generalization

Poor ability to generalize something learned in one setting to another setting is characteristic of mentally retarded pupils. For instance, a pupil may know how to compute $\begin{array}{r} 2 \\ + 2 \\ \hline 4 \end{array}$ but may not recognize that $2 + 2 = 4$ is the same thing. Once a skill has been mastered, relate the skill to as many areas of practical use as possible.

For example, when the concept of negotiation to settle disputes between countries is presented in Social Studies class, other applications of the negotiation process can be discussed or role played. Examples might be negotiating:

• The purchase of a car

• A reinforcement menu for a behavioral project

• The selection of physical education activities

Good teachers seem to intuitively interrelate skills learned in school with the use of the skills in other situations. Pointing out the initial sound *st* on the large stop sign at the end of the school driveway, walking around the block to discover the functional use of odd and even numbers, and relating the feeling of driving around a sharp curve to centrifugal force are examples of helping pupils generalize school knowledge to other settings. Field trips provide excellent opportunities to reinforce generalization–application activities.

Hints to Improve Memory

One characteristic associated with mental retardation is difficulty with memory. Information must be maintained in short–term memory, encoded in a meaningful organization, and transferred to long–term memory. Transfer from immediate short–term to long–term memory appears to be the problem with mentally retarded. Lerner (1981, p. 186) states that "many factors have an effect on memory: the child's intensity of attention, meaningfulness of material, interest in the subject, and the amount of drill and overlearning." These factors have definite implications for teachers in regard to improving memory.

Attention to task can be stimulated in several ways:

1. *Active involvement.* Perform a science experiment instead of reading about a scientific principle.
2. *Using movement.* Walk and verbalize a number line instead of verbalizing only.
3. *Working for a goal.* Have pupils set a goal before the task such as proposing to learn five specific spelling words.
4. *Working for a reward.* Specify a reward (star, point, game playing) contingent upon successful completion of a task.
5. *Varying the rate of the presentation.* Present material at varying rates instead of using a monotonous pattern of presentation.
6. *Varying speech patterns.* Vary the pitch of the voice, the rate of speech, and inflection in speaking to prevent monotony.

Several techniques can be used to make the material to be learned more meaningful. Material becomes more relevant when it is related to past knowledge and experience:

1. *Using applications.* Loosen a tight metal jar top by running hot water over it instead of reading about how metals expand when heated.

2. *Practicing imagery.* Have pupils close their eyes and form a mental picture of the attributes of a word such as number of letters and configurations, or form a mental picture associating a word with experience such as relating the word *pouring* to the act of pouring.

3. *Applying verbal association.* Construct a verbalization to relate facts. ("In 1492 Columbus sailed the ocean blue.")

4. *Reconstructing verbalizations.* Describe an event in the pupils' own words instead of restating the event exactly as presented in the book or in your own words.

Focusing skills and content to be learned on something of interest to pupils will facilitate memory. Refer to Chapter Two for suggested activities.

Drill and overlearning are necessary for most school learning. Practice should be spaced over a period of time, with more frequent repetition in the beginning stages. Practice should continue until pupils can retrieve the information with ease. Continued periodic practice will aid retention.

Most of the preceding suggestions have involved some form of rehearsal. Other techniques related to rehearsal have proven useful:

1. *Recognizing a pattern.* See the similarity in the names *Dan* and *Jan*. Notice that all building numbers on one side of the street are odd.

2. *Enhancing mental imagery.* Use color, size, and shape in visual presentations. Use variation in auditory presentations.

3. *Cumulative repetition.* Examples are 2—24—246—2468; 1—loo—look.

4. *Chunking.* This is repetition of units or syllables. For a phone number, 646-2858, this could be 646—28—58.

5. *Oral rehearsal.* Have pupils vocalize or tell the information to themselves during practice.

6. *Written or haptic rehearsal.* Pupils write, copy, or trace the material to be learned.

Tips for Teaching Reading and Language Arts

The goals and instructional sequences for reading and other language arts subjects are the same for slow-learning pupils as they are for average pupils. The major differences are in regard to extended readiness training, gradual introduction of new skills and concepts, shorter segments of material, presentation of instruction from the concrete or semiabstract levels to the abstract level, and providing repetition for overlearning. As discussed earlier, mentally retarded pupils will need a longer readiness period before introducing reading skills. Reading instruction will begin with sight words. Sight words can be taught by labeling objects in the classroom, associating words with pictures, acting out the meanings of the words, and other activities that associate meanings with the visual symbols.

Kolstoe (1976) recommends that phonics be introduced in two-sound words such as *so*. Three-, four-, and five-sound words are presented as each earlier skill is mastered. Individual letter sounds are taught next, followed by sound blending.

Compound words, affixes, and syllabication are among the structural analysis skills taught. The idea of finding the little words that make up the big words is a helpful approach to introducing compound words. The most commonly used prefixes, such as *un-*, *in-*, *im-*, and *de-*, should be taught. A game format is useful and motivational for teaching affixes. The vowel–consonant–consonant–vowel (VCCV) rule and the vowel–consonant–vowel (VCV) syllabication rule should be taught, as well as pointing out that each sounding vowel represents a syllable (Kolstoe, 1976).

Vocabulary and comprehension should be stressed in all reading lessons. Use of context clues should be emphasized.

The suggestions for teaching grammatical language structures in Chapters Five and Six are appropriate for working with the mentally retarded. Other activities are described at the beginning of this chapter.

Conventions of punctuation are best taught by a functional approach. Language experience stories provide an excellent format. The following example has been used effectively.

A pupil generates a story, which is written on the chalkboard without capital letters, periods, or commas:

> our class went on a study trip to the marine science center when
> the bus came to take us joe and kurt were missing they got to
> school just when mr smith said we had to leave they told us there
> was a wreck on the bridge so their father had to wait

Next, you read the story without expression and then ask the pupils for punctuation to "make the story sound right." The use of capitalization for beginning sentences and proper nouns is elicited. Activities like this help pupils recognize the purposes for using these conventions.

For practice, choose paragraphs from high-interest, low-reading-level materials (usually the school newspaper), and type them without the punctuation feature the group is learning. Next, pupils correct the passages. Then they use the original materials for self-checking.

While the preceding example focuses on the use of the language experience approach for one type of language arts activity, all aspects can be taught this way. It can be a very effective method of integrating the teaching of reading and language arts in a meaningful fashion.

Commercial writing programs can be used successfully with mentally retarded pupils. Current series have an extensive selection of materials, aids, and activities from which to choose.

Teaching Arithmetic

The goals of the mathematics program for mentally retarded pupils should focus on the applications of arithmetic to everyday living and working. The curriculum should include instruction in the computation processes, time, money, measurement, and consumer arithmetic.

Effective instructional techniques should utilize the same principles that have appeared repeatedly in this chapter. Instruction should be:

1. Structured
2. Developmental and sequential
3. Concrete
4. In short segments with limited changes between steps
5. Repetitive
6. Practical

The major difficulties encountered in teaching arithmetic to mildly retarded pupils are the level of abstraction and the level of reading. Both of these hindrances can be accommodated by modifying instructional techniques and reading requirements.

Other practices that will facilitate the learning of arithmetic by mildly retarded pupils are using consistent language, routine formats, and color coding, and providing reference charts or personal dictionaries. Because these slow learners do not "shift gears" readily, consistent language will prevent confusion. For example, "times," "multiply," and "find the product" are some of the terms you might use to explain a multiplication problem. It is best to use the same term until pupils have a thorough understanding of the process. Different language can then be paired with what was previously used; for example, "12 times 11" can be restated as "11 multiplied by 12."

Material should be developed in a standard format until pupils master the concept. For instance, when the pupils' accuracy level is satisfactory with $+ \frac{2}{2}$, then $2+2 =$ can be introduced.

Color coding can be an effective technique in teaching arithmetic. One way to use color is to show each step in a different color:

yellow = division	6 4	yellow
blue = multiplication	6)3 8 4	
purple = subtraction	3 6	blue
brown = bring down	purple 2 4	brown
	2 4	blue

Of course, color cues can be used in many other ways.

Reference charts or personal dictionaries might include such things as addition, subtraction, multiplication, and division facts; illustrative examples; process signs with common words associated with the signs; clock faces with word and arrow cues; and measurement equivalencies. These charts or dictionaries help pupils to function independently.

Memory difficulties will be improved by the meaningfulness of the material. Many of books with practical activities suitable for slow learners have been published. Newspaper advertisements, application forms, checking materials, and similar items can usually be obtained without cost. Addresses for materials are presented later in this chapter.

Manipulative materials are readily available. Examples of appropriate aids follow:

- Counting blocks
- Abacus
- Number lines including tactile models
- Place value and equivalency rods
- Clock faces
- Realia
- Marbles
- Cups

- Thermometers
- Money

Kolstoe (1976) suggests a list of desired outcomes in arithmetic from preschool through vocational levels. Reisman (1972) provides a mathematics inventory, analysis of some common errors, and suggestions for remediation.

Teaching Social Skills

Many mentally retarded individuals often develop poor self-concepts. This would seem to be a natural consequence because the mentally retarded are more subject to failure in the academic setting than more competent pupils. A positive learning environment that provides successful experiences is helpful. Much of this low esteem might be prevented if instruction could be modified for pupils who learn more slowly and need more repetition and concrete experiences than average pupils. This is not to imply that these pupils should never experience failure or criticism. They must learn to deal with failure and criticism just as all children must.

While an individual's pattern of social behavior is somewhat dependent on self-concept, you can be instrumental in helping pupils to develop acceptable social skills.

Many mentally retarded pupils will be unaware of the nuances of emotional reactions of other individuals. To facilitate recognition, understanding, and proper response of emotional reactions, use pictures or role playing of situations such as the following:

- Happiness
- Sadness
- Anger
- Fear
- Disgust

The "teachable moment" should be capitalized on when situations that demonstrate these and other emotions occur in the school setting. For instance, if a pupil has some good fortune, such as going on an exciting trip, guide the other pupils in making appropriate reactions. Another example might be related to a death in a pupil's family. Many pupils benefit from instruction in the proper way to behave in such situations.

Numerous opportunities to develop responsibility and self-management are available in the classroom. A few suggestions follow:

- Caring for plants and animals
- Cleanup activities
- Being prepared to start activities
- Being on time
- Completing tasks
- Role playing an employer

Social interaction skills may be deficient in mildly and moderately mentally retarded pupils. Opportunities to develop more appropriate social skills include the following:

- Exchanging proper greetings
- Engaging in play activities
- Seeking alternative strategies to fighting
- Developing a sense of humor
- Knowledge of whom to trust
- Participating in small group work
- Engaging in social conversation

Slower-learning pupils generally benefit from role playing or sociodrama to learn proper behavior. It is helpful to role play alternative responses when an inappropriate occurrence has taken place in the school setting.

MODIFYING THE CURRICULUM

The curriculum for mildly and moderately mentally retarded pupils is similar to the regular curriculum. At the elementary level, reading, mathematics, language arts, science, and social studies are included in the curriculum. At the secondary level, attention to certain areas will probably help these pupils function better in the classroom. Goals will need to be modified to individual needs for these slower-learning pupils.

Using the Unit Approach

The unit approach to organization of the curriculum has long been advocated for mentally retarded pupils. In using the unit approach, a theme, concept, or interest is selected, with all school subjects being taught based on this topic. For instance, the grocery store might be a selected topic. Reading, language arts, mathematics, career education, and social skills lessons would be developed around the grocery store theme. Objectives in these subjects will need to be individualized to each pupil's functional level.

Since mentally retarded pupils perform poorly in seeing interrelationships and perform better and benefit more from practical application of skills, the unit approach appears useful for this group of pupils. This approach to curriculum organization is appropriate for other pupils as well; therefore, units can be planned for the class with activities at the lower functional levels of the unit being selected for the mentally retarded.

SELECTING MATERIALS

As mentally retarded pupils progress in school, most textbooks will be written on a reading and conceptual level above the pupils' abilities. Although curriculum content can be taught through specialized teaching techniques, appropriate materials are readily available. Materials that are appropriate for mentally retarded pupils should have the following features:

1. Materials should be written on a lower reading level than average.
2. Materials should have simple and consistent directions.
3. Materials should be ordered in shorter than average segments.
4. Skill development should be sequential in nature.
5. Only one skill should be introduced in each segment with enough practice exercises to ensure mastery.
6. Frequent opportunities for feedback should be provided.
7. There should be provisions for assessing pupil progress.
8. Content should be relevant and practical.
9. Suggestions for concrete and semiabstract learning activities should be available.
10. Periodic review should be provided.

Materials listed below are representative of the wide variety that is available. Reading programs that are used extensively with mentally retarded pupils include the following:

Distar Reading
Science Research Associates
259 East Erie Street
Chicago, Illinois 60611

Remedial Reading Drills
Hegge, Kirk, and Kirk
George Wahr Publishing Company
Ann Arbor, Michigan 48106

Sullivan Reading Series
Behavioral Research Laboratories
Box 577
Palo Alto, California 94303

Commonly used arithmetic programs include:

Distar Arithmetic
Science Research Associates
259 East Erie Street
Chicago, Illinois 60611

Pacemaker Arithmetic Program
Fearon Publishers
6 Davis Street
Belmont, California 94002

Stern Structural Arithmetic
Houghton-Mifflin Company
53 West 43rd Street
New York, New York 10036

Me Now and *Me and My Environment* are science curricula designed for the mentally retarded. They are available from:

Hubbard Science
1946 Raymond Drive
Northbrook, Illinois 60062

The publishers below have numerous materials to meet the special needs of mentally retarded pupils:

Frank E. Richards Publishing Company, Inc.
P.O. Box 66
Phoenix, New York 13135

Janus Book Publishers
2501 Industrial Parkway West
Haywood, California 94505

Many multimedia teaching kits designed for the average pupil can be modified to meet the special needs of mentally retarded pupils. Supplemental activities to provide more repetition are the most common modifications needed.

FOSTERING ACCEPTANCE OF THE MENTALLY RETARDED

The fact that mentally retarded individuals are less well accepted has been documented repeatedly. An overall negative attitude toward these slower-learning pupils is a reflection of the larger society. How do these pupils react to subtle messages of rejection, such as not being selected by peers for group work, and not so subtle messages, such as being called "retard," "nitwit," or "moron"? Of course, they are sensitive to these messages and frequently develop a poor self-concept.

What can you do to foster acceptance of these pupils? Simulations can help develop empathy and understanding of the feelings and problems of the mentally retarded. Have the pupils remember and perform a set of simple directions such as:

- Stand up.
- Clap twice.
- Say your name.
- Hop on one foot.
- Say the first line of the Pledge of Allegiance.
- Sit down.

Repeat the directions once. When they realize how difficult it is to remember and carry out these commands, a guided discussion should be conducted to elicit feelings about what it would be like to have these difficulties constantly. A simulation has been used with college students who were given a difficult mathematics problem to solve with a time limit. Success has been rare. After a discussion about their feelings during the activity, they were asked how they would get help in solving the problem. The two most frequent responses are that they would go to a textbook and that they would get someone to help them.

When posed from the viewpoint of mental retardation, they soon realize that the textbook would have little value and that the best method is assistance from another person. This has been an effective technique.

Class discussions of the pupils' feelings when they were "left out" can be useful. Exclusion from adult conversations or not being allowed to accompany an older brother or sister are examples of these situations.

Another technique for fostering acceptance is to conduct a unit on the sensory nervous system in regard to how learning occurs. Individual abilities in learning can be compared to individual abilities in other areas such as art or athletics.

Literature can be helpful in developing understanding. *He's My Brother* (Lasker, 1974), *Like Me* (Brightman, 1976), and *One Little Girl* (Fassler, 1969) are typical of books available about the mentally retarded.

Guest speakers can include parents who have a mentally retarded child and speakers from agencies and organizations such as the Association for Retarded Citizens. Volunteer assistance in conducting a Special Olympics can be a valuable activity.

Special interest stories from newspapers and television programs can serve as the basis for class discussions. Occasionally, television programs and films like *They Call Me Names* can be secured for class viewing. (For information about this film, contact BFA Educational Media, 2211 Michigan Avenue, Santa Monica, California 90404.)

Perhaps the greatest influence on acceptance of the mentally retarded pupil comes from the attitudes and behaviors modeled by you, the teacher. Equal opportunity to perform favored tasks should be provided. Other pupils will be aware if you have genuine respect for the slower learning pupil.

SUMMING UP

Identification of mentally retarded pupils is based on two equally important factors: intellectual ability and adaptive behaviors. Functional ability results from the interaction of these factors. Adequacy of adjustment determines which slow-learning pupils will be mainstreamed in the regular classroom.

Slow rate of learning and poor memory, abstract conceptualizing ability, and generalizing ability are among the characteristics that lead to identification of mildly and moderately mentally retarded pupils.

Other characteristics include slow language and social development, as well as limited creative abilities. As with any group of pupils, each pupil will have strengths on which you can capitalize to enhance learning.

Many of these pupils will benefit from an extended readiness period. Academic achievement should be satisfactory if meaningful material is presented in a "learning by doing" manner with provisions for generalization of knowledge and skills. Multisensory learning experiences can be effective for some mentally retarded pupils. It is also suggested that cognitive learning involve motor movements.

Materials for mentally retarded pupils should provide concrete and semiabstract learning activities to develop concepts in a sequential manner. Teaching practical and relevant material will ensure future success for these pupils. Representative materials have been suggested.

REFERENCES AND SELECTED READINGS

Bannatyne, M., and A. Bannatyne. *Body-Image/Communication.* Rantoul, Ill.: Learning Systems, 1973.

Bereiter, C., and S. Engleman. *Teaching Disadvantaged Children in the Preschool.* Englewood Cliffs, N.J.· Prentice-Hall, 1966.

Brightman, A. *Like Me.* Boston: Little, Brown, 1976.

Cegelka, P. A., and W. J. Cegelka. "A Review of Research: Reading and the Educable Mentally Handicapped." *Exceptional Children* 37 (1970): 187–200.

Cratty, B. J. *Active Learning.* Englewood Cliffs, N.J.: Prentice-Hall, 1971.

Cratty, B. J. *Motor Activity and the Education of Retardates.* Philadelphia: Lea and Febiger, 1969*a*

Cratty, B. J. *Perceptual Motor Behavior and Educational Processes.* Springfield, Ill.: Charles C. Thomas, 1969*b*.

Ebersole, M., N. C. Kephart, and J. B. Ebersole *Steps to Achievement for the Slow Learner.* Columbus, Ohio: Charles E. Merrill, 1968.

Fassler, J. *One Little Girl.* New York: Human Sciences Press, 1969.

Frostig, M., and P. Maslow. *Learning Problems in the Classroom.* New York: Greene and Stratton, 1973.

Gillespie, P. H., and L. E. Johnson. *Teaching Reading to the Mildly Retarded Child.* Columbus, Ohio: Charles E. Merrill, 1974.

Grossman, H. J. (ed.). *Manual on Terminology and Classification in Mental Retardation.* Washington, D.C.: American Association on Mental Retardation, 1977.

Guerin, G., and K. Szatbcky. "Integration Programs for the Mentally Retarded." *Exceptional Children* 41 (1974): 173–179.

Halpern, A. S. "General Unemployment and Vocational Opportunities for EMR Individuals." *American Journal of Mental Deficiency* 78 (1973): 123–127.

Kirk, S. A., J. M. Kliebhan, and J. W. Lerner. *Teaching Reading to Slow and Disabled Learners* Boston: Houghton-Mifflin, 1978.

Kolstoe, O. P. *Teaching Educable Mentally Retarded Children.* New York: Holt, Rinehart, and Winston, 1976.

Lasker, J. *He's My Brother.* Chicago: Albert Whitman, 1974.

Lerner, J. *Learning Disabilities,* (3rd ed.) Boston: Houghton-Mifflin, 1981.

Lowenbraun, S., and J. A. Affleck. *Teaching Mildly Handicapped Children in Regular Classrooms.* Columbus, Ohio: Charles E. Merrill, 1976.

Permenter, N. "Retardate for a Week." *Journal of Rehabilitation* 39 (1973): 18–21, 41.

Reisman, F. K. *A Guide to the Diagnostic Teaching of Arithmetic.* Columbus, Ohio: Charles E. Merrill, 1972.

Spache, E. B. *Reading Activities for Child Involvement.* Boston: Allyn and Bacon, 1976.

CHAPTER FOUR

Giftedness

Who are the gifted? When you're distributing worksheets, one pupil asks, "What do I do now? I'm finished," before the worksheets have reached the last row in the classroom. All of his answers are correct. Another pupil annoys you and her classmates by always suggesting another way to solve a problem. The "lockstep" flow of activities in a typical classroom is disrupted by pupils whose attention is totally focused on a project in which they are interested. Each of these behaviors could mark a pupil with superior abilities. These pupils make positive contributions to the class. Enthusiasm for learning and receptiveness to new ideas can result in other pupils being "sparked" to greater achievement. Gifted pupils who are not achieving well in school present a more complex problem in identification than these examples.

This chapter presents characteristics of gifted pupils, acceptance of pupils with superior abilities, teaching methods, sources of materials, and fostering understanding of the gifted.

IDENTIFYING THE GIFTED

Definitions and concepts of giftedness vary greatly. Discussion of the following terms will help to clarify the focus of this chapter.

Intellectual giftedness can be described as an unusual ability to deal with abstract and symbolic learning. Individuals with intellectual superiority are able to relate facts and ideas about numbers, time, and space in unusual ways. Pupils with intellectual superiority may or may not do well in school.

Academic giftedness involves the skills and abilities necessary to perform well in school-related tasks. Among these skills and abilities are memory, logical reasoning, and ability to make meaningful associations of facts and ideas. Facility in convergent thinking is characteristic of this group of students.

Creativity can be referred to as unique or original production of ideas or products. Creative thought processes result in responses that are unexpected and may be regarded as novel or peculiar. Ideational fluency, flexibility of thinking, originality, and elaboration are elements of creativity. Ideational fluency involves being able to generate a flow of ideas, while flexibility means the ability to modify the flow of information. Originality is the ability to come up with uniquely different relationships or creations. The ability to extend and embellish ideas is elaboration. Redefinition involves finding new uses for products. Divergent thinking is associated with creativity.

Talent can be defined as an unusually high aptitude, ability, or level of performance in a particular field. The most commonly mentioned talents are artistic, musical, physical, mechanical, social, and leadership. The great masters provide examples of the artistically and musically talented, while professional and Olympic athletics exemplify the physically talented. Mechanical talent is illustrated by youngsters who have expert problem-solving abilities with mechanical problems. The socially talented are those who have intuitive sense of appropriate behavior in varied personal interactions. Charismatic qualities are evident in those with leadership talent. They have a knack for influencing followers.

There is much overlapping of these abilities and aptitudes. The academically gifted are usually intellectually gifted; however, the intellectually gifted may not be academically gifted. Controversy continues about the relationship between creativity and intellectual giftedness. Both areas appear to require many of the same abilities. Talent involves a specific ability, while intellectual giftedness and creativity are more global. However, one may be talented, intellectually gifted, and creative. These pupils will have strengths and weaknesses. It is unlikely that they will be superior in all areas. While intellectual giftedness, academic giftedness, creativity, and talent are generally addressed separately in professional literature, they will be treated in a generic manner in this chapter as superior abilities. It is assumed that the talented are receiving appropriate educational training from specialists in their specific talent areas.

Eighteen Clues That Indicate Giftedness

1. Learning commensurate with that expected of older pupils; often reading at an earlier than average age
2. Knowing about things of which other pupils are unaware
3. High ability for abstract and symbolic thinking
4. Curiosity, asking many questions
5. Large vocabulary for age and mature expressive ability
6. Requiring limited exposure and fewer repetitions to learn
7. Extraordinary memory
8. Ability to apply knowledge to unfamiliar situations
9. Good problem-solving ability
10. Attention span long for age
11. Dislike of rigid time schedule
12. Annoyance with details
13. Intense interest in one area
14. Spontaneous and diverse interests
15. High energy level (physical and intellectual)
16. Unusually high standards and goals, self-critical
17. Often thinking faster than they write (can result in sloppy work)
18. Poor study habits that may result in careless work

No student should be expected to exhibit all of these characteristics. Some can be observed more readily in structured academic tasks, while others are best observed in informal settings. Observations of pupil behaviors should therefore be carried out in a variety of settings.

Gifted pupils usually exhibit abilities more advanced than those expected of pupils at their age and grade level. They often learn to read before starting first grade. They are usually curious, ask many questions, and carry on mature dialogue about diverse topics.

Gifted pupils are often bored with repetitious assignments. Sloppy work may result from eagerness to get on to other things. They may be independent and nonconformist.

Ineffective study habits can be a problem for gifted pupils as with any other group of pupils. It is important to remember that gifted pupils can also have any of the handicapping conditions described in other chapters of this book, with the exception of mental retardation. However, some mentally retarded individuals do have innate talents in particular areas such as art, although by definition they do not have the high abstract conceptualization ability that characterizes gifted pupils. There have been numerous cases in which pupils undergoing referral and screening procedures for special services for the handicapped were found to be intellectually gifted, with or without the suspected handicap. We need to employ sophisticated observation skills to try to recognize various implications of pupils' behaviors.

Recognizing the Culturally Different Gifted Pupil

Identifying culturally different gifted pupils is complicated by several factors. Most intelligence tests are biased in favor of those with standard verbal and language facility. Classroom expectations, academic and behavioral, are based on white middle-class values. The following characteristics may indicate superior abilities in people from different cultural backgrounds:

1. Performing better in solving specific problems than abstract problems
2. Performing better on tasks that require reasoning ability
3. More action-oriented
4. Participating and producing more work in individual or small groups than in whole-class activities
5. Often aspiring to higher-status occupations
6. Being motivated by physical activities (games, movement, manipulation of concrete objects)
7. Learning better by visual rather than auditory means
8. Possibly oriented to short-term goals

Most culturally different gifted pupils are "turned on" by visual and physical activities related to the here and now, yet schools tend to focus on sedentary, aural activities with the goal of preparing for the future. Some culturally different pupils lack the skills necessary to succeed in a typical school setting. The structure of many activities does not allow these pupils to demonstrate their superior abilities. These pupils tend to differ from middle-class pupils in the areas of interests and attitudes rather than physical ability and personality. Others hide their abilities because success in traditional schools is not valued in their culture. In fact, they may be ostracized if they cooperate and display their superior abilities in schoolwork. Environmental and sociological differences in pupils' cultures must be considered. Skill is required to observe and correctly interpret the subleties of these pupils' classroom behaviors.

USING SPECIAL TEACHING METHODS

Special teaching methods and enrichment activities are techniques that you can use in the regular classroom to enhance education for gifted pupils. While the focus of this chapter is on pupils with superior abilities, the following suggestions are also beneficial for other pupils in the regular classroom. A discussion of each technique is presented, followed by an illustrative example.

Hints for Counseling Gifted Pupils

While classroom teachers are not trained in counseling techniques, there are some factors that can be addressed in an informal manner. The following are several factors concerning gifted pupils of which you should be aware:

1. *Feelings of isolation.* These result because pupils vary in their rates of development in different areas (physical, social, mental) and may be grouped with pupils at a different developmental level. The gifted pupil may feel left out, although there may be a feeling of superiority as well. Pupils with superior abilities tend to feel like spectators to what is going on even though they are in the middle of it. An analogy might be "feeling alone in a crowd." An observant teacher can use flexible grouping patterns to match more nearly the different developmental levels within the individual pupil. Grouping pupils with similar interests will also benefit these pupils.

2. *Self-criticism.* Many gifted pupils have high goals and become self-critical. This may result, in part, because everyone has expected

them always to know the correct answer. They often find it difficult to admit they don't know an answer and frequently resort to rationalization in this situation. You can help these pupils to set more realistic expectations and to be more accepting of their performance. An atmosphere that reduces the anxiety of making errors is helpful.

3. *Grading.* Most schoolwork is evaluated on a conformity of one right answer. Confusion can result for pupils who spend part of their school time in a regular program and part in a resource program for the gifted. Convergent thought is rewarded in the regular school program, but divergent thought is rewarded in the special class. It would be helpful for pupils with superior abilities, as well as other pupils, to recognize that there is more than one way to approach a situation. This will better prepare all pupils to live in the real world.

4. *Concern over moral and social issues.* Gifted pupils may tend to be unusually concerned about human problems such as hunger and injustice. Providing opportunities for discussion and problem-solving activities may provide some outlet for this anxiety. Another outlet may be involvement in local projects designed to relieve some of these problems. It is a good practice to help pupils develop value systems and recognize them as their own. Be careful not to try to indoctrinate pupils with your values.

5. *Self-concept.* Pupils who generate and express unusual ideas may be looked upon as odd. This may result in feelings of inferiority. Fostering an attitude of acceptance of individual differences in the classroom and an attitude of self-worth will help these pupils to feel better about themselves.

6. *Critical attitudes toward others.* Pupils with superior abilities may view other individuals in a condescending manner. They may show little tolerance for those with lesser ability. Counseling can help these pupils to realize that their superior abilities are a gift, an accident of birth. When pupils acknowledge the fact that they had no control over the fact that they have intellectually superior abilities, they can accept responsibility for the wise use of their abilities and talents.

7. *Emotional problems.* Pupils with superior abilities are subject to the same types of emotional distress as all pupils. In addition, these pupils must cope with the fact that they are different. Pupils

usually respond positively when you use an honest and straight-forward approach. Help these pupils to recognize and accept this difference from the norm. Because they are bright, they can use their insight to deal with problems they may experience.

Motivating the Underachieving Gifted

Underachievement is a complex problem; consequently, there is no simple solution. One common technique used by parents and teachers for trying to motivate underachieving gifted pupils is to admonish them to try harder. "You could do better if you would try harder." This statement implies failure. Since low performance of many gifted pupils appears to be partly the result of poor self-concept, the problem is compounded by this constant urging to trying harder. Attempts to improve motivation in this way have proven to be ineffective. Counseling and other such procedures for remediating these psychological difficulties are not within the realm of the regular classroom teacher, although there are things you can do to improve motivation.

Perhaps the most influential force in motivating underachieving gifted pupils is the relationship with the teacher. Teacher characteristics that may be helpful in establishing the desired relationship are acceptance of pupils, genuine interest in pupils, concern for pupils and their academic progress, and flexibility in dealing with pupils and classroom events. These characteristics are useful in establishing an atmosphere of trust and mutual respect. The positive effects of this relationship on motivation and learning can be understood by recalling your own experience with your favorite teacher. In all probability you felt secure and encouraged to risk (try) within the atmosphere created by this teacher.

Factors within the educational program, other than this special relationship with the teacher, that may stimulate motivation for academic improvement include a variety of available materials, self-selection of alternative learning activities, consideration of preferred learning style, attention to special interests, improvement of study skills, remediation of basic skills, and behavior modification techniques.

The textbook is the basic source for teaching in the typical classroom. Overreliance on the textbook can curtail motivation. The challenge to meet unique educational needs of pupils with superior abilities can be fulfilled in part by access to a variety of materials. A desire for self-selection of alternative learning activities is a characteristic of pupils with superior abilities. Flexibility on your part in providing alternative learning activities can be rewarding. Pupils feel some control over their fate when they are given choices.

Many pupils are motivated by an action-oriented approach to learning, yet an auditory–verbal approach with emphasis on reading is most frequently used in the average classroom. Attention to preferred learning style may stimulate pupil effort.

Providing the opportunity to pursue individual interests can have a positive effect on unmotivated pupils. Pupils with superior abilities usually have a wider range of interests than average students; therefore, the regular curriculum without enrichment can be constraining.

While some gifted pupils achieve moderately well even with poor study skills, a detrimental effect is experienced by others. Inefficient study habits prevent achievement commensurate with ability. A poor foundation in the basic skills can limit achievement for this group of pupils as well as with other pupils. Teachers assume that pupils with superior abilities readily master basic skills and characteristically these pupils will not ask for help. Nevertheless, astute observation will reveal any impediment to learning. Remediation of basic skills is a prerequisite to achievement for this group.

The use of behavior modification techniques may provide motivation for underachieving pupils. Substituting aversive tasks with those more preferred by the pupils may result in improved attitudes toward learning. When pupils reach a satisfactory level of task involvement, previously attempted tasks may be gradually reintroduced. The use of external rewards may prove to be effective. Grandma's Law, "If you clean your plate, you can have dessert," is in effect in numerous classrooms at the present time. A written or verbal contract states that if pupils satisfactorily complete certain tasks, they can have a specified reward. Reward systems can be planned with the pupils.

As stated earlier, these pupils have unusual abilities and are therefore capable of providing insight into solutions for their own problems. Cooperative problem solving may be possible if a positive relationship with you, the counselor, or a peer support group is established.

The suggestions for motivating underachieving pupils with superior abilities can also be effective with other nonachievers in the classroom. While many of these suggestions appear to effect short-term results, once the pupils begin to have academic success, habits and attitudes conducive to school progress are being developed.

Using Cooperative Planning

Several factors lend credence to cooperative planning of educational activities between pupils with superior abilities and the teacher. Among these factors are that pupils with superior abilities:

- Usually dislike drill and repetitious activities.
- May be resistant to specific and limiting directions.
- Are motivated by cooperative determination of learning activities occurring simultaneously.
- Motivated by alternative choices.

Cooperative planning offers an alternative that may prevent development of problems related to these factors. Many pupils with superior abilities become bored with the amount of repetition required by typical pupils in the classroom. This may lead to "tuning out" and underachievement. Many of these pupils are independent and resist being told what to do and how to do it. Adherence to rigid conformity prevents pupils with superior abilities from developing their potential; therefore, cooperative planning is an educationally sound practice.

As a unit of work is being planned for a class, it is wise to involve gifted pupils in planning additional activities, especially on a higher cognitive level. Varied interests can be taken into account. This approach also relieves you of the time and effort required to develop these extra activities.

How to Use Brainstorming

Brainstorming is a method of encouraging the development of creative ideas. It requires divergent production. The basic process in brainstorming is to pose a problem and then generate as many ideas for solution as possible.

Proper atmosphere is essential if brainstorming is to be successful. An emotional climate that nourishes imagination is necessary. Pupils must feel free to express creative thoughts without fearing ridicule. The following rules are helpful in establishing an appropriate atmosphere for brainstorming activities:

1. No idea can be criticized.
2. All ideas are acceptable, no matter how unusual.
3. Pupils are urged to generate as many ideas as possible.

A simple way to conduct a brainstorming session is to write a problem on the chalkboard. Next, pupils are encouraged to jot down as many ideas as they can. These ideas are then compiled and reviewed for possible solutions. The best solution is selected. For instance, the problem might center on solutions for a chewing gum company that had overproduced 1 million pieces of gum. Possible solutions might include new advertising or marketing procedures as well as new uses for chewing gum.

You are probably thinking that brainstorming is a desirable activity, but how can another thing be added to the school day? Brainstorming is suitable for such times as:

1. The extra time when your class is ready to proceed to the lunchroom and you are notified that the lunch line is running 25 minutes late.
2. A rainy Friday afternoon when both you and the pupils are anxious for the bell.
3. After a long testing period to release tension.

After pupils with superior abilities have practiced the rules for brainstorming, they can engage in these activities without teacher supervision. This provides creative enrichment and effective and productive use of class time by these pupils. Brainstorming is a viable method for solving classroom problems.

Developing Problem-Solving and Thinking Skills

Problem solving is an active process of searching for alternative solutions through which pupils can be guided. Problem solving can be an ongoing activity in the regular classroom. It is an excellent way to provide indepth learning and should be an integral part of the school experience. Basic skills, such as the use of reference books, can be taught in conjunction with problem-solving activities. Extra time is required only to check on pupils' progress and to provide guidance for the next step. The steps in problem solving are as follows:

1. The problem must be identified and described. Pupil interests, subject matter, and the daily news are only a few sources for identification of problems. There are usually controversial events occurring in the school or on the local, national, or international level that provide stimulating problems on which to focus.

2. The next step involves finding facts related to the problem. Relationships among these facts are identified.

3. Possible solutions to the problem are generated by the pupils.

4. Pupils now evaluate each of the proposed solutions. This involves much cause-and-effect reasoning. The most favored solution is selected by the pupils.

5. Verification by testing reveals the worth of this solution or the need for modification.

The following illustration is provided as an example of the problem-solving process.

Problem: A learning disabled pupil has just been put into the classroom and is being ostracized by his peers.

Facts: Facts are gathered from several sources.

  1. A learning disabled adult invited as a guest speaker explains problems she had in school and the types of modifications that helped.

  2. Library research reveals what learning disabilities are and how they affect different pupils.

  3. The special education teacher explains the specific problems of the new pupil in the class. The following facts that appear to be causing most of the problem are identified.

    a. The new pupil will need help reading some of the textbooks.

    b. The new pupil has difficulty finishing tests in the same time allotted to other pupils.

    c. The new pupil has poor motor coordination resulting in lack of skill in certain games.

Solutions: 1. Classmates can read assignments for the new pupil.

  2. Books can be recorded.

  3. Time to complete tests can be extended.

  4. The number of test items can be limited for the new pupil.

  5. A remedial physical training program to improve motor coordination can be planned for the new pupil.

Evaluation of solutions:
6. Games in which the new pupil is successful will be played when competitive scores are involved.

1. Reading to the new pupil seems impractical.
2. Recorded books are available.
3. The new pupil can be allowed extended time for tests.
4. Allowing the new pupil to answer fewer test items will seem unfair and will cause jealousy.
5. The physical education teacher can plan a remedial program.
6. If winning or losing is important, games will be chosen in which the new student performs best.

Verification: The above solutions will be tried for a month to see if acceptance of the new pupil improves.

Teaching thinking skills sounds rather esoteric; however, activities that require engaging in certain types of mental processes can be used effectively in the regular classroom to develop thinking skills. Among the processes involved in thinking are becoming aware, meditation, reflection, forming a mental image, and inductive reasoning. Activities that require the following types of skills are included among those that facilitate development of thought processes:

Cause and effect Why do interest rates of money borrowed by U.S. citizens affect the value of foreign currency?

Comparison Compare music forms of the eighteenth and nineteenth centuries.

Prediction If the inflation rate of the present year continues, what will the quality of life be like in 2020?

Analysis How many ways are a mushroom and a housefly alike and different?

Evaluation Is it right for government employees to strike?

"How" and "why" questions are excellent for fostering thought processes.

Planning Inquiry and Research Projects

During his preschool years, David was curious and excited by discovery of "his world." He busily explored the unknown. His inquiries about what, why, and how were frequent. Then David went to school. Something changed dramatically, for now the teacher decided what was to be explored and asked most of the questions. David's experience is not uncommon. Schools, in general, have not fostered an attitude of enthusiastic inquiry for knowledge. The present emphasis on basic minimum-level skills supports this fact. If preparation for the future is one goal of schools, it would be wise to prepare pupils to search for knowledge and inquire into new ideas when the teacher is no longer present to ask the questions. Also, with the proliferation of information, no one today can know everything. It is more important to know how and where to look for information.

Quantitative subjects such as science and mathematics provide excellent opportunities to develop inquiry lessons and research skills. Performing an unexplained science experiment is probably the most commonly used type of inquiry lesson. Pupils are expected to discover and evaluate possible explanations for why the response occurred. In order to do this, pupils must engage in searching (for facts), observational, interpretational, and evaluational strategies. Some teachers hesitate to encourage experimental activities because the outcome may not be what was expected. If this occurs, it provides additional opportunities for pupils to engage in problem solving. Basic steps for planning inquiry projects are listed below:

1. A problem is identified. The teacher may identify a general principle to be learned.
2. Hypotheses are proposed.
3. Possible ways to gather data are identified. These can include readings, films, experiments, and observations.
4. These data-gathering methods are evaluated, and plans are made to carry out the most valid methods.
5. Data are gathered and interpreted. Research skills are an integral part of this step.
6. Scientific explanations are formulated.

A simple illustration for developing inquiry and research skills is presented in Table 4-1.

Organizing Independent Study Projects

Independent study is a viable learning technique for pupils with superior abilities because they tend to have a wide range of interests,

TABLE 4-1

The problem is identified.	Pupils propose hypotheses (about why the balloon zoomed down the string).	Possible ways to gather data are identified.

The teacher releases a balloon that has been blown up and loosely tied to a string stretched between two chairs.	1. Gravity caused the movement.
	 2. The string was lower at one end than at the other.
	 3. Air coming out of the balloon caused it to move.
		1. Experiment to observe:
		   a. Lower one end of the string.
		   b. Repeat the experiment with the balloon blown up to different levels.
		   c. Push the balloon.
		 2. Read:
		   a. About gravity.
		   b. About air.
		   c. About balloons.

Decisions are made about data gathering	**Data are gathered and interpreted.**	**Explanation.**
1. Conduct experiments a, b, c. 2. Read a, b. 3. No films on subject available.	1. Results of experiments a, b, c. 2. Facts from reading a, b.	The air coming out of the balloon caused it to move.

favor self-determination of learning activities, and can successfully engage in more ongoing projects than average pupils. This is not to imply that independent study benefits only advanced pupils, but it is one alternative method of providing enrichment.

The basic components in organizing independent study projects are:

1. Identifying the topic to be studied
2. Locating resources to carry out the study
3. Determining the end products of the study
4. Evaluating accomplishments

A proposal for the project is presented to you for approval and suggestions to make sure the pupil has a well-planned study. A common problem relates to the selection of a topic. If the topic is too narrow, there is little to be studied. Consequently, if the topic is too broad, the study will lack focus, and success will be more limited.

The inclusion of a time line for projecting pupil–teacher conferences and the completion of the study is helpful for many pupils. The pupil–teacher conferences, used for checking on pupils' progress and to offer suggestions, should be short.

Numerous opportunities to apply research skills, such as library use, note taking, and organizing material, are provided by independent study projects. Experiences in interviewing, public speaking, and art work are also an integral part of independent study.

An illustration of an independent study is shown in Table 4-2.

Some independent study projects are more complex and require far more time than the above example. A "chaining reaction" often occurs; that is, additional topics for study are discovered during the activities.

TABLE 4-2

Topic	Resources
(What I want to know)	(What I plan to do).
Sign language	1. Read
	a. _____
	b. _____
How did sign language used by American Indians develop? Is Indian sign language like sign language used by deaf people?	2. Interview Dr. Robert Anthony, who teaches sign language.

Product

(What I will do with my new knowledge)
1. Written report
2. Oral report and demonstration of signs for the class
3. Chart comparing American Indian signs and signs for deaf people

Time line	Evaluation
(When I will complete my study)	(How well I did)
Week 1 (Sept. 9–16) Read.	1. Completed.
Week 2 (Sept 16–23) Write summary.	2. Not completed.
Week 3 (Sept. Exam Week)	3. Survived.
Week 4 (Sept. 30–Oct. 6) Interview Dr. Anthony.	4. Completed—great experience.
Week 5 (Oct. 6–13) Write report.	5. Outline completed; paper not written.
Week 6 (Oct. 13–20) Complete chart; prepare demonstration.	6. Finished paper; chart not written.
Week 7 (Oct. 20–27) Turn in paper; give oral report.	7. Completed! Teacher and class liked my project.

Activities for Developing Creativity

The regular curriculum can provide numerous opportunities for creative development. It is assumed that experiences in music, art, drama, dance, and physical movement are available to all pupils. It has been heartening to see the recent shift in emphasis from trying to copy the teacher's example in these art forms to encouragement of creative expression. While these creative subjects are offered at a specific time, creative development cannot be turned on and off by a schedule. Your attitude and approach to teaching all subjects can provide an environment in which creative thought can be expanded. There are numerous opportunities while teaching content subjects to incorporate creative activities involving the arts, creative writing, constructions, and creative problem solving. Sample activities for developing creativity while teaching reading and science are presented.

The teacher's manuals for many basal reading series contain suggestions for enrichment activities. While many of these suggestions do provide experiences for developing creativity, some are quite limiting in scope. It would be helpful for the teacher to evaluate each suggestion in relation to the elements of creativity. Does the activity provide for experience in original thought, ideational fluency, or flexibility (redefinition or elaboration)? The following suggestions will provide ideas for appropriate activities:

1. How many different things could the title of a story mean?
2. While looking at a picture, describe as many things as you can that might have happened before the scene in the picture.
3. Pretend that you are one of the characters in a story. Imagine what you are thinking as each event happened in the story.
4. Read to a critical point in a story; then make up as many different endings as you can.
5. Develop awareness of sensations by imagining sounds, smells, tastes (if reasonable), and visual images that might be associated with a story.
6. Make drawings, diagrams, and constructions related to a story.
7. Dramatize the plot or alternative events that you have proposed. Dramatization may include design and construction of puppets, costumes, props, and sets.
8. Create or select music to reflect the mood of a story or poem.
9. Develop as many solutions as possible for a mystery story.

The subject matter of the sciences provides unlimited opportunities to develop creativity. Sample activities follow:

1. Provide as many explanations as possible for the Bermuda Triangle.
2. Write a story based on the Bermuda Triangle.
3. Engage in creative problem solving based on ecological problems in disposing of toxic wastes.
4. Use a discovery approach with science experiments as opposed to performing only those experiments suggested in the science unit under study.
5. Suggest as many explanations as possible for black holes in outer space.
6. Create art work to depict several interpretations of the inside of a black hole.
7. Write a fantasy using a black hole as the setting.
8. Build scientific models. Change one element in the model, and describe ramifications of the change. Change another element in the model, and tell what the result would be.
9. Suppose all the electricity in the world was inoperable for 24 hours. List as many things as you can that would be affected. Include human feelings and emotions.
10. Pretend you are a butterfly. Write a diary of your life through the cycles of metamorphosis to your demise.

Scientific subject matter provides an excellent background for how and why questions, creative problem solving, creative art work, and imaginary thought based on reality.

The preceding suggestions are easily adaptable for other subject areas such as language arts and social studies. Once you have the mind-set of constantly analyzing what mental processes will be developed or reinforced by each learning activity, providing varied experiences becomes quite easy.

Hints for Dealing with Mathematics

It appears that many teachers are reluctant to expand their mathematics program to be more suitable for superior pupils. The basic reason is insecurity about their own knowledge and abilities in mathematics. There are some ways to compensate for an insufficient background.

While the modern or new math movement tended not to be an overwhelming success for the average pupil, it was most appropriate for pupils with superior mental abilities. The focus is on the underlying nature and structure of math. It deals with abstraction and theory—the why of mathematics—and requires logical ways of thinking. A discovery approach is emphasized. The availability of math lab manuals and materials is an advantage for the regular classroom teacher.

Types of mathematics experiments that may be provided include the following:

- Games for drill
- Games involving problem solving
- Number puzzles
- Design puzzles
- Geometry
- Figural relationships
- Analysis of attributes
- Logic problems
- Calculator experiences
- Discovery through the use of rods
- Construction of graphic visualizations
- Comparative diagrams
- Flow charts
- Timetables
- Maps
- Fractional parts
- Brain teasers
- Riddles
- Magic squares and other configurations
- Games with coins, playing cards, spinners
- Geoboard activities

Word problems of the following types can be beneficial:

- Whole numbers
- Mixed processes
- Percents

- Decimals
- Fractions
- Analysis of relevant and irrelevant information
- Probability

While much mathematics instruction is taught at the knowledge and comprehension levels, it is not difficult to structure learning activities to require higher levels of cognitive thinking. (See Table 4-3.) The underlying structure of mathematics provides an appropriate base for abstract and symbolic thinking, which is characteristic of pupils with superior abilities.

The use of materials designed to develop higher-level cognitive abilities is another way to expand and enrich the mathematics program. Representative materials are presented in this chapter. A sample of suggested activities is presented below. Familiar "trick" questions require logical reasoning and other types of thinking skills appropriate for pupils with superior abilities. The following riddles will probably be familiar to you. Perhaps you can think of others.

TABLE 4-3

Level of thinking	Ability	Example
Knowledge	Ability to identify facts, terminology, generalizations, and theories	Defining addition as more
Comprehension	Ability to translate, interpret, and extrapolate (stating a word problem in conventional form)	Stating a word problem
Application	Ability to apply mathematical principles to real-world situations	Determining how much artificial turf is needed to cover a football field
Analysis	Ability to recognize elements and their organizational relationship	Figural analogies
Synthesis	Ability to organize elements into a logical whole	Designing and constructing a math game
Evaluation	Ability to make judgments based on evidence	Debating the value of adding a music teacher to the staff, expanding library holdings, or buying computers for the math department when the school budget limits the choice to one option

1. On which side of a cup is the handle? (outside)
2. What is black and white and read all over? (newspaper)
3. What do you answer that does not ask a question? (doorbell or phone)
4. What goes up and down at the same time? (stairs)
5. What has eyes but cannot see? (potato)
6. What is always behind time? (back of the clock)
7. Which weighs more, a pound of cotton or a pound of lead? (both weigh the same; a pound is a pound)
8. What is the difference between a nickel and a dime? (five cents)
9. What has legs but cannot walk? (chair)
10. A wooden crate weighs 20 pounds when it is empty. What can you put into it to make it weigh 18 pounds? (holes)
11. What number is larger when it is turned upside down? (6 becomes 9)

Compare the following word problems to the typical drill format found in textbooks and worksheets; that is, rows of examples to be solved. The problem-solving approach is more challenging to pupils who have superior abilities.

1. Profit of $150.00 from the candy sale at school was divided among three groups—the band, the service club, and the school patrol unit. The band received 50 percent, the service club received 30 percent, and the school patrol unit received 20 percent. How much money did the service club get?
2. The swimming pool in the gymnasium measures 60 feet by 40 feet. (A) How much paint would be required to paint the bottom of the pool if 1 gallon of paint covers 350 square feet? (B) How much more paint would be required to paint the sides of the pool, which are 4 feet high?
3. Fred was riding his motorcycle west at 50 miles per hour. Scott started out at the same time, 219 miles west, on the same highway as Fred. If Scott traveled at 40 miles per hour to the east, how far would Fred have gone when he met Scott?
4. Sue has 5 pairs of school shoes. If she decides to wear them on a different day each week, how many possible sequences does she have?

5. Erik sells computers. The company receives 10 percent profit on each computer. Erik gets 5 percent of that 10 percent profit. How much would Erik receive from the sale of a computer that costs $2700.00?

The magic squares and other configurations presented below are representative of types available.

1. Have pupils add each row, then each column, and then each diagonal. Ask what they discover about each answer.

1	8	3	12
6	4	2	12
5	0	7	12
12	12	12	12

12   12

2. Have pupils complete the magic square.

18			15
	13	12	
	9	8	
6		17	3

3. Have pupils place the numbers 1 to 5 so that each diagonal line totals 9.

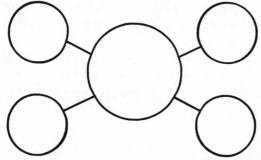

The use of computers in classrooms is becoming more commonplace daily. Computer languages, program writing, using computers to solve problems, and computers in the world of work are among the knowledge and skills that are considered in computer literacy. Experience with computers is a necessary component in the education of pupils with superior abilities. For a more complete discussion of the use of computers in the classroom, refer to Chapter Nine.

MODIFYING THE CURRICULUM

It is unrealistic to expect additions to the regular class curriculum for the diverse interests of pupils with superior abilities. Most teachers experience the pressure of time to "cover the basics." In addition, many teachers lack confidence in their ability to teach in general education or some other specific subject area. When a pupil shows interest in an area unfamiliar to you, it often help to say, "Let's learn this together." Pupils respect honesty from a teacher who admits lack of knowledge in a particular field.

Fortunately, specialized instructional techniques and independent study, which provide enrichment, rather than modification in the regular classroom curriculum, help to meet the needs of gifted pupils. However, because of the unique characteristics of these pupils, informal counseling may help to prevent or overcome some difficulties they may experience.

SELECTING MATERIALS

Regular classroom teachers are more fortunate today than previously in the availability of suitable teaching materials for pupils with superior abilities. Most textbooks have enrichment activities to develop high levels of cognitive ability and creativity. After using these suggestions for a while, it becomes easy for the teacher to generate similar ideas for other units.

Learning center idea books and materials also provide a ready source. The following are representative of these materials. Learning center books, idea books, and games are available from:

Engine-Unity, Ltd.
P.O. Box 1610
Phoenix, Arizona 85068

Incentive Publications
P.O. Box 12522
Nashville, Tennessee 37212

Midwest Publications
P.O. Box 448
Pacific Grove, California 93950

Other sources for appropriate teaching activities are also readily available. The following examples are representative:

Creative Publications
P.O. Box 10329
Palo Alto, California 34303

Growing Up Green,
Alice Skelsey and Gloria Huckaby

Workman Publishing Company
New York, New York 10018

Innovative Sciences, Inc.
300 Broad Street
Stamford, Connecticut 06901

Using Community Resources

Every community provides valuable resources to enrich the educational program. Resources can include study trips, guest speakers, specialized educational facilities, and mentor relationships. Since each geographic area is unique, it would be impractical to describe typical opportunities. Instead, here is a listing of sites for study trips used one year by the authors while teaching gifted pupils:

- Marine science center
- Arts and Sciences museum
- Art gallery
- Planetarium
- Computer center
- Botanical garden used for pharmaceuticals
- Chemical company
- Automated bakery
- Potato chip factory
- Home for the aged

- Medical laboratory
- Architectural firm
- Newspaper
- Zoo
- Advertising company
- Paper manufacturing company
- Historical fort

An integrated unit approach was used for each trip; that is, knowledges and skills in language arts, mathematics, history, economics, career education, and social skills were developed. Pupils were of junior high school age, so they were able to assist in making arrangements within both the school and the community for the study trips. Pupils were prepared with background information and appropriate learning activities so that the trip would be meaningful. Follow-ups after the trips included discussions and academic activities.

Inviting and making arrangements for guest speakers also allows pupils to develop responsibility as well as knowledge in the academic areas mentioned above. Guest speakers to the authors' classes included in the following:

- Broadcast journalist
- Religious leaders
- Artist
- Nutritionist
- Forester
- Juvenile probation officer
- Actor and actress
- Veterinarian
- Author
- Naval officer stationed in Antarctica

Preparation and follow-up learning activities were an integral part of these experiences.

Mentor relationships, where a pupil is placed in an apprenticeship with an adult who is an expert in some area, is an excellent way to meet the needs and interests of pupils with superior abilities. Many college and university professors, business people, artists, athletes, and professionals are amenable to taking a pupil under their wings and providing valuable training and insights into their particular field, which is of interest to the pupil.

Materials designed to develop higher-level cognitive abilities offer another way for regular classroom teachers to expand and enrich the program. Representative materials have been presented in this chapter.

FOSTERING UNDERSTANDING AND ACCEPTANCE OF PUPILS WITH SUPERIOR ABILITIES

Acceptance of pupils with superior abilities can be a problem in the regular classroom. If these pupils are always singled out as being "smart" and allowed to have more privileges than others in the classroom, they will receive the reputation of being the "teacher's pet." Selection of alternative learning activities, game formats, and other suggestions that are made for pupils with superior abilities should be available to all pupils in the classroom. Your attitudes and treatment of all pupils can provide a model for acceptance and respect for individual differences. Monitor your comments to be sure that praise, smiles, and selection of pupils for desirable tasks are equally distributed among pupils in the class.

Guest speakers can help pupils understand differences in levels of cognitive functioning. Teachers of the gifted, adults who are gifted, and parents of gifted children are among the types of resource persons who are available. Members of Mensa, an organization of intellectually gifted individuals, may be appropriate speakers. These speakers can share insights into problems they have experienced because of their superior abilities, as well as the positive aspects.

Simulations can be used to help develop understanding of those with superior abilities. For instance, you can use an arithmetic activity in which you require the computation of row upon row of simple addition examples. The task seems never-ending and extremely boring. At the conclusion of the activity a discussion of feelings and emotions is conducted.

A discussion that has been positively received revolves around feelings and resentment when someone helped us complete a task or did it for us. What is implied is that one isn't capable of doing the task. Over time, poor self-concept can result. Acceptance of the independence that most of these pupils with superior abilities are capable of can be facilitated by such discussions.

Recognition that each person has strengths and weaknesses can occur as a result of the following activity. Have pupils make a list of their strengths. Next, have pupils list a weakness opposite each strength. Everyone has strong and weak points.

To facilitate the acceptance of individual differences, classify class members by physical attributes, such as eye color, height, sex, length of little finger, and so on. Guide the discussion to show how each pupil is included and excluded in various groupings. The object is to help pupils avoid the rigid stereotyping characteristic of our culture. This activity can be followed by having pupils think about a friend in the class and note that differences do not interfere with friendship.

To enhance the esteem of each pupil in the class, a bulletin board focusing on the pupil of the week is helpful. Highlights emphasizing each pupil's interests and skills is another way of displaying the worth of each individual. Frequently, similar hobbies and interests are identified by pupils of varying ability. These common interests can form the basis for true integration of all pupils in the classroom.

Values clarification and Magic Circle activities (see Chapter Two) are techniques that can be used to foster acceptance of pupils with superior abilities in the classroom. An atmosphere that encourages frank discussion and discovery is essential.

SUMMING UP

Confusion about terminology and concepts of giftedness create some uncertainty about which pupils are gifted. Teachers, however, can identify academically gifted pupils rather easily. Other pupils who are unusually divergent in their thought processes, those who are underachieving or culturally different, and those with handicapping conditions are not as easily recognized in the regular classroom. Various characteristics of these pupils have been described to improve your observational skills.

Superior pupils who are mainstreamed require little modification in the regular curriculum. Some areas in which counseling these pupils might be beneficial have been presented.

There are many teaching strategies that will facilitate the development of the special abilities of superior pupils. Most textbooks provide enrichment activities to supplement the educational program. It has been suggested that these methods and activities are appropriate for other pupils in the class, although they will not be able to achieve comparable levels of cognitive thought or production.

The availability of materials suitable for pupils with superior abilities is a boon to the regular classroom teacher. In addition to materials, the local area provides sites for study trips and varied resource persons to expand and enrich the educational program.

Every pupil with superior abilities will have strengths and weaknesses. Be cautious about expecting these pupils to be "good" in all areas and to be free of personal problems. Each possesses unique characteristics, like every individual.

A thought to keep in mind when preparing for pupils with superior abilities is that they do not need more of the same learning activities. Your focus should be on providing experiences to develop higher levels of cognitive abilities. Having these pupils in the regular classroom can provide challenge and stimulation for other pupils as well as for you.

REFERENCES AND SELECTED READINGS

Barbe, W. B. and J. S. Renzulli (eds.). *Psychology and Education of the Gifted*, 3rd ed. New York: Irvington, 1981.

Bishop, W. "Successful Teachers of the Gifted." *Exceptional Children* 34 (1968): 317–325.

Bloom, B. S., M. D. Englehart, E. Furst, W. Hill, and D. R. Krathwahl. *Taxonomy of Educational Objectives, Handbook I: Cognitive Domain.* New York: David McKay, 1977.

Clark, B. *Growing Up Gifted*. Columbus, Ohio: Charles E. Merrill, 1979.

Cutts, N., and N. Moseley. *Teaching the Bright and Gifted*. Englewood Cliffs, N.J.: Prentice-Hall, 1957.

Davis, G. A., and J. A. Scott. *Training Creative Thinking*. New York: Holt, Rinehart, and Winston, 1971.

DeHaan, R., and R. Havinghurst. *Educating Gifted Children*. Chicago: University of Chicago Press, 1957.

Dirkes, M. A. "Only the Gifted Can Do It." *Educational Horizons* 59 (1981):138–142.

Dudek, S. Z. "Teachers Stifle Children's Creativity: A Charge Too Easily Made." *Learning* 5 (1976):98–104.

Dunn, L. M. (ed.). *Exceptional Children in the Schools*. New York: Holt, Rinehart, and Winston, 1973.

Frierson, E. "Upper and Lower Status Children: A Study of Differences." *Exceptional Children* 32 (1965):83–90.

Gallagher, J. J. *Teaching the Gifted Child*, 2nd ed. Boston: Allyn and Bacon, 1975.

Gallagher, J. J., M. Aschner, and W. Jenne. *Productive Thinking of Gifted Children in Classroom Interaction.* Reston, Va.: Council for Exceptional Children, 1967.

Gallagher, J. J., and T. H. Crowder. "Adjustment of Gifted Children in the Regular Classroom." *Exceptional Children* 23 (1957):306–312, 317–319.

Ginsberg, G., and C. H. Harrison. *How to Help Your Gifted Child: A Handbook for Parents and Teachers.* New York: Monarch, 1977.

Gowan, J. C., G. D. Demos, and E. P. Torravice (eds.). *Creating: Its Educational Implication.* New York: John Wiley and Sons, 1967.

Guilford, J. P. *Intelligence, Creativity, and Their Educational Implications.* London: Robert R. Knapp, 1968.

Hobbs, H. "Feyerstein's Instrumental Enrichment: Teaching Intelligence to Adolescents." *Educational Leadership* 37 (1980): 566–568.

Karnes, M., G. M. McCoy, R. P. Zehrbach, J. Wallersheimy, and H. F. Clarizio. "The Efficacy of Two Organizational Plans for Underachieving Intellectually Gifted Children." *Exceptional Children* 29 (1963): 438–446.

Kirk, S. A., and J. J. Gallagher. *Educating Exceptional Children.* Boston: Houghton-Mifflin, 1979.

Levy, P. S. "The Story of Marie, David, Richard, Jane, and John: Teaching Gifted Children in the Regular Classroom." *Teaching Exceptional Children* 3 (1981): 139–142.

MacKinnon, D. H. "The Nature and Nurture of Creative Talent." *American Psychologist* 17 (1962): 484–495.

Osborn, A. F. *Applied Imagination.* New York: Charles Scribner's Sons, 1963.

Passow, S. H. (ed.). *The Gifted and Talented: Their Education and Development.* Chicago: University of Chicago Press, 1983.

Pegnato, W., and J. W. Birch. "Locating Gifted Children in Junior High School." *Exceptional Children* 26 (1959): 303–304.

Ralph, J. B., M. L. Goldberg, and A. H. Passow. *Bright Underachievers.* New York: Columbia University Teachers College Press, 1966.

Renzulli, J. S. "Talent Potential in Minority Group Students." *Exceptional Children* 39 (1973): 437–444.

Renzulli, J. S., and R. K. Hartman. "Scale for Rating Behavioral Characteristics of Superior Students." *Exceptional Children* 38 (1971): 243–248.

Renzulli, J. S., and L. H. Smith. *A Guidebook for Developing Individualized Educational Programs for Gifted and Talented Students.* Louisville, Ky.: Creative Learning, 1979.

Sato, I. S. "The Culturally Different Gifted Child—The Dawning of His Day? *Exceptional Children* 49 (1974): 572–577.

Shaw, M. C., and J. T. McAven. "The Onset of Academic Underachievement in Bright Children." *Journal of Educational Psychology* 51 (1960): 103–108.

Shlesinger, B. E., Jr. "I Teach Children to Be Inventors." *Educational Leadership* 37 (1980): 572–573.

Sisk, D., K. Bierly. "Every Child in a Gifted Program? Yes!" *Instructor* (April 1979): 84–86, 90, 92.

Telford, C. W., and J. M. Sawrey. *The Exceptional Individual.* Englewood Cliffs, N.J.: Prentice-Hall, 1981.

Torrance, E. P. *Discovery and Nurturance of Giftedness in the Culturally Different.* Reston, Va.: The Council for Exceptional Children, 1977.

Torrance, E. P. *Encouraging Creativity in the Classroom.* Dubuque, Iowa: W. C. Brown, 1970.

Torrance, E. P., and J. Khatena. "What Kind of Person Are You? *Gifted Child Quarterly* 14 (1970): 71–75.

Torrance, E. P., J. Khatena, and B. F. Cunnington. *Thinking Creatively with Sounds and Words.* Lexington, Mass.: Personnel Press, 1973.

Torrance, E. P., and J. P. Torrance. *Is Creativity Teachable?* Bloomington, Ind.: Phi Delta Kappa, 1973.

Whimbey, A. "Students Can Learn to Be Better Problem Solvers." *Educational Leadership* 37 (1980): 560–562.

Whitmore, J. R. *Giftedness, Conflict, and Underachievement.* Boston: Allyn and Bacon, 1980.

Williams, F. *Classroom Ideas for Encouraging Thinking and Feeling.* Buffalo: Dissemination of Knowledge Publishers, 1970.

CHAPTER FIVE

Speech and Language Impairments

Speech and language impairments are among the easiest atypical pupil behaviors for the regular classroom teacher to identify *if* you (1) know the sequence of normal speech and language development, (2) have some knowledge of the types of speech and language impairments, and (3) have "a good ear." Speech and language development and disabilities are frequently discussed simultaneously in professional literature; therefore, clarification of the following terms will be helpful:

- *Speech* (articulation) is the production or vocalization of sounds that form words.
- *Language* is the underlying meaning of sounds, words, or combinations thereof.
- *Oral language* is the ability to express ideas verbally in a comprehensible manner as well as to understand ideas that have been spoken.

Speech is a way to express or transmit the meaning of language. The discussion of language in this chapter focuses on two areas:

1. The abilities to listen to and understand oral language. These abilities are often called *receptive and associative language.*
2. The ability to form correct spoken language messages. This ability is often called *expressive language.*

This chapter will address clues to identifying speech and language impairment, teaching methods to accommodate the needs of speech and language impaired pupils, curriculum modification, materials adaptation, and encouraging acceptance of pupils with speech and language impairments.

IDENTIFYING SPEECH AND LANGUAGE DIFFICULTIES

What is defective speech? While this seems to be a simple question, there is a fine line between acceptable speech and that which is defective. This is because of the great variations in speech that are viewed as acceptable. For instance, you only have to compare the speech of many Southerners, New Englanders, and Midwesterners to see that different pronunciations of the same word are all acceptable. Everyone experiences periods of speech disfluency, yet few are classified as stutterers. It will be helpful in this discussion to consider a common definition that clarifies the parameters of defective speech (Van Riper, 1972, p. 29):

> Speech is defective when it deviates so far from the speech of other people that it calls attention to itself, interferes with communication, or causes the possessor to be maladjusted.

As with other atypical characteristics described in this book, it is the degree of the behavior related to age expectancy that determines whether a characteristic is an ability or a disability. The parameters specified by Van Riper can also be applied to language disabilities. Gearheart and Weishahn (1976, p. 99) state that "language problems should be considered significant if they interfere with communication, if they cause the speaker to be maladjusted, or if they cause problems for the listener."

Five Clues to Watch for in Spotting Speech Problems

1. Faulty articulation
   a. substitutions ("wabbit" for "rabbit")
   b. omissions ("ome" for "home")
   c. distortions ("ship" for "sip")
2. Unpleasant voice quality
   a. nasality
   b. hoarseness
   c. harshness
   d. breathiness
3. Inappropriate voice quality
   a. too high or too low
   b. too loud or too soft
   c. inflexible (monotonous)
4. Inappropriate fluency, stuttering
5. Language problems
   a. difficulty in understanding the meaning of spoken words or sentences
   b. difficulty in forming oral sentence structures

Faulty articulation is mispronunciation of part or all of a word. The term "baby talk" is derived from the fact that the speech of many young children is characterized by faulty articulation. Speech and language development is incomplete for many pupils in kindergarten and first grade; therefore, it is critical that you know the sequence and age expectancy of normal speech and language development. Developmental stages of normal speech and oral language are presented in Table 5-1.

Substituting, omitting, and distorting sounds are common types of *articulation impairments*. A pupil may exhibit one or a combination of these types of articulation impairments:

1. *Substitutions.* Common substitutions of sounds by young children include the following:

W for R	("wabbit" — "rabbit")	Th for S	("yeth" — "yes")
W for L	("yewo" — "yellow")	F for Th	("free" — "three")
K for T	("cree" — "tree")	B for V	("Bolkswagen" — "Volkswagen")
T for K	("take" — "cake")	P for F	("punny" — "funny")

TABLE 5-1

NORMAL SPEECH AND EXPRESSIVE LANGUAGE DEVELOPMENT*	
Speech sounds adequate	**Expressive language stages**
AGE (months)	
1–3	Prelinguistic vocalization—crying and cooing
4–6	Babbling—imitates and initiates sounds for pleasure
7–10	Repetitive sounds—puts two sounds together—inflected vocal patterns
11–12 *a e, i, o, u*	First words—"bye-bye," "mama," "daddy"
13–18	One-word sentences (usually nouns), jargon or made-up language
18–23	Two-word sentences (usually noun and verb); begins to use other parts of speech
AGE (years)	
2 *m, n, p, h, w*	Three-word simple sentences; uses some possessives and pronouns; begins singular and plural agreement
2½ *b*	Expanded use of other parts of speech in addition to nouns and verbs; uses contractions
3 *k, g, d, f, y, wh*	Uses three- or four-word sentences; can tell stories, sing songs, repeat rhymes
4 *ng*	Expanded grammatical forms using four- or five-word sentences; complex sentences begin to appear
4½ *r, l*	May talk excessively; uses past and future tenses; asks why questions
5 *s, u, ch, sh, th, z, j, v*	Mastery of structure of native language
6 *zh*	

*Development may vary six months in either direction.

The substituted sounds may not be used consistently in each word. Substituted sounds are usually those the child has mastered perfectly and therefore are easy to use. Substitutions may occur in the initial position of a word but not in the medial or final position.

2. *Omissions.* Sounds may be omitted from the beginning, middle, or end of a word. Occasionally, pupils will omit so many sounds that their speech is unintelligible.

3. *Distortions.* Distorted sounds differ from substituted sounds in that they are not identifiable as consonants or vowels. Distorted sounds may be associated with older pupils more than substituted or omitted sounds.

The *s* sound is frequently distorted. Mushy *s*, slushy *s*, or whistling *s* are descriptions resulting from the incorrect formation of this sound. The air flow usually comes out of the sides of the mouth to cause the distortion.

A word of caution might be useful in reference to identifying articulation problems. You should be aware that regional speech patterns may lead to confusion. For example, in one region, some pupils say "skrawberry" for "strawberry." Assessments by speech therapists will invariably show that pupils can hear and pronounce the *str* sound correctly; they simply learned an incorrect pronunciation for the name of the fruit. It is interesting to note that, even after individuals have been in speech therapy to correct a defective sound, the words they have said since early childhood containing the defective sound will be the last words to show carryover to correct production.

Quality of voice disorders involves the production of sounds. Sounds are produced by air vibrating the vocal folds of the larynx and passing through the throat, mouth, and nose. Voice disorders are more commonly treated in adults than in children. Nasality, hoarseness, harshness, and breathiness can be classified as voice disorders:

1. A nasal twang—*hypernasality*—results when too much of a sound passes through the nose instead of the mouth. Hypernasality may be associated with cerebral palsy or cleft palate. Denasal sounds—*hyponasality*—are the opposite of hypernasal sounds. Denasality causes sounds to have a muffled quality, such as when one has a head cold. Denasality can be simulated by talking with one's nose pinched.

2. *Hoarseness* is temporarily experienced by most individuals on occasion during certain types of respiratory infections, overexuberant yelling, or a period of extreme tension. Chronic hoarseness should be assessed by a speech therapist or medical doctor.

3. *Harshness* describes a voice quality that is grating, discordant, and irritating. A harsh voice has a jarring and unpleasant effect on the listener.

4. *Breathiness* describes a voice quality sometimes thought to be sexy in females. A "Marilyn Monroe voice" is an example of breathiness. An excess of air is used during the production of voiced sounds, accompanied by less than normal use of the vocal folds.

Suspected voice quality disorders are best referred for proper diagnosis. If correction is indicated, it must generally be carried out by a qualified speech therapist. These disorders can lead to or be caused by physical pathologies in the vocal track. The speech therapist may make suggestions for the regular classroom teacher.

Vocal pitch, intensity, and flexibility can be characteristic of certain types of speech impairments:

1. *Pitch* is how high or low the voice is in relation to age expectations. There is usually a natural voice change commensurate with age. Occasionally, appropriate pitch is not developed.

2. *Intensity* refers to loudness or softness of speech. The amount of energy expended in speech production is reflected in voice intensity. Competent assessment may be necessary to determine if voice intensity is related to a speech impairment or to psychological factors. Attention seeking and insecurity can be manifested by a voice that is too loud or too soft.

3. *Flexibility* is the variability usually present in a normal speaking voice. A monotone voice may also indicate an individual's emotional state.

Stuttering is a problem of speech rhythm which is characterized by hesitations, disruptions, repetitions, prolongation of words or parts of words, or interjection of extraneous sounds. There appears to be a struggle to speak. Of particular importance to the regular classroom teacher is the fact that stuttering appears to be developmental in nature. Preschool children will alternate periods of fluent speech with stuttering. Usually after second grade, tension may be observed in the facial area and/or the throat. There may be some secondary symptoms such as slapping the knee, squinting, or snapping the fingers. Stuttering periods become longer and may affect more important words in a sentence. Increased periods of disfluency should serve as indicators to refer the pupil for assessment by a specialist. The cause of stuttering is not yet clearly understood, although many theories have been proposed.

Oral language is the vehicle of thought. While a linguist might describe the components of language as phonology, morphology, semantics, syntax, and pragmatics, the discussion here will be addressed in more simplistic terms:

1. Some pupils have *difficulty in comprehending the meaning of words or sentences.* Some pupils are unable to understand oral messages. Despite the fact that they may hear the communication, they still do not make appropriate responses because they lack comprehension. The spoken language of these pupils may not be sensible.

2. *Problems with the formation of correct oral sentence structures* is a characteristic of some pupils with oral language impairment. They do not arrange words in proper order ("help you me?" for "Will you help me?"). This type of oral language impairment is quite easily recognized where lack of understanding oral communication is more subtle. Caution should be exercised in regard to making judgments about forming improper sentence structures. This is a prevalent pattern of speech in some regions.

DEFINING THE CLASSROOM TEACHER'S ROLE

There are several ways in which you can facilitate improvement of speech and language impairments:

1. Refer pupils for assessment by a speech therapist.
2. Implement procedures suggested by a speech therapist.
3. Provide a good speech and language model.
4. Integrate speech and language activities throughout the school day.

If you feel that any element of speech or oral language deviates enough from the norm for age expectancy, referral should be made for assessment by a speech therapist. Assessment by a therapist is critical because some types of problems result from physical deviations and are organic in nature. Classroom teachers are not trained to determine whether the cause of the problem is functional or organic. Attempts at remediation might compound the problem unless correct assessment has been made.

After assessment by a speech therapist, any adjustments in instruction or implementation of remedial activities suggested by the speech therapist can be made. You can assume a major role in dealing with problems that are functional in nature. For instance, activities for teaching phonics are appropriate for remediation of some articulation impairments.

Your own correct speech and oral language have a great influence on the pupils in the class. Your attitude can shape an atmosphere that generates respect for correct speech and language usage. Strive for an atmosphere in which correct speech and language usage are respected, but at the same time the atmosphere must be such that pupils will risk making possible mistakes. You have to "walk a tightrope" in this regard.

You have opportunities throughout the school day to integrate speech and language activities with whatever subject is being taught. Any skill taught in isolation must be generalized and reinforced in other settings; therefore, capitalize on every chance to use skills being taught.

Providing a Good Speech Model

Your attitude toward and production of oral communication will have an impact on the pupils in the classroom. Your respect for correct speech serves as a model for pupils. You have only to become aware of how much teacher verbalization occurs in a typical classroom to realize that there is consistent bombardment of speech and oral language being correctly or incorrectly produced and used. Since speech "begins in the ear," the quality of oral production is bound to influence pupils' speech and language.

Another consideration of your role as a model concerns the classroom climate. If pupils have a supportive climate where they are not subjected to criticism and ridicule for errors or differences, they will risk verbalizing more readily. Speech and oral language are learned by talking; therefore, pupils need opportunities to make mistakes without the implication that the production is unacceptable. Otherwise, feelings of failure and poor self-concept develop. Create a classroom climate in which pupils feel comfortable and secure in their learning efforts.

SPECIAL TEACHING METHODS

Hints for Improving Oral Language

Difficulties with oral language have been described as an inability to comprehend the meaning of spoken words or sentences, and difficulty in forming sentence structure:

1. If pupils appear to have difficulty in comprehending the meaning of spoken words or sentences, try the following suggestions—
   a. Use short phrases, sentences, and questions when speaking to the pupils.
   b. Use concrete experiences such as role playing the meaning of words, sentences, and stories.
   c. Provide visual cues such as illustrative pictures during oral activities.
   d. Provide enough time for pupils to "gather their thoughts" before expecting an answer to oral communication.
   e. If pupils understand written communication better than oral communication, give them written material before oral questioning.

Activities that might be helpful include the following—

   a. Simon Says and other games that are based on oral commands provide excellent opportunities to practice and demonstrate meaning associated with spoken language.
   b. Give verbal directions such as "Stand up," "Stretch as high as you can," "Touch your toes," "Sit down."
   c. Riddles that involve verbal descriptions are fun. For example, "It is green; it hops; it is a movie star. What is it?"
   d. Display an interesting picture. Ask pupils to locate items such as the part of the dock that extends over the water, the boat that is towing a water skier, and the boat with fishing equipment.
   e. Read a short story aloud. Ask questions concerning the story. Begin with simple recall of detail questions; then, as soon as possible, include questions that require higher-level skills. Many teachers feel that the job is done when they quiz for immediate recall of detail. They do not ask questions that require higher levels of comprehension such as sequence of time, cause and effect, or prediction.
   f. Repeat sentences stressing different words. Ask pupils if the sentences are the same or different.
      "The boy rode a *motorcycle*."
      "The *boy* rode a motorcycle."
      "The boy *rode* a motorcycle."
   g. Use analogies.
      "A dog is to a cat as a tree is to _____."
      "A shirt is to a boy as a sheet is to _____."
      "An apple is to an orange as a bean is to _____."

"A road is to a car as a track is to _____."
"A touchdown is to football as a homerun is to
_____."

h. Use oral sentences with words that refer to emotions. Have pupils act out the emotions as they are spoken. For instance, "John was laughing at Sue's joke" or "Wanda was angry when her new skates broke."

i. Have pupils tell how these are alike and different.
  flower—tree
  salt—pepper
  horse—dog
  chair—table

j. Have pupils generate alternative hypotheses by presenting sentences with negative statements. Ask questions that require pupils to generate hypotheses.

"The tree is not *tall*. What do you think the tree looked like?" "The car was not in the *garage*. Where do you think the car was?"

2. Try the following types of activities with pupils who have difficulty in forming oral sentence structures—

a. Provide a folder with pockets containing word cards with different parts of speech. Have pupils select words to make sensible sentences. Be sure that the pupils read the sentences orally.

b. Vary the activity above by using phrase cards.

c. Another variation of this activity could be to have pupils form questions and other types of sentences as their usage improves.

d. Prepare *oral* cloze exercises. Cloze exercises are sentences in which certain words have been omitted. Begin by omitting nouns for the pupils to supply. Later, omit verbs, and then adjectives and adverbs.
"The big fat _____ was squealing."

e. Have pupils role play telephone conversations, such as ordering a pizza or inviting several other pupils to a skating party.

f. Use a comic strip without words. (You might cut the pictures to delete the words and then mount them on cards.) Have pupils supply the conversation that they think is occurring.

g. The Language Master can be used to vary the activities above. Provide picture cards. Have pupils record what is happening, using complete sentences.

h. Have pupils view a filmstrip and then tell the story. Short, simple stories should be used with one- or two-sentence summaries expected in the beginning stages.

i. Provide two pupils with a toy catalog. Have each pupil in turn select a toy she would like and tell the other pupil why she would like it. Attention span may be increased with this activity by varying the number of toys each pupil is allowed to select.

j. Play "I Spy." A pupil describes some object in the environment for one or more other pupils to identify.

k. Have pupils give directions for a game or activity. Let them prepare what they are going to say in advance. It is often helpful to have pupils demonstrate as they speak. The focus is shifted from their talking to the action.

l. The use of puppets, drama, and music are other ways to shift emphasis from the speaker to the action.

m. Have pupils describe their artistic creations (painting, construction, athletic routine, etc.).

n. Have pupils expand sentences.

> "Sharon had a horse."
> "Sharon had a big horse."
> "Sharon had a big black horse."
> "Sharon had a big black horse with a saddle."

o. Have pupils provide a definition.

> "A patriot is _____."

p. Have pupils describe their ideal day.

q. Provide pupils with opportunities to generate alternative thoughts or strategies.

r. Have pupils prepare and present oral reports (books, field trips, television programs) to other pupils from a lower grade.

Language activities suggested in Chapter Six will also be helpful.

Tips for Modifying Reading and Spelling Instruction

Spoken language is the basis for written language (reading and spelling). In most cases, pupils must be able to hear sounds accurately in order to produce sounds accurately. Pupils must associate the correct sound with the correct visual symbol.

If phonics is the foundation of the reading program, some speech impaired pupils will be at a decided disadvantage. Emphasis on auditory factors as the primary decoding method will penalize these pupils.

Correct pronunciation is a decided asset in spelling. Teachers tend to emphasize the phonic elements learned in reading lessons with beginning spellers.

This relationship between phonics and reading and spelling alters the purposes of phonics instructions for some pupils. Pupils with good auditory and speech skills will benefit from phonics instruction as a help in decoding written language and for production of correct spelling. Phonics instruction will be remedial in nature for those pupils with auditory and some type of speech impairments. In addition to phonics exercises found in reading materials, books such as *The Big Book of Sounds* (Flowers, 1980) provide hints for instruction as well as practice exercises.

The implication for reading instruction is that phonics should be taught, but the visual aspects of structural analysis and use of context clues should be emphasized as the primary modes for decoding written language for pupils with some types of speech impairments.

The use of structural analysis clues such as configuration and affixes should be stressed for correct spelling production.

Using Music to Remediate Speech Problems

Music can serve as the basis for remediating several types of speech problems:

1. Remediation of articulation problems may be enhanced by musical activities. Simple songs that feature particular sounds can be identified. "Do-Re-Mi" from *The Sound of Music* (Rodgers and Hammerstein) is an example of a song that might be used. Pupils can also compose songs using sounds being learned. This is a particularly good activity.

2. Many stutterers experience little disfluency while singing. This provides a "success" experience as well as another channel of communication. As Turnbull and Schulz (1979) point out, this ability to sing without disfluency may lead to membership in the school chorus or similar activities.

3. Pitch, intensity, and flexibility have been described as voice disorders. Music provides an excellent vehicle for improving

these areas. Also, the structured rhythm of musical exercises may benefit pupils who experience breathiness in vocal production.

The relaxed atmosphere in which most musical endeavors occur may also help speech impaired pupils. This is especially true if the pupil has become sensitive and self-conscious about speech production. A comfortable environment tends to relieve some of the stress felt in more formal and open situations.

Steps in Remediating Articulation Problems

Substitutions, omissions, and distortions have been described as articulation problems. As stated earlier, the regular classroom teacher can deal effectively with functional articulation problems. It is wise to consult the speech therapist before beginning remedial activities. The major steps in remediation of articulation errors follow:

1. *Isolating the sound.* First, pupils must learn to isolate the sound from the whole word. For example, have pupils name objects in the classroom that contain the sound. Then you say the word emphasizing the sound, followed by pupils saying the word and omitting the sound.

2. *Bombardment of sound.* Next, the sound is presented repetitively. For example, pupils can color as long as you are producing the sound. When you pause, pupils must stop coloring.

3. *Associating the sound.* The sound is paired with some type of picture, symbol, or concept. The *v* sound could be identified with a picture of a violin and called the "*vibrating violin*" sound.

4. *Discriminating the sound.* Pupils must learn to discriminate correct and incorrect sounds. It is easier to discriminate sounds through visual cues. Teach the discrimination of the sound with visual cues; that is, with a view of your mouth. Later, remove visual cues by covering your mouth as discrimination improves. Produce the correct and incorrect sound with pupils signaling by raising their hands for each incorrect production. Learning to hear the error is essential, and no further work should be attempted until this step is accomplished.

5. *Producing the sound.* Pupils must learn to produce the sound. Attempts may be inaccurate at first but should move slowly toward correct production. It may be necessary to show some pupils how to position the articulators. Sometimes a mirror is helpful.

6. *Incorporating the sound.* Once the sound can be correctly produced, it must be incorporated into syllables and then words. Pupils will need to practice the sound in the initial, medial, and final positions.

7. *Integrating the sound.* Next, pupils must integrate the correct sound in their regular speech. A good transition exercise to go from producing the sound in words to sentences is to use a sentence such as "Linda lost her little ___." The student repeats the sentence, ending with a different word each time. You have a definite advantage over the speech therapist by being able to monitor and reinforce the correct sound. Integration of the correct sound will usually occur gradually.

If there is more than one pupil in the classroom who has the same problem, remediation can occur in a group setting. Some of the remedial activities can be carried out during reading instruction. Aides, peer tutors, volunteers, and tape recorders can be used to assist you. Activity books are also available (Blockcolsky, Frazer, and Frazer, 1979; Dexter, 1972; Egland, 1970; Fairbanks, 1960; Flowers, 1980; Griffith and Miner, 1979).

Deemphasizing Oral Activities

Some pupils may be self-conscious about their speech and oral language production. Often, the stress of speaking in the presence of a large group may compound the problem. In these cases, the pupils still need opportunities to talk, but they may need a more private setting. For instance, it may be beneficial to conduct oral lessons with a severe stutterer in a secluded area of the classroom.

The ultimate goal is to have all oral activities occur in the normal interactions of the classroom. However, your judgment will be required in determining what setting is best for a particular speech or language impaired pupil while remediation is in progress.

MODIFYING THE CURRICULUM

The regular curriculum usually requires little modification for speech and oral language impaired pupils. Speech therapists are available in most schools, at least on an itinerant basis, to provide assessment and remediation for specific problems. The activities that therapists suggest can usually be incorporated into normal curriculum offerings. Additional emphasis on teaching phonics skills may benefit pupils with articulation problems.

Emphasizing Phonics

Heilman (1976, p. 2) defines phonics instruction as "a facet of reading instruction which (1) leads the child to understand that printed letters in printed words represent the speech sounds heard when words are pronounced; (2) involves the actual teaching of which sound is associated with a particular letter or combination of letters." It is the phrase "speech sounds heard" that will benefit speech impaired pupils. The first step in remediation of articulation errors is for pupils to recognize the correct sound. They must be able to distinguish between correct and incorrect pronunciation of the sound. Reading readiness materials are replete with exercises for this.

Sounds are generally introduced in isolation. However, remember that sounds may be somewhat dependent on their position in a word. Sounds before and after the specific sound may change that sound slightly. Steps in remediating articulation errors as well as sample activities have been presented in this chapter.

SELECTING MATERIALS

It is unnecessary for you to modify materials used in a typical classroom. The deemphasis of oral work, the use of phonics work as remediation of certain types of speech problems, and books with drill exercises have been discussed in earlier sections.

Many activity and drill books for speech and oral language exercise are available. Selected books have been mentioned previously in the chapter, and additional selections appear in the reference list. Adequate sources for securing materials can be suggested by a speech therapist, a librarian, or numerous educational publication catalogs.

HINTS FOR ACCEPTANCE OF
SPEECH AND LANGUAGE IMPAIRED PUPILS

Pupils tend to reflect an overall societal rejection of atypical individuals. The regular classroom teacher has unlimited opportunities to further the acceptance of pupils who are "different." While pupils tend to be "up front" with their comments and opinions, they also appear to be able to modify their attitudes more readily than adults. Understanding and acceptance of human variability can be fostered in the classroom.

Your attitude will determine to a large extent the atmosphere in the classroom. Most pupils tend to be aware of subtle nuances of irritation and rejection if there is no overt teacher rejection of a particular pupil. For example, finishing words for stutterers, telling them that they are "thinking faster than they talk," or telling them to slow down are inappropriate comments that have negative connotations. Being patient with a stutterer's speech difficulty would be a positive response that other pupils can emulate.

Your attitude can usually be improved with increased confidence in dealing with atypical pupils. The teacher's acceptance is usually reflected in the pupils' attitudes and treatment of others.

If the speech and oral language of a pupil causes negative (and often cruel) reactions in the classroom, try these suggestions:

1. Have a speech therapist make a presentation to the class.

2. Invite an adult who has or has had speech or oral language problems to share his or her experiences and feelings with the class.

3. Use literature such as *A Certain Small Shepherd* (Caudill, 1965) to foster understanding and acceptance.

4. Use films and filmstrips such as "The Story of Helen Keller" as a basis for class discussions.

SUMMING UP

The overview of speech and oral language that has been presented here indicates that regular classroom teachers can identify, provide some types of remedial activities, and modify the learning situation if they are aware of speech and language development and disabilities. Speech impairments are among the easiest atypical conditions to identify. The major types of speech impairments are articulation, voice quality, and inappropriate fluency. Oral language problems include difficulty in understanding and/or forming appropriate oral language communication.

Your role in regard to speech and language problems focuses on referral for proper assessment and implementing strategies suggested by the therapist. You can provide a good speech and language model as well as integrate speech and language activities throughout the school day.

The regular classroom curriculum will require little modification. The role of phonics in reading instruction may be remedial in nature if pupils have articulation problems. Undue emphasis on phonics may not be the most effective approach to teaching reading for these pupils.

Activities to improve oral language reception and expression have been suggested. These activities will be appropriate for many other pupils in the typical classroom. Much extra time and energy will not be required to meet the needs of speech and oral language impaired pupils in the regular classroom.

REFERENCES AND SELECTED READINGS

Ashlock, P., and M. Grant. *Educational Therapy Materials.* Springfield, Ill.: Charles C. Thomas, 1972

Blockcolsky, V. D., J. M. Frazer, and D. N. Frazer. *30,000 Selected Words Organized by Letter, Sound and Syllable.* Tucson: Communication Skillbuilders, 1979.

Bloom, L., and M. Laney. *Language Development and Language Disorders.* New York: John Wiley and Sons, 1978.

Broman, B., and S. Shipley. "Language Development." *Instructor* 79 (1969):132.

Burne, M. C. *The Child Speaks.* New York: Harper and Row, 1965.

Bush, W. J. and M. T. Giles. *Aids to Psycholinguistic Teaching.* Columbus, Ohio: Charles E. Merrill, 1969.

Caudill, R. *A Certain Small Shepherd.* New York: Holt, Rinehart, and Winston, 1965.

Collins, N., G. Czuchna, G. O'Betts, M. Stahl, and D. Pushaw. *Teach Your Child to Talk.* New York: CEBCO/Standard, 1975.

Dexter, B. L. *The Speech Tree.* Johnstown, Pa.: Marex Associates, 1972.

Egland, G. *Speech and Language Problems: A Guide for the Classroom Teacher.* Englewood Cliffs, N.J.: Prentice-Hall, 1970.

Fairbanks, G. F. *Voice and Articulation Drillbook* , 2nd ed. New York: Harper and Row, 1960.

Flowers, A. M. *The Big Book of Language Through Sounds.* Danville, Ill.: Interstate Printers, 1963.

Flowers, A. M. *The Big Book of Sounds* 3rd. ed. Danville, Ill.: Interstate Printers, 1980.

Gearheart, B. R., and M. W. Weishahn. *The Handicapped Child in the Regular Classroom.* St. Louis: C. V. Mosby, 1976.

Griffith, J., and L. E. Miner. *Phonetic Context Drillbook.* Englewood Cliffs, N.J.: Prentice-Hall, 1979.

Heilman, A. W. *Phonics in Proper Perspective* , 3rd ed. Columbus, Ohio: Charles E. Merrill, 1976.

Karnes, M. B. *Helping Young Children Develop Language Skills: A Book of Activities.* Reston, Va.: Council for Exceptional Children, 1974.

Mowrer, D. "Speech Problems: What You Should Do and Shouldn't Do." *Learning* 6, no. 5 (January 1978): 34-39.

Turnbull, A. P., and J. B. Schulz. *Mainstreaming Handicapped Students: A Guide for the Classroom Teacher.* Boston: Allyn and Bacon, 1979.

Van Riper, C. *Speech Correction: Principles and Methods* , 5th ed. Englewood Cliffs, N.J.: Prentice-Hall, 1972.

Van Riper, C. and R. A. Erickson. "A Predictive Screening Test of Articulation." *Journal of Speech and Hearing Disorders* 34 (1969):214–219.

Wiig, E. and E. Semel. *Language Disorders in Children and Adolescents.* Columbus, Ohio: Charles E. Merrill, 1976.

CHAPTER SIX

Hearing Impairment

Students with mild to moderate hearing loss are apt to go undetected in the classroom. The subtle behaviors of these students elicit comments such as "lazy," "doesn't pay attention," "can hear when he wants to." In reality such behaviors could be caused by not hearing enough of what is going on to stay involved, becoming tired because of the extra effort required to hear, or being able to hear conversations when they are close and not being able to hear conversations when they are at distance. Erratic hearing results. Such children often may not know that they are not hearing normally. This is particularly true when onset of the hearing loss is gradual. Often teachers suspect other problems such as mental retardation or behavior disorders.

This chapter presents methods of identifying pupils with hearing impairment, modification and considerations in the classroom, general teaching principles, special teaching methods, curriculum modification, materials adaptation for hearing impaired pupils, use of aids and services, and fostering acceptance of hearing impaired pupils.

CLUES FOR RECOGNIZING HEARING IMPAIRMENT

How can teachers identify pupils who might have a mild or moderate hearing loss? The following pupil behaviors may indicate possible hearing difficulty.

Three Physical Clues to Watch for in Spotting Hearing Disabilities

1. Frequent earaches or fluid discharge coming from ear
2. Frequent colds and sore throats
3. Difficulty with balance

Middle ear infection is quite common among school pupils. Pus accumulates in the ear; this inhibits the passage of sound impulses along the auditory path resulting in muffled sounds. Most people experience diminished hearing from middle ear infection at some time in their lives. Pressure from pus in the middle ear can also cause tiny holes in the eardrum, resulting in runny ears. Scar tissue will form around these perforations in the eardrum and interfere with the passage of sound impulses.

Frequent colds and sore throats may also lead to hearing difficulty. All teachers have observed pupils who blow their noses with extreme pressure. Another common habit of pupils is to sniff nasal discharge back into the nasal passage. Either of these habits can force fluid into the ear, resulting in infection and/or diminished hearing.

Difficulty with balance might be another clue related to hearing difficulty. The vestibular area, the center for balance, is located in the ear. Pressure in this area can cause trouble in maintaining balance.

Twelve Behavioral Clues to Watch for in Spotting Hearing Difficulties

1. Inconsistency in following directions
2. Asking "What?" with unusual frequency
3. Paying particular attention to the speaker's face or lips
4. Speech problems
5. Limited vocabulary and immature language development
6. Responding differently to slapstick and verbal humor
7. Inattention

8. Appearance of being lazy
9. Restlessness
10. Acting out
11. Withdrawal
12. Performing better using machines with earphones

If hearing problems are suspected, one simple technique you can use for informal assessment is to address the pupil with his back to you. Try standing at different distances from the pupil when he is unaware of your presence. If response of the pupil diminishes with distance, a portable audiometer could be used to screen for possible hearing loss. The speech therapist in the school will have access to an audiometer and will be qualified to give the screening examination. If behaviors persist, screening testing should be repeated over a period of time because of the erratic effects of some types of hearing loss. An examination by a physician or audiologist may be needed.

The terms "deaf" and "hard of hearing" need clarification in order to understand the educational needs of hearing impaired pupils. Hearing impairment refers to both the deaf and the hard of hearing. Deaf individuals do not benefit from speech sounds, while the hard of hearing do. The age at which the deafness occurred has significant impact on the individual's development in relation to educational needs. If deafness occurred at birth, speech and language development will be severely impaired. Conversely, if deafness occurred after speech and language development are advanced, the pupil will be able to function more easily in the regular school environment.

Hard of hearing individuals can benefit from the sense of sound with or without a hearing aid even though hearing is defective. Speech and language development are more normal for hard of hearing individuals although usually delayed. Thus, the greatest educational disadvantage of hearing impairment is the underdevelopment of speech and language.

MODIFICATIONS AND CONSIDERATIONS IN THE CLASSROOM

There are certain modifications and considerations in the classroom environment that will benefit hearing impaired pupils. Pupils with a hearing impairment need a favorable location in the classroom. Allow and encourage them to move to be close to oral or visual activities. Care must be exercised, however, so that these pupils will not be looking toward the ceiling lights.

How to Improve the Environment for Effective Speech Reading

Hearing impaired pupils may utilize lipreading or speech reading with auditory clues to facilitate communication. These pupils concentrate on the speaker's lips, facial expression, and body gestures to help them understand what is being said. Consideration of the following factors will result in more effective speech reading:

1. Speech reading can be hampered by hairstyles, mustaches, beards, and jewelry. Distractions such as these should be avoided so that pupils can use subtle cues to understand what is being said.

2. When reading aloud, be sure the book does not cover your face. Eye contact aids in oral communication.

3. When speaking, be sure your face is not at an awkward angle to the hearing impaired pupil. The hearing impaired pupil's ability to benefit from speech reading is limited by having to look up into the speaker's face. If the speaker's face is turned at an angle of more than 90 degrees, speech reading is hindered.

4. Light must shine directly on the speaker's face. Don't stand in front of windows or other light sources, which causes your face to become shadowed or silhouetted.

5. Be careful not to talk while facing the chalkboard. This bad habit puts hearing impaired pupils at a definite disadvantage since they cannot speech read. Try to remember to stand still while talking.

There are misconceptions about the degree to which hearing impaired individuals can benefit from speech reading. Speech reading cannot be equated with hearing for understanding oral messages. Some sounds such as *k*, *g*, and *h* do not appear on the lips. Other sounds such as *f* and *v* look exactly alike on the lips. We are always amused when mystery book authors employ speech reading as a mechanism to solve a crime. Typically, the hero speech reads a conversation between the villain and his cohorts which explains the plot. It is not unusual for the villain to be making a phone call from a booth across a busy street from the hero who is speech reading the message. This is a very unrealistic portrayal of the utility of speech reading.

Ways to Prevent Fatigue

Since pupils with hearing difficulty must concentrate with great energy, they may become fatigued more quickly than other pupils. Some ways to prevent fatigue are:

1. Short periods with activities that do not require complete dependence on oral communication
2. Combining visual illustrations with oral activities
3. Worksheets and individual games for variation
4. Physical activities and relaxation exercises

Extended use of vision is more tiring than extended listening. You can relate to having had "tired eyes" more often than "tired ears."

How to Use Hearing Buddies

A "hearing buddy" is a hearing pupil from the class who looks out for the hearing impaired pupil's needs. Here are some ways a hearing buddy can help:

1. Be sure the hearing impaired pupil is keeping up with the class in large group work.
2. Take notes for the hearing impaired pupil.
3. Point to the person who is speaking during large group work.
4. Help the hearing impaired pupil in situations that are likely to be confusing, such as physical education.

Hearing buddies can help hearing impaired pupils keep the correct place in the material on which the whole class is working. We have all experienced losing our place because of some distraction; therefore, it is understandable that pupils who miss part of the oral message might have this problem. Imagine the strain on hearing impaired pupils in keeping up with the following transitions that might occur in a typical classroom: a member of the group is reading a chapter aloud from the social studies book, there are spontaneous interruptions for discussion, someone comes to the classroom door with a message, and a class member has to leave for speech therapy. Hearing buddies could help hearing impaired pupils get back to the correct place in the lesson.

Another valuable service of the hearing buddy is to take notes. Since hearing impaired pupils must depend on looking and listening simultaneously, it is impossible to take notes. Using carbon paper under the buddy's own notes makes this a simple process.

During class discussions the hearing buddy can point to the person who is speaking. This helps the hearing impaired pupil focus on the source of sound so that speech reading can be effective. Hearing buddies can be most helpful to hearing impaired pupils during large group activities at school. Remember the effect of noise from large groups in compounding the hearing difficulty. During physical education, in the cafeteria, at assemblies, and during other school events, hearing buddies can help hearing impaired pupils to participate more fully. In physical education they can clarify the rules of games and specific vocabulary involved. Terms that require fine discrimination in meaning and terms with multiple meanings often need clarification related to the context in which they are used. An example is the difference in the terms *dash* and *run* as used in physical education. Think of the meanings of *basket*. Hearing impaired pupils would probably know the word *basket* to mean a container with a handle, but it has a separate meaning in the game of basketball.

There are advantages and disadvantages in using hearing buddies. A disadvantage of the buddy system can be dependence of the pupils on this supportive relationship. To prevent such dependence, the buddy role can be rotated among the pupils in the class. When possible, the situation should be structured so that hearing impaired pupils assume the initiative for self-help. Hearing buddies can be used for certain activities and not for others in order to lessen hearing impaired pupils' dependence on others. Help during certain activities can be phased out as hearing impaired pupils become familiar with the routines and expectations of the events. These actions will help hearing impaired pupils learn and practice independence in the mainstream of the school. Observations of each pupil's skills in different types of situations should be the guide for deciding whether a buddy is needed or not. There will probably always be some need for assistance. The issue is not that the person is a success only when completely independent. The goal should be for these pupils to maintain a high level of functioning. Conversely, the alert teacher will perceive opportunities for the hearing impaired pupil to serve as a helper. This is important for such students.

Social interaction among pupils is one of the main advantages of using the buddy system. Integration into the mainstream of the school involves more than physical proximity. Participation and acceptance in school activities are the intents of integration.

Providing Speech and Language Models

Provide good speech and language models by considering the following:

1. Speech sounds should not be exaggerated.
2. Speak in a normal manner.
3. Do not speak fast.
4. Use correct sentence structure and correct vocabulary to provide reinforcement for hearing impaired pupils.

EMPLOYING GENERAL TEACHING PRINCIPLES

Several general principles apply to the instruction of pupils who have any type of handicap. The most important of these principles is to capitalize on pupils' strengths. Examples follow:

1. Combine a visual presentation with oral materials for hearing impaired pupils.
2. Write assignments on transparencies for an overhead projector as well as reviewing them orally or providing a handout sheet of the day's announcements that typically come over the school's intercommunication system.
3. A hearing buddy could make a brief outline of the announcements for hearing impaired pupils.
4. Machines such as Language Master or System 80, where there are simultaneous visual and auditory presentations, are helpful.
5. Use other learning modalities such as tactile and kinesthetic. Using a multisensory approach provides pupils with additional channels for learning. For example, pupils can say vocabulary words while they trace and look at the printed copy.

Another important principle deals with the way a lesson is presented. The following sequence is suggested:

1. Some type of activity to focus the pupils' attention is needed to clue them to the fact that a particular subject lesson is about to begin.

2. There should be a clear, concise introduction to the lesson.

3. Teach the major portion of the lesson itself.

4. A summary or review of the important points should conclude the lesson. Summary charts written like experience charts provide a permanent reference.

This format is educationally sound for all pupils but especially helpful for handicapped pupils.

Hearing impaired pupils cannot attend to two visual activities at the same time. For instance, if a filmstrip is being used with the teacher providing commentary, these pupils cannot look at both. They would have to look at the visual filmstrip. This problem can be alleviated by the teacher sitting near the screen and facing the class.

To assist hearing impaired pupils to use speech reading in following oral discussions and conversations, someone needs to point out who is speaking at the time. Pupils with diminished hearing have difficulty keeping up with who is talking because of the rapid shift of speakers in spontaneous discussion and conversation.

One helpful technique is to give visual clues when changing activities or subjects during the school day. Examples follow:

1. Hold up the textbook for the next lesson.

2. Use transition sentences.

3. Flip the light switch to indicate lunch time.

Such environmental clues facilitate understanding of what is being said and what is going on in the classroom.

Be sure that you have the hearing impaired pupils' attention before giving instructions or beginning a lesson:

1. Verbalizations should be short and simple in order to be easily understood.

2. Ask questions to check understanding.

3. Rephrase if pupils have difficulty understanding the communication.

Rephrasing directions and explanations to clarify understanding is often necessary. An automatic nod of assent is common with hearing impaired pupils when they are asked if they understand. To be sure that the pupils know what to do or what has been said or read, ask questions that cannot be answered with yes or no. Require students to answer with complete sentences so that they can practice correct language usage.

Hearing impaired pupils perform better when studying or being tested on spelling words or vocabulary words if the words are used in meaningful sentences. Sentences that are relevant to the pupils' experience are especially helpful.

Workbook pages and other school activities may lack clearly written directions or explanatory examples. Hearing impaired pupils may not understand the oral explanation. Providing such information in written form helps them know how to proceed with the lesson. A hearing buddy could prepare simple written directions or an example to illustrate what is expected and also to serve as a permanent reference.

When hearing impaired pupils are called upon for an oral response, give them adequate time to answer. Many hearing impaired pupils develop the habit of outwaiting teachers. Regular students also do this. Teachers will usually supply the answer if pupils hesitate long enough, so pupils should be encouraged to attempt answers.

One practice you will find useful is to give hearing impaired pupils vocabulary lists, fact sheets, outlines, and assignments before introducing new material in class. These can be sent home for family members to review with the pupils. Hearing buddies, aides, and volunteers can also help to prepare hearing impaired pupils for new material. Such advanced preparation will assist these pupils to progress at a rate commensurate with the rest of the class.

SPECIAL TEACHING TECHNIQUES

Ways to Facilitate Language Development

Language development is probably the greatest educational disadvantage experienced by hearing impaired pupils. Language reception must precede language expression just as with normally hearing individuals. These pupils are often described as concrete thinkers. Since learning for all individuals originates at the concrete, experiential level, this type of exposure is indicated for hearing impaired pupils. Role playing the meanings of words, phrases, sentences, and stories leads to understanding. Simple examples of role playing are the actions associated with *over* and *under, fast* and *slow*. Phrases such as "in the box" or "around the curve" are easy to experience at the concrete level. Many far more abstract concepts can also be taught at the concrete level. For example, what about the concept of constitution in relation to government? This concept is difficult for most pupils to understand, especially when they are asked to derive the real meaning of *constitution* by reading the Constitution printed in their social studies books. It can be made meaningful for pupils by having them develop a set of rules and regulations by which the class will be guided as an analogy to the Constitution. Procedures of this type relate abstract concepts in a relevant manner to the pupils' real world. This type of activity can facilitate understanding of science vocabulary and concepts quite effectively. For instance, understanding cell structure and function is difficult for most normal pupils as well as handicapped pupils. Groups of pupils can role play the parts of a cell. One group of pupils forms the entire cell wall, with other pupils forming other parts of the cell. Each group or individual describes the function of that structure at whatever level of sophistication the class could understand. When you have "been" a cell wall, or vacuole, or mitochondrion, you don't forget very rapidly what one is or how it functions.

The representation or semiabstract level is the next highest level of presenting vocabulary and concepts. A common technique at this level is the use of pictures. This is essential since hearing impaired pupils rely on visual presentations. If pictures, filmstrips, or films are not readily available to explain the particular vocabulary or concepts being studied by the class, a simple exercise is to have class members illustrate the vocabulary or concepts. The best of these illustrations can be used as examples to help the hearing impaired pupils.

Pupils can also construct illustrative cards for permanent reference and study. This technique is helpful in understanding synonyms, antonyms, homonyms, and multiple meanings. Figures 6-1, 6-2, 6-3, and 6-4 show how illustrative vocabulary and concept cards can be made.

Each pupil should draw her own illustrations so that you can be sure that she has a clear understanding of the concepts. After the hearing impaired pupil has mastered her set of cards, she can form a study team with another pupil so that they can practice from both sets of cards. Examples and wording on these cards should be used when teachers construct tests. Remember how important it is for wording used on tests to be consistent with what hearing impaired pupils have been studying.

FIGURE 6-1

FIGURE 6-2

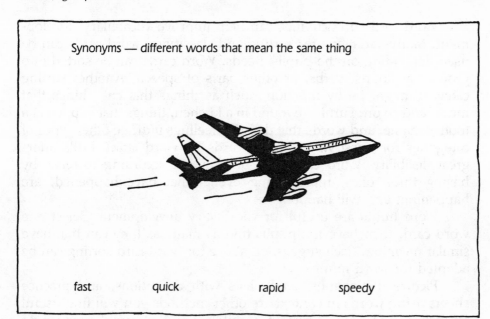

FIGURE 6-3

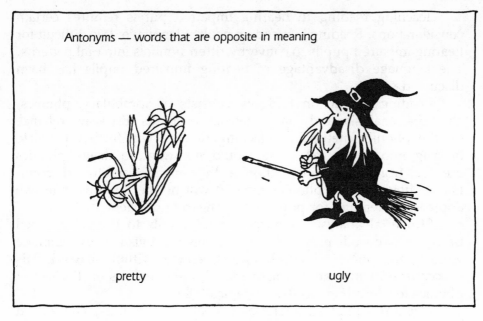

FIGURE 6-4

Word card sort activities can help improve vocabulary development. Many variations for sorting and classifying word cards can be used depending on the pupils' needs. Word cards can be sorted into groups by nouns, verbs, or other parts of speech. Another sorting category might be by function, such as things that cut, things that move, and so on. Furniture found in a kitchen, things that happen at a football game, and words that describe feelings indicate other types of categories for classifying. Sorting cards by word attack skills offers great flexibility. Word cards can be grouped according to tense by having three piles, representing events that have happened, are happening, and will happen.

Word hunts are useful for vocabulary development. Select one word card, then have the pupils find as many as they can that have similar meaning. Each suggestion above for word card sorting can be adapted for word hunts.

Picture dictionaries, study lists with definitions, and practice sheets using words in context are other methods you will find useful for facilitating language growth. Capitalize on the pupils' experiences as much as possible.

Adapting Reading Instruction

Teaching reading to hearing impaired pupils requires certain considerations. Reading is based on spoken language. It is difficult for hearing impaired pupils to convert written symbols into oral patterns. The language disadvantage of hearing impaired pupils has been discussed earlier.

Reading instruction typically consists of vocabulary, phonics, structural analysis, and comprehension exercises. Excessive reliance on the phonics method in teaching reading will further penalize hearing impaired pupils. You would not want to delete phonics exercises from reading instruction, as they enhance auditory discrimination; however, the phonics method will not be the most effective approach to reading for pupils with a hearing deficiency.

Structural analysis exercises induce pupils to use their visual processes to decode printed symbols. They must visually discriminate word configuration and morphological elements within the word. This procedure provides an alternative to undue emphasis on the use of phonics for decoding words. Examples follow.

Structural analysis includes inflectional endings, compound words, plural forms, affixes, syllabication, and contractions. Since instructional materials for teaching these skills are readily available, only sample activities will be presented.

1. Inflectional endings:
   a. Sue's mother is ~~make~~ making a cake.
   b. Circle the root word.
      softer   slowly
      brightest   darkest
      lonely   shorter
   c. Make new words by adding *s, ed,* and *ing* to these words. Pronounce each word and tell how the ending changes the meaning of the word.

Word	s	ed	ing
jump			
show			
bark			
call			

2. Compound words:
   a. Each of these words is a compound word. Write the two words found in each compound word on the lines provided.

   notebook   _____   _____

   homework   _____   _____

   baseball   _____   _____

   railroad   _____   _____

   teapot   _____   _____

   breakfast _____   _____

   b. Add another word to each of the following words to make a compound word.

   foot   _____ (ball)

   pea   _____ (nut)

air   _____

tooth   _____

bath   _____

sail   _____

3. Plural forms:
   a. Write the correct word on the line below each picture.

Here is one _____. Here are three _____.

Here is one _____. Here are two _____.

Here is one _____. Here are two _____.

   b. Find ten plural words in the newspaper.
4. Affixes:
   a. Circle the root word in each of these words.
      looks   interested
      lovely   useless
      playing   playful
   b. Circle the root word in each of these words.
      review   indirect
      unpack   prepaid
      disagree   misinform

5. Syllabication:
    a. Say each to yourself. Write the number of parts or syllables you hear.

rabbit	_____	train	_____
dog	_____	banana	_____
unhappy	_____	spider	_____

    b. Draw a slash between the syllables in the words below. (fur/ni/ture)

    sudden   yellow
    basket   pilot
    tomorrow   elephant

6. Contractions:
    a. Draw a line from each word in column 1 to the matching contraction in column 2.

1	2
cannot	I'm
I am	I'd
I had	can't
they are	they're

    b. Write a contraction for each of the following.

    I have   _____

    here is   _____

    will not   _____

    he is   _____

Cloze exercises may be helpful in developing comprehension. This technique has been used to assess pupils' understanding during silent reading. It can also be used as an instructional technique. Fill in the blank sentences that are typical cloze exercises. In the simplest form, a choice of words to fill in the blank is supplied: "The dog (ran, barked)." The difficulty level can progress as the pupils' ability to use context clues improves. At the highest level you would require pupils to supply correct words for each blank.

You may find matching simple and complex sentences to be an appropriate activity. Here is an example: "The boy is tall. The boy has red hair. The boy, who is tall, has red hair."

The language experience approach has proven to be an effective way to teach hearing impaired pupils to read. Any common experience can form the basis of a story dictated or written by the pupils. Since the pupils compose the story, it matches their level of language usage. Variations of reading activities such as word matching, locating parts of speech, and oral reading can be developed in relation to the story.

A set of pictures that can be arranged in some logical sequence can be used quite effectively as a basis for pupils to compose a story. Sets of pictures are available commercially. Comic strips without words are often appropriate. A series of photographs of pupils participating in some event can provide the focus for creating a story of special interest to the pupils.

Teaching Written Expression

Hearing impaired pupils often experience difficulty with written expression. Because of difficulty in language usage, sentence structure can be quite confused. Pupils may write words out of sequence so that the sentence makes no sense. Arranging words in phrases, clauses, and sentences so that correct meaning is conveyed is called *syntax*. Children develop the syntactic process as they experience words and events in their environment. Hearing impaired children frequently do not develop this syntactic process naturally because of their limitations in receiving spoken language.

Semantics refers to the meaning system of language. If pupils know one meaning of a word, they may not understand when the word is used in a different sense or as a different part of speech. For instance, compare the meaning and use of the word *run* in these simple sentences: "You may run in the race." "You have a run in your stocking." Be aware that confusion may result when hearing impaired pupils do not understand the transition in meaning that occurs when words are used differently in sentences.

Several types of activities help to remediate these language problems:

1. Give pupils a list of several simple sentences and a set of word cards including all of the words in the sentence. Have pupils sequence the word cards in correct order to match the sentences. As they practice the matching exercise, help them to understand the function of the words; that is, the function of the parts of speech.

2. After students are proficient with the matching exercise, provide a story with key words left out. Initially, omitted words should be

nouns. When pupils are successful in supplying nouns correctly, nouns can be included in the sentences and verbs omitted. This progression can be continued to include grammatically complex sentences. The following is a simple example:

"The _____ came to town yesterday. A train
with pictures on the cars brought many _____.
A _____ was roaring. Men
were putting up the big _____."

3. Give pupils word cards to arrange in correct order. Initially, pupils should be given only two cards, a noun and a verb to sequence. When pupils master this step, other parts of speech or phrases can be added. Typically, articles, adjectives, helping verbs, and adverbs are learned in that order. As pupils master each step, sentence expansion exercises can be used. Here is an example: "The boy runs. The tall boy runs. The tall boy will run. The tall boy will run tomorrow."

4. Use questions about who, what, when, where, and how many to help hearing impaired pupils organize words in correct sentence form. When pupils have difficulty sequencing words to convey the meaning they want, help by asking questions. When you ask, "What are you going to write about?" the pupil answers or writes, "My dog."
"What did your dog do?"
"My dog barked."
"When did your dog bark?"
"My dog barked yesterday."

5. After pupils are familiar with this technique, charts can be made to hang in the room. Each chart should have words known by the pupils that refer to one of the questions. For instance, "in the lunchroom," "on the playground," "at my house," and similar words and phrases might be listed on the "where" chart. This procedure allows pupils to formulate sentences independent of constant supervision.

Mathematics

Hearing impaired pupils do not have any more difficulty in learning arithmetic computation than hearing pupils. However, the language element in story problems may present difficulty. Hearing impaired pupils have the ability to conceptualize at higher levels needed for problem solving; however, it is not uncommon for hearing pupils to experience difficulty with problem-solving skills, and they need instruction here.

Teaching the meaning of the language in story problems is essential. An understanding of key phrases such as "less than," "how many more," and "how many all together" will need to be established before pupils can analyze the problems for computation. In other words, the language of the story problem will need to be taught before hearing impaired pupils can proceed.

The same techniques that have been suggested earlier apply to the teaching of mathematics:

1. Use abacuses, plastic chips, coins, and other small objects to bring learning to the concrete level.

2. Use place value boxes, number lines, playing cards, and other semiabstract materials to facilitate learning.

HOW TO MODIFY THE CURRICULUM

Pupils with hearing difficulty require few modifications of the regular curriculum unless there are other factors such as lower intellectual ability and other sensory deficiencies involved. The range of intellectual ability among hearing impaired pupils is the same as in the hearing pupil population when tested with nonverbal instruments. However, academic achievement is often lower then average because of retarded language development. You will find that the hearing impaired pupil can usually be grouped with other pupils in the classroom who have similar achievement needs. There may be variations from one subject to another just as with hearing pupils. Most pupils achieve better in some subjects than in others, and this holds true for hearing impaired pupils.

Tips on Auditory Training

One curriculum modification that may be required for pupils with hearing difficulty is increased emphasis on auditory training. Auditory training involves teaching discrimination between sounds, training auditory memory, and the skills necessary to listen for pitch, rhythm, and intensity. You do this when teaching reading. The same principle of progressing from grossly different sounds (hard *c* and *m*) to sounds of fine discrimination (short *e* and *i*) applies to auditory training with hearing impaired pupils as with pupils who have normal hearing. Auditory training should not be confined to one class period. Use every opportunity throughout the school day to help hearing impaired pupils to discriminate sounds.

Overcoming Language Deficit

Hearing impaired pupils benefit from language development programs. The greater the hearing loss, the more it interferes with normal language development. To assist you there are many commercial vocabulary development programs and workbooks available. The following are representative:

Peabody Language Developmental Kit
American Guidance Service
Publisher Building
Circle Pine, Minnesota 55014

Language Training for Adolescents
Educators Publishing Service
75 Moulton Street
Cambridge, Massachusetts 02138

Appletree Language Program
Dormac, Inc.
P.O. Box 622
Lake Oswego, Oregon 97034

These may be quite useful for general language development, but pupils will also need help with language concepts in subjects being taught to the class.

Considering Conceptual Difficulty of Hearing Impaired Pupils

While the normal curriculum may not need to be modified for hearing impaired pupils, the conceptual level of the language and the method of presentation often need to be adjusted. Hearing impaired pupils may not understand the language associated with abstract concepts. They may have difficulty understanding relationships such as cousins. Idioms such as "in hot water" may present problems. Literal interpretation of idioms often occurs. However, hearing impaired pupils are not deficient in the *ability* to conceptualize abstractly.

Reinforcing Speech Therapy Procedures

If hearing impaired pupils are receiving speech therapy, you can reinforce the sounds and speech patterns learned in therapy sessions. Close communication with the speech therapist will result in consistent and concentrated programs.

SELECTING MATERIALS

There are two major considerations in regard to selecting or adapting materials for hearing impaired pupils:

1. Concept level of the language
2. Involvment of input modalities other than auditory

Ways to Modify Concept Level of Materials

A pupil's ability to conceptualize is closely related to language associated with direct experiences. Young children function at the concrete level, conceptualizing objects or events that can be observed. A child may attend several birthday parties. If the child did not hear or associate any words with the event, she would need to see pictures with explanations or have to be involved in a birthday party to be aware of the concept or idea of birthday party.

Young children normally learn to connect specific words with specific objects or events. Over time, experiences with the same object or event will evoke a word or words associated with that object or event. For example, after a child has experienced several birthday parties that have been labeled as birthday parties, she forms a mental picture of a birthday party. The mind perceives and remembers what has been seen by the eyes. This mental picture can be recalled by hearing the words "birthday party." It is then possible to describe concepts by definition. At this point the experience can evoke the name, or the name can evoke the concept of the experience. Children can function at the abstract level of conceptualization as they store more memories that can be recalled by words.

This chapter has stressed that language and conceptualization must be considered in all educational activities involving hearing impaired pupils. This is true in the selection or adaptation of materials. If available materials are not appropriate for the needs of certain hearing impaired pupils, instructional strategies will need to be used to mediate difficulties with comprehension. These strategies have been discussed in the section on teaching techniques.

Materials can be rewritten in language familiar to the pupils; however, few teachers have time for this. You can use fact sheets, summaries, diagrams, and illustrations if materials are inappropriate.

Textbooks and materials designed for a lower grade level may be used. This is particularly true for content subjects such as science and social studies and especially if the lower-level books are ones not used in the school and therefore unfamiliar to the pupils. Separate the units from the cover, and make booklets on each topic. Manila folders make durable covers for the booklets. Attractive designs can be created by pupils on these covers. This procedure removes some of the stigma of grade level numbers or "secret codes" on the spines of textbooks.

Using Materials Incorporating Varied Learning Modalities

Another consideration for material selection and adaptation involves the use of learning modalities other than auditory. Books should be selected that use pictures and illustrations liberally. Many books have accompanying pictures, charts, maps, filmstrips, and other media available. You will find that these multimedia programs provide effective instructional materials for hearing impaired pupils. Select materials that minimize reliance on the auditory channel.

Captioned films are available for hearing impaired pupils. These films have verbal statements printed on the bottom of each frame to provide accompanying narrative or dialogue.

Information can be obtained from the following organizations:

Captioned Films for the Deaf Distribution Center
5034 Wisconsin Avenue, N.W.
Washington, D.C. 20016

National Captioning Institute, Inc.
5203 Leesburg Pike
Falls Church, Virginia 22041

HEARING AIDS AND SPECIAL SERVICES

Using Hearing Aids and Manual Interpreters

Pupils with hearing disabilities may wear hearing aids. A demonstration of the aid will help both teachers and other pupils in the class.

Hearing impaired pupils, parents, resource teachers for the hearing impaired, or speech therapists could demonstrate how the hearing aid works and simple maintenance procedures. A few maintenance procedures can be performed quite easily by teachers or responsible pupils:

1. Every morning the battery should be checked to see if it is working.
2. Cords and cord connections should be checked if the pupil wears a body aid.
3. The earmold should be cleaned of wax.

The school should furnish a simple meter to test the battery. Such meters are commonly available as science equipment. Parents should provide extra batteries to keep at school. You will notice quite a difference in the hearing impaired pupil's performance when the aid is dysfunctional. Occasionally the earmold will become loose and slip, which causes a squeaking or squealing sound. Learning to insert the earmold or fit it securely in the pupil's ear to remedy the problem is a simple procedure.

A hearing aid does not enable a hearing impaired pupil to hear normally. While the aid amplifies sound, it is seldom free from distortion. Remember that the aid will amplify all classroom sounds, so background noises are louder. Unexpected sounds such as slamming the door or throwing books down can be unpleasant for pupils wearing aids. Pupils who wear hearing aids still need favorable seating. Again, a hearing aid does not enable a person to have normal hearing. It helps but does not completely eliminate the hearing impairment.

Some regular classrooms will have profoundly deaf pupils as class members. These pupils will be unable to benefit from oral communication whether they wear a hearing aid or not. They will communicate with some form of manual communication, usually finger spelling or sign language. (An interpreter is required to translate spoken language into manual code. Deaf pupils and the interpreter should be allowed to select the most appropriate seating arrangement.) There should be no cause for alarm in having a profoundly deaf pupil in the regular classroom, because adequate intelligence and learning strategies will have been demonstrated before they are placed in regular classrooms. You can expect these pupils to achieve quite satisfactorily. Incidentally, hearing pupils are usually intrigued with manual communication and become quite proficient in using it when provided with basic instruction and practice.

Using Ancillary Service

Ancillary services are available for hearing impaired pupils. Interpreters who translate spoken language into a manual code were mentioned above. Oral interpreters translate manual communication of deaf pupils into spoken language for hearing individuals. Aides, tutors, and note takers may be supplied by the school district. Itinerant teachers for hearing impaired pupils are a source of help for regular classroom teachers. In addition to audiometric screening and speech therapy, the speech therapist can supply other information and suggestions for the education of hearing impaired pupils.

PREPARING THE CLASS TO RECEIVE HEARING IMPAIRED PUPILS

It is important for teachers to prepare the class for a hearing impaired member. Your attitudes and treatment of hearing impaired pupils provide the model for acceptance and integration into the class. These pupils should be treated the same as all pupils, including the same expectations, provided proper accommodations have been made for the disability.

One technique is the use of simulations to help pupils understand hearing impairment. Tape recordings of cafeteria noise played while oral communication is occurring, and holding a book in front of your face while reading with a low voice are examples of simulation activities.

The use of children's literature depicting hearing impairment correctly can be useful. *Lisa and Her Soundless World* (Levine, 1974) is an example of a book that would provide a realistic explanation of hearing impairment. The attitude to be developed should reflect the philosophy that the class members need to understand the nature of hearing impairment and to make appropriate accommodations instead of fostering the philosophy that the hearing impaired pupil has the problem.

You may also use preparation of the class to receive hearing impaired pupils as the stimulus to introduce a science unit on sound.

Hearing impaired pupils also benefit from the science unit by learning about their disability. Surprisingly, pupils are apt to have little factual knowledge related to their own disability. An activity for social studies would be a discussion of the social or environmental difficulties that hearing impaired individuals encounter. Pupils find investigations of the lives of historical figures who were hearing impaired, such as Thomas Edison, interesting and relevant.

Be aware of the individual differences in each hearing impaired pupil. Hearing impairment refers to only one of the many traits of these pupils. Often we focus on the disability and forget the whole child. Factors such as social experiences, physical condition, family background, and intelligence influence the educational performance of these pupils just as it does with all pupils. A cold can further diminish the hearing of hearing impaired pupils just as it can affect the hearing of other pupils. Keep all of these factors in mind when planning the educational program for hearing impaired as well as normal pupils.

SUMMING UP

Identification of mild to moderate hearing loss requires careful observation of physical and behavioral characteristics of pupils. These behaviors do not always manifest themselves in ways that cause teachers to suspect a hearing loss. Poor academic achievement, immature language development, inattention, or behavior problems may be symptomatic of diminished hearing.

Language development and attention to the conceptual level of vocabulary and ideas will require specific teaching techniques. Language should be made relevant to the pupils' world.

The regular classroom curriculum may require little modification. Auditory training and language development may need to be emphasized. Some attention to the conceptual level of language used by the teacher and in the materials will probably be necessary.

Two additional points should be made. First, the suggestions in this chapter have focused on the needs of pupils with deficit hearing; however, these techniques are also applicable to the educational needs of other pupils in a typical classroom. Most culturally, economically, or educationally disadvantaged pupils can benefit from these modifications. There is usually a group of pupils in every classroom who can profit from these educational considerations; thus, the teacher's time is used effectively.

The second point is a reminder to focus on the whole pupil rather than on the hearing impairment. Like every hearing pupil, each pupil with a hearing loss has strengths and weaknesses that are unique. Regular classroom teachers have a challenge and an opportunity to provide an appropriate education for all pupils in the class, including the integrated hearing impaired pupils.

REFERENCES AND SELECTED READINGS

Birch, J. W. *Hearing Impaired Children in the Mainstream*. Minneapolis: Leadership Training Institute/Special Education, University of Minnesota, 1975.

Bitter, G. B., and E. G. Mears. "Facilitating the Integration of Hearing Impaired Children into Regular Public School Classes." *Volta Review* 75 (1973): 13–22.

Bothwell, H. "What the Classroom Teacher Can Do for the Child with Impaired Hearing." *NEA Journal* 56 (1967): 44–46.

Braddock, M. J. "Integrating the Deaf and Hard of Hearing Student." *Volta Review* 64 (1962): 500–501.

Caniglia, J., N. J. Cole, W. Howard, E. Krohn, and M. Rice. *Apple Tree*. Lake Oswego, Ore.: Dormac, 1972.

Dunn, L. M. (ed.). *Exceptional Children in the Schools*. New York: Holt, Rinehart, and Winston, 1973.

Faas, L. A. *Children with Learning Problems: A Handbook for Teachers*. Dallas: Houghton-Mifflin, 1980.

Fitzgerald, E. *Straight Language for the Deaf*. Washington, D.C.: Volta Review, 1972.

Frick, E. "Adjusting to Integration: Some Difficulties Hearing Impaired Children Have in Public Schools." *Volta Review* 75 (1973): 36–46.

Gearheart, B. R., and M. W. Weishahn. *The Handicapped Child in the Regular Class*. St. Louis: C. V. Mosby, 1976.

Hedgecock, D. "Facilitating Integration at the Junior High Level." *Volta Review* 76 (1974): 182–188.

Hewett, F. M., and S. R. Forness. *Education of Exceptional Learners*. Boston: Allyn and Bacon, 1974.

Kirk, S. A., and J. J. Gallagher. *Educating Exceptional Children*. Boston: Houghton-Mifflin, 1979.

L'Abate, L., and L. T. Curtis. *Teaching the Exceptional Child*. Philadelphia: Saunders, 1975.

Leckie, D. J. "Creating a Receptive Climate in the Mainstream Program." *Volta Review* 75 (1973): 23–27.

Levine, E. S. *Lisa and Her Soundless World.* New York: Human Sciences Press, 1974.

McGee, D. I. "The Benefits of Educating Deaf Children with Hearing Children." *Teaching Exceptional Children 2.* (1970): 133–137.

Nix, G. W. *Mainstream Education for Hearing Impaired Children and Youth.* New York: Grune and Stratton, 1976.

Northcott, W. H. "A Hearing Impaired Pupil in the Classroom." *Volta Review* 74 (1972): 105–108.

Pollock, M. B., and K. C. Pollock. "Letter to the Teacher of a Hard of Hearing Child." *Childhood Education* 47 (1971): 206–209.

Rister, A. "Deaf Children in a Mainstream Education." *Volta Review* 77 (1975): 279–290.

Telford, C. C., and J. M. Sawrey. *The Exceptional Individual.* Englewood Cliffs, N.J.: Prentice-Hall, 1972.

Turnbull, A. P. and J. B. Schulz *Mainstreaming Handicapped Students: A Guide for the Classroom Teacher.* Boston: Allyn and Bacon, 1979.

Wallace, G., and J. M. Kauffman. *Teaching Children with Learning Problems.* Columbus, Ohio: Charles E. Merrill, 1978.

CHAPTER SEVEN

Visual Impairment

One pupil has difficulty copying from the chalkboard; another pupil has difficulty keeping his place when reading. One pupil has difficulty playing baseball; another pupil complains of headaches. Any of these behaviors could be symptomatic of a mild to moderate visual impairment. Most individuals with severe visual impairment are identified during their preschool years or during initial screening for entry into school. However, pupils with mild to moderate vision loss may go undetected in the classroom, particularly if the loss is gradual in onset.

This chapter presents clues for identifying vision difficulties, hints for spatial orientation and other environmental considerations, special teaching methods, suggestions for curriculum and materials adaptation, ancillary services, and tips on integrating visually impaired pupils into the regular classroom.

DEFINING VISUAL DIFFICULTIES

Visual impairment can be defined in two ways. There is a medical–legal definition and an educational definition. The *National*

Society for the Prevention of Blindness Fact Book (1966, p. 10) includes the following definitions:

> Blindness is generally defined in the United States as visual acuity for distance vision of 20/200 or less in the better eye, with best correction; or visual acuity of more than 20/200 if the widest diameter of field of vision subtends an angle no greater than 20 degrees.
>
> The partially seeing are defined as persons with a vision acuity greater than 20/200 but not greater than 20/70 in the better eye with correction.

This is a medical–legal definition largely based on tests of visual acuity. These numbers are most commonly derived from testing with the Snellen Chart. While the exact meaning is somewhat more complex, the following description is often used to explain symbols in visual acuity testing. The numbers 20/200 mean that the individual can distinguish at 20 feet the symbol or letter that the normal eye can distinguish at 200 feet. The phrase "with best correction" generally means that visual acuity can be improved with the use of eyeglasses, or by surgery or therapeutic exercises. The reference to the width of the visual field relates to those who might be described as having a visual field loss or loss of the ability to see clearly through the complete visual field. While this loss sometimes results in pinpoint or tunnel vision, often vision in the center of the visual field is lost while peripheral vision remains intact. Therefore, any type of visual field loss of 80 percent or more is classified as medical–legal blindness. Individuals who fall between the 20/200 and 20/70 classifications have enough residual vision to function normally in most situations and are therefore classified as partially sighted.

While the above definition was and is widely used, it became apparent that a definition more practical for the educational environment was needed. Two basic factors directed attention to this need for an educationally relevant definition:

1. Research findings have shown that a large percentage of individuals who were classified as legally blind learned to read print.
2. The medical–legal definition is based on an individual's distance visual acuity, while elementary grade school activities (increased reading and writing) rely more on near-point vision.

For visual screening to be adequate, tests for near vision, muscle balance, and visual perception must be included. The Massachusetts Vision Test is often recommended. The American Optical, Bausch and Lomb Optical, and Titmus Optical are among the companies that manufacture binocular instruments that test various elements of vision. Individuals who may be available to administer a vision screening program include the school nurse, teachers of the visually impaired, other special education teachers, and trained parent volunteers. Results of initial screening are used to recommend further testing by ophthalmologists or optometrists.

The functional use of residual vision indicated a shift in the belief that most visually impaired pupils required Braille instead of print materials. Therefore, an educational definition evolved. Bateman (1967, p. 258) has stated the following:

> Educationally speaking, blind children are those visually handicapped children who use Braille, and partially seeing are those who use print.

The majority of visually impaired pupils are educated in public schools, with many pupils receiving a major portion of their education in regular classrooms with or without support services.

TWELVE CLUES TO WATCH FOR IN SPOTTING VISUAL DISABILITIES

Teachers have the opportunity to observe signs and behaviors that might indicate a pupil who has a possible vision problem. Observations of different types of activities should be conducted in a variety of settings.

Five physical clues:

1. Frequent encrusted eyelids, watering eyes, reddened eyes or eyelids, or sties
2. Crossed eyes
3. Blurring of vision
4. Frequent headaches, nausea, dizziness, or burning of the eyes
5. Constantly jerky eye movements

Some of these physical clues are obvious. Disorders such as crossed eyes or drooping lids are easily detected. Encrusted eyelids, watering eyes, and conditions of this type prompt you to look for chronic recurrence.

Other physical clues are brought to your attention by pupils' complaints. Repeated complaints of blurred vision, headaches, and burning eyes are examples.

Seven behavioral clues:

1. Body rigidity or thrusting the head forward or backward while looking at distant objects
2. Frowning or losing the place while reading or writing
3. Frequent rubbing of eyes
4. Closing or covering one eye or tilting head to one side
5. Avoiding close visual tasks or placing the head unusually close to learning material
6. Difficulty in copying from the chalkboard
7. Bumping into people or objects or poor performance on tasks requiring eye–hand coordination

Awkward positioning of the head or body when using distance vision or near vision may be a warning signal. A personal experience illustrates this point. Throughout elementary and secondary school a pupil was teased by peers for "looking funny" when she viewed films or engaged in similar activities. She had glasses prescribed by a doctor for a refraction problem. However, it was not until she reached adulthood that a doctor discovered a visual defect that caused her to hold her head in a contorted position in order to improve her ability to see.

Difficulties in orientation during spatial activities, such as those engaged in at recess time or physical education, may suggest a vision problem. Performance in penmanship or writing exercises, such as poor spacing and inability to stay on the line, could be another indication. However, these behaviors could be caused by other conditions such as perceptual or motor problems instead of visual acuity difficulties.

A teacher with keen observational skills may notice a discrepancy in a pupil's ability to perform distance vision tasks such as copying from the chalkboard and near-point vision tasks such as reading. A pupil's avoidance of or complaints about certain kinds of tasks may trigger the need for you to concentrate on seeking a reason for this behavior. As with all types of atypical behavior, if you look for a consistent pattern of pupil behavior, most problems that need further testing or referral can be identified in the classroom.

MOBILITY AND ORIENTATION

Overcoming Difficulties with Spatial Orientation

The visually impaired pupil may not experience the same degree of independence in moving about as pupils with normal sight. Orientation difficulties can impose one of the greatest limitations to mobility. Mobility is travel from place to place using strategies, particularly sound and remaining vision. Canes, dogs, and sighted guides may also be used. Orientation means awareness of where one is in relation to objects and in what direction one needs to go in order to get to other people.

Blind pupils receive training in mobility and orientation from a specialist. If the training is proceeding while the pupil is enrolled in a regular classroom, you should receive information from the specialist so that you will understand the nature of the training.

Several types of mobility and orientation training programs and aids are available. Determination of the most appropriate training should receive consideration from the parents, the blind individual, and the mobility and orientation specialist.

Independent travel without personal assistance or use of an aid means teaching the blind individual to use environmental objects or sound as orientation for movement and to use the hands and arms to protect other parts of the body during movement.

A sighted guide is one mobility technique employed by blind individuals. The impaired individual walks one step behind and to the side of the sighted guide, grasping the guide's arm just above the elbow. Movement of the guide provides cues that direct the travel of the blind individual.

A long cane to sweep the area that the visually impaired individual is approaching is one of the many cane travel techniques. Several types of canes are available. Cane techniques are most often taught to adolescents.

Electronic devices generally use sound or tactile vibration to guide movement. Some of these devices use laser, ultrasonic, and infrared rays in the conversion to sound or vibration.

The use of a guide dog may appear to be a rather dramatic solution to travel difficulties experienced by the blind. In reality, a small percentage find the use of guide dogs a practical technique for independent travel. Among the disadvantages are cost, training, constant care of the dog, maturity of the owner, and inconvenience for other people. A dog is often impractical in a school setting. The blind must know how to get to the desired location, with the guide dog serving to indicate the clarity of the path to that location. Despite the disadvantages, guide dogs will be a viable alternative aid to travel for some blind individuals.

Visually impaired pupils may need assistance in mastering the school environment. A tour of the school is common for all new pupils in a classroom or school. This tour takes on added dimensions and is significantly more important for visually impaired pupils. If possible, before school enrollment these pupils should come in to get familiar with the classroom, school buildings, and playground. If that is not possible, orientation and mobility activities should be conducted when other pupils are not around. This allows the visually impaired pupils to gain confidence in addition to benefiting from a quieter environment. The following activities should be helpful:

1. Guide the pupil around the classroom. Explain the layout of furniture and architectural structures such as bookshelves and closets.

2. Have the pupil practice walking around the classroom until he is comfortable.

3. Repeat the same procedure of guiding the pupil while explaining the layout for other areas of the school such as restrooms, cafeteria, main office, gymnasium, library, and playground.

4. Concentrate on movement to one area at a time. The pupil may need to be guided several times before independent practice begins.

5. Be sure to rehearse fire drill routes.

6. Give specific verbal descriptions. For example, "To get to the nurse's office, when you leave the classroom turn west in the hall and go all the way to the end. Then turn east in Hall A. The nurse's office is the second door on the right." Compass directions are more practical than left and right because they do not change.

7. Use the pupil's name when speaking to him, as he may not know you are looking at him.

8. Use a buddy as a guide if there is an event such as a field trip that is not part of the normal routine.

9. Familiarize the pupil with any changes that are made in the school environment at a later date.

Some visually impaired pupils find walking into crowds when changing classes disturbing. You can arrange to have these pupils go earlier or later than the rest of the group. This is particularly helpful when pupils have to walk down stairs.

In summary, emphasis on the following techniques will help pupils with visual impairment to overcome difficulties with spatial orientation. Guidance and practice in new settings and using specific oral communications assist pupils in effective management of the environment.

HINTS FOR MODIFICATION AND CONSIDERATION IN THE CLASSROOM

Several factors in the classroom must be considered and possibly modified to provide the most appropriate environment of *maximum opportunity* for partially sighted pupils. Illumination, contrast, size, distance, and color are among the most important factors.

1. *Illumination.* The source and quality of brightness may need to be controlled. Some visually impaired pupils need more light, while others need less. Light from all sources should be diffused. Glare and shadows should be avoided. Of course, pupils should have favorable seating in regard to glare and the chalkboard. In some cases a desk lamp is helpful.

2. *Contrast.* The degree of contrast betwen the figure and the background can be a significant factor for partially sighted pupils. A gray-green chalkboard appears to reduce glare. Some combinations of colors are better than others. Off-white paper is usually preferable. Using a yellow highlighting marker over print will improve contrast. If material cannot be marked, place a sheet of yellow acetate over print. Black stencils are better than purple stencils for duplicated materials such as tests and handout materials. Dark felt-tip pens provide better contrast than pencils or ballpoint pens. Looking at forms, objects, or symbols on the stage of an overhead projector is another technique for obtaining

contrast. This is especially useful when learning letters, numerals, and other symbols.

3. *Size.* Size of print is another factor to be considered. Up to a point, the larger the print, the better; however, if the print is too large, pupils cannot see all of it. Cursive writing may be harder to read than manuscript writing. The goal is to write large enough and clearly enough for pupils to be able to read the material. Several sources of magnification are available. Addresses for agencies that provide large-print books and materials are presented later in this chapter. Primary typewriters can be used to produce worksheets and tests. Magnifying glasses, overhead projectors, microfiche viewers, rearview projection screens, microcomputer graphics, and telescopic lenses (which can be designed as glasses or monoculars) are examples of optical aids that are available. Monoculars are particularly useful for chalkboard work, reading directional signs, and other tasks of similar nature. Remember that these aids help, but they do not completely solve the vision problems.

4. *Distance.* Seating with regard to distance from what is being viewed is a consideration. Pupils with visual impairment should be encouraged to move about until a place for favorable viewing is located. Desks with adjustable tops may help these pupils achieve optimum distance for their particular needs.

5. *Color.* The color of educational materials is another important factor. Multicolored chalk, blue and white stencils or other reproduction materials, as well as gray pencil lead may be difficult to see.

Another helpful practice is to call visually impaired pupils by name when talking to them. They may be unaware that you are looking at them. Also remember to combine verbal explanations with visual activities, such as when you are writing or drawing an illustration on the chalkboard.

Considerable energy is expended when one must "look harder." Therefore, you will want to vary class activities to prevent fatigue. It may be prudent to record directions, rules, and other things that require repetitious viewing. This reduces the stress of concentrating for long periods of time on visual tasks.

Longer spaces for answers may be needed to accommodate the pupils' handwriting. Allow pupils to type answers as soon as they master the rudiments of typing; insist on correct finger placement from the beginning.

There is a tendency to talk more loudly to visually impaired individuals. This is unnecessary because blindness does not affect hearing. The manner in which sensory compensation occurs is a common misconception. The degree of auditory acuity is the same for visually impaired individuals; blind people do not have better than average hearing. They may develop their listening skills quite well from more reliance on this mode of learning, but this does not necessitate louder speech. You may relate this fact to the not uncommon occurrence of trying to traverse a bedroom on a dark night without illumination. You try to rely on sounds to help determine direction.

Another factor to consider is the level of noise in the classroom. Since the visually impaired depend so much on sound to understand what is occurring, who is present, and many other things, it is important to keep background noise to a minimum.

It is also important to take into account all aspects of each pupil (intelligence, background experience, aptitudes, etc.) when determining expectations for visually impaired pupils. If appropriate modifications have been made, expectations are the same for pupils with visual impairment as for pupils with normal vision.

How to Use Seeing Buddies

A "seeing buddy" is a pupil with normal vision who looks out for the visually impaired pupil's needs. There are several ways to use seeing buddies:

1. To assist the pupil with visual disabilities during emergency situations such as fire drills or severe storms
2. To take notes for the visually impaired pupil
3. To serve as a reader or peer tutor
4. To help the visually impaired pupil be aware of what is happening

We have all had the experience of asking someone near us what is going on or who came in when we realize we have not been aware of changes that occurred. How much more important it is to have a buddy during these situations if we are unable to see clearly. A tremendous learning experience is provided for a sighted pupil who has the opportunity to serve as a buddy.

SPECIAL TEACHING METHODS

Using Unifying Experiences to Overcome Conceptual Difficulties

Vision tends to unify the multitude of sensory stimulations experienced by pupils daily into some type of meaningful organization. Understanding the interrelatedness of these various inputs might be called a conceptual framework. We can hear, smell, and touch a horse, but the concept of horse is clarified and unified by seeing a horse. Naturally, the more severe the visual difficulty, the more conceptualization is affected. Many partially sighted pupils will have no more trouble with conceptualization than other pupils in the classroom.

Verbalism in the blind is another consideration. This refers to the tendency for blind individuals to articulate concepts verbally without concrete conception as a foundation for the words. The individual may talk very intelligently about a subject without real understanding. Concrete experiences and application activities facilitate understanding.

Several factors promote conceptual development for visually impaired pupils as well as for sighted pupils:

1. Use concrete experience. The more pupils can touch and manipulate with guided language, the more attributes they can unify into a meaningful whole. You help pupils to associate words with tactile experience.

2. Structure activities where pupils can learn by doing. Actually experiencing a situation helps pupils put together bits of information and improves conceptualization. Compare a description of a factory with a field trip to a factory. See Chapters One and Six for other examples.

3. Teach by study units. The unit method organizes learning activities into a meaningful whole. Various aspects of a topic are related by the systematic structure of study units.

4. Integrate study units. Integrating reading, writing, number work, the arts, and physical activities offers an excellent opportunity to help pupils experience the wholeness of life.

These ideas are not new to classroom teachers, but they take on added importance for visually impaired pupils. However, it must be emphasized again that these methods will benefit other pupils in the typical classroom.

Tips for Modifying Reading Instruction

The question of whether pupils with visual impairment should be taught through the use of Braille or print materials is of concern for young children. This decision will be made by vision specialists and parents rather than the regular classroom teacher. If the pupil is to learn Braille, the resource or itinerant vision teacher will be responsible for the instruction. Regular classroom teachers do not have to learn Braille, although with sight it is not difficult. On the other hand, learning the rudiments of Braille can be a motivational activity for the whole class because sighted pupils enjoy learning "secret codes." This also fosters understanding and acceptance of pupils with visual impairment.

If the partially sighted are to learn to read print material, several environmental factors warrant attention:

1. Be sure that proper aids (magnifiers, glare shields) have been selected and that pupils know how to use them.
2. When depending on oral instructions from the teacher, be sure to keep background noise to a minimum. This is especially important when teaching phonic elements.
3. Fatigue may result from an awkward position that the pupil may assume to improve the visual field. In most cases, special adjustable desk tops can be used to achieve good posture and maximum visual efficiency.

Determine the developmental level of reading readiness for each pupil. Occasionally, visually impaired children have not been encouraged to explore and experience the environment as freely as sighted children. You may need to provide concrete experiences and other readiness activities to prepare the pupils to proceed in reading instruction. As previously stated, there is usually a group of pupils in every classroom who have similar needs, so you do not have to prepare solely for the visually impaired pupils.

Pupils with visual impairments may have slightly more speech defects than the average pupil population, particularly articulation problems. This probably results from inability to clearly observe facial expressions and speech articulations, which is one of the ways young children learn to speak. It is important to recognize speech defects and recommend therapy from the speech clinician. These pupils will be hindered somewhat in reading instruction because speech sounds form the basis for work with phonics.

It has also been pointed out that the visually impaired rely on sound to a great extent. Listening skills play a vital role in adult life. Evaluate the importance of listening skills to success in your own professional and private life. Although instruction in listening skill should be part of the curriculum for all pupils, it takes on added significance for pupils with visual disabilities.

Visually impaired pupils must learn to focus attention on all letters of a word. Observe the confusion that could easily result from words of similar configuration. *When–where* and *went–wet* are examples of words that require letter by letter discrimination. Recognition of vowel shapes should be emphasized. It is also wise to teach pupils to rely on context—that is, what makes sense—as a decoding tool.

Pupils with vision impairment may require more time than sighted peers for activities involving use of a dictionary or telephone book. The length of the assignment may need to be modified to prevent fatigue.

Some pupils with visual impairment will require large-print materials. Auditory aids such as talking books, audio tapes, and strips are available. Both fiction and textbooks are available. Talking books have become a major aid for the blind and partially sighted. Compressed speech recorders are also available. These machines increase the rate of speech up to twice as fast without distortion (the Donald Duck sound). More recent are the breakthroughs using microcomputer speech synthesizers. These audio aids have enabled visually impaired individuals to attend colleges and graduate schools. Two major sources of reading materials, as well as mathematics, science, social studies, and other teaching aids for the visually impaired, are:

American Printing House for the Blind
1839 Frankfort Avenue
P.O. Box 6085
Louisville, Kentucky 40206

Division for the Blind and Physically Handicapped
Library of Congress
1291 Taylor Street
Washington, D.C. 20542

A magazine advertising such products is:

Creative Computing
P.O. Box 789-M
Morristown, New Jersey 07960

There are also regional libraries in all major population areas. These services are free for legally blind individuals.

Teaching Mathematics

Many tactile and manipulative devices are easy to make or to obtain for the teaching of mathematics. Typical activities for developing number readiness and teaching mathematical concepts are helpful for teaching visually handicapped pupils. Suggestions follow:

1. Use chips, spools, beans, and other objects to teach number readiness.

2. Arrange manipulatives in different patterns to avoid confusion between the pattern and the concept. For instance, $0^0 0$ can represent three, as well as 000.

3. Magnetic boards are useful teaching devices. Arrangments can be varied, but pieces do not fall off or blow away as readily as paper or felt boards.

4. Provide a desk copy of illustrative work that is to be placed on the chalkboard.

5. Teach mental arithmetic. Pupils may discard numerals from previous steps as they progress with mental computation. They can write down key numerals for a process that requires several steps if this seems necessary.

6. Time may be reduced by having answers only written or recorded on tests. If the problem is incorrect, the pupil could be asked to write it for the teacher to detect the error.

7. Use an adapted abacus. The beads are slightly more resistant to movement, which facilitates a clearer understanding of the work. Lightweight portable models are available.

8. Use two- and three-dimensional models for teaching when possible.

9. Darken the lines of illustrative drawings

10. Embossed graph paper, tables of numbers in Braille, adapted protracters, rulers, slide rules, and other equipment used in mathematics are available.

11. A typewriter can be used for algebra because it is primarily oriented in a linear fashion. It is not useful for arithmetic because the alignment is primarily oriented in columnar fashion.

12. Talking calculators are available. As the pupil pushes the buttons $2 + 2 =$, the machine gives information orally, "Two plus two equals four." This lets the pupil know what buttons she has pushed, as well as the answer.

13. Use clock faces with raised numerals.

Techniques for Teaching Writing

Many pupils with partial vision can develop moderate to good handwriting production. There are several aids and techniques that may be useful in teaching handwriting to visually impaired pupils:

1. Use tactile materials such as wire, rope, or modeling clay to form letters and numbers.

2. Have pupils use a stylus to write letters and numbers in a pan with a thin sheet of clay in the bottom. Kinesthetic feedback is provided by this exercise.

3. Some pupils may benefit from training templates.

4. Use dark writing pencils or pens and widely lined paper with a dull surface.

5. Use paper with raised lines, or make the lines by attaching thin strips of tape to the paper or running a thin line of glue on the paper.

Some visually impaired pupils may have experienced considerable difficulty with handwriting performance. In this case, emphasis should be on having the pupils write their names and addresses. A guide for writing a signature can be made from thin cardboard or plastic. An illustration follows:

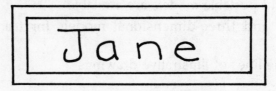

Signature guides can also be purchased.

Typewriting has been discussed earlier. Typewriting will be an important asset to visually impaired pupils as the number and length of written assignments increase with progress through school. Typewriters that say words aloud are available.

Ways to Facilitate Spelling Skills

Spelling is a rather complex skill. It has been suggested that to learn to spell a word pupils must be able to:

1. Read the word.
2. Apply phonic and word analysis techniques.

If pupils are going to write the word, they must also:

3. Remember the visual aspects of the word.
4. Use controlled motor movements.

Difficulty in spelling experienced by some visually impaired pupils may be compounded by the following:

1. Braille readers may lack visual meaning of the graphic form of the word.
2. Auditory discrimination may not be developed to a high degree, or a speech problem may interfere with proper auditory discrimination.
3. Spatial orientation may cause difficulty.

The following suggestions for learning to spell a word may be helpful:

1. Articulate the words clearly.
2. Point out the visual aspect of the words (length of words, letters that go below the line, etc.).
3. Give oral spelling tests until pupils can write proficiently or type.
4. Have pupils practice spelling lists on a typewriter. This repetition improves both spelling and typewriting skills.
5. Allow pupils to type spelling tests. The words can be recorded on an audio tape for your convenience.

Considerations for Physical Education

Occasionally, young children with visual difficulties have not been allowed or encouraged to engage in physical activities such as climbing, throwing balls, hopping, and running. If pupils come to school without skill in these "readiness" activities, they should be given supervised guidance to master activities of this type. Overprotected pupils may need to develop muscle tone and improve coordination and spatial orientation abilities.

Some visually impaired pupils will benefit from a physical education program that minimizes group organized games and emphasizes calisthenics. A few pupils may need manual guidance; that is, manipulating the body through the correct movements. Others may produce acceptable responses through the use of verbal guidance. Simple, specific, and exact verbal descriptions should be used. Be sure to call pupils' names before passing them the ball or when it is their turn to participate.

A buddy system is quite helpful during physical education activities. The buddy can let the visually impaired pupil know when it is her turn, keep her in the proper location, and assist in teaching rules and correct physical movements.

Numerous aids for the visually impaired are available for physical activities. Balls with beepers or audible devices to indicate the side of a swimming pool are examples of equipment that serve as orientation guides.

MODIFYING THE CURRICULUM

Curriculum needs of partially sighted and blind pupils who are mainstreamed are determined in the same manner as for normally sighted pupils. Look at the "whole child" before deciding if curriculum modifications are warranted. Current research points to a few curriculum modification areas on which attention might be focused.

Utilizing Typewriting and Braillewriting

Handwriting may present difficulty for pupils with poor vision. Most visually impaired pupils who are mainstreamed into regular classrooms will be able to achieve moderate proficiency in handwriting. Pupils who experience the most difficulty should be taught to write commonly used words such as their names and addresses.

Typewriting is an essential skill for the visually impaired. It provides an excellent method for sharing written communication with seeing individuals. It is also necessary for the increased requirement for written assignments as pupils progress in school.

Typewriting is usually introduced between the third and fifth grades, dependent on such factors as muscle control and coordination. Electric typewriters with large or primary type are especially beneficial for young typists. Bold black print is easier to read than some of the fancier types of print that are available. Recorded lessons can be secured.

Since visually impaired pupils are frequently poor spellers, teaching typewriting and spelling concurrently strengthens both skills through the necessary repetition for mastery. The goal for typewriting should be accuracy rather than speed because of reduced visual feedback in detecting errors.

Some visually impaired pupils have been trained to read Braille and use a Braillewriter. Braille involves reading a system of raised dots by touching them with the fingers. Different combinations of up to six dots form a cell which represents a letter, punctuation mark, mathematical or scientific number or notation, or musical symbol. Figure 7-1 shows a sampling of Braille characters.

A Braillewriter is easier for young pupils to operate than a typewriter. However, pupils are switched to typing as soon as it is feasible because of the advantages when communicating with sighted individuals.

The regular classroom teacher will not need to learn Braille. Usually you send assignments to the itinerant or resource vision specialist, who prepares them in Braille. This specialist may grade the assignments or write above the Braille dots for you.

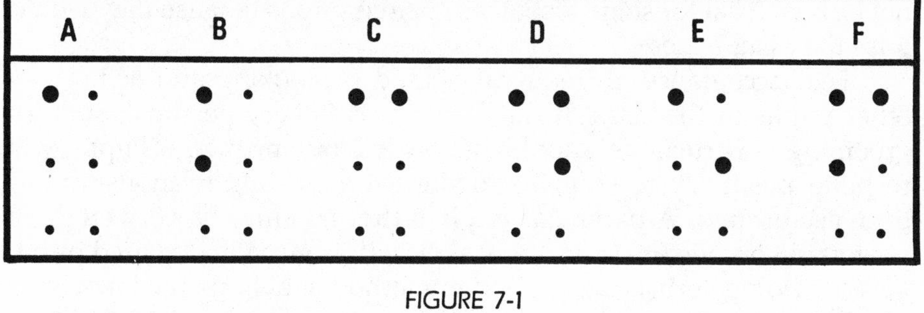

FIGURE 7-1

Today, it is feasible for pupils to use a microcomputer with a typewriter keyboard that projects letters, words, and sentences on a television screen or monitor in large type. The letter size is adjustable.

Some modification in the length of the assignment may be necessary because of the slower speed at which Braille can be read. The average reading speed for Braille is 60 words per minute, while the average speed for reading print is 300 words per minute. Braille is also very bulky.

A student at the University of Florida recently took his computer programming lessons using a program that gives students a choice of regular, medium, or large text; tall narrow text or short wide text; and so on. The time is coming soon when such materials will be commonly available to help the teacher who is mainstreaming atypical pupils.

Teaching Social Skills

Occasionally, pupils with visual impairment may exhibit some deficiency in areas such as grooming or proper response in a particular situation. This may result from lack of experience in social situations because of overprotectiveness or from the fact that they are unable to see details. Often, visual cues and body language give a more accurate indication of the nature of a particular situation than words, yet visually impaired pupils may miss these subtle clues. When pupils do well in classsroom activities, they are often rewarded by a smile and the relaxed appearance of the teacher instead of verbal communication. Visually impaired pupils may be unaware of this positive feedback. Pupil behavior is also controlled to a considerable degree by visual cues, such as "The Look," when the teacher stops talking and adopts a rigid and blank appearance. A ripple effect takes place around the classroom, with the whispered comment, "She's got 'The Look.'" Soon the class gets back to acceptable behavior. This technique would not be beneficial for some visually impaired pupils because they would miss the visual cues.

Peer acceptance is frequently based on looking and acting like other pupils in the class. If the deficit area is very personal, such as grooming, instructions should be carried out privately. Pupils will respond positively to your instructions if a trusting relationship has been established. A particular pupil in the class may be very effective in working on personal and social skills with a visually impaired pupil.

Providing verbal cues is another method of helping the low-vision pupils to be aware of what is happening. An example might be when the principal makes an unanticipated visit to speak to the class. The teacher would say, "Pupils, Ms. Jones has come to make an announcement." This helps pupils who might be unaware of the principal's presence to discontinue their tasks and direct their attention to the area indicated by the teacher's voice. It is often helpful to have a buddy provide these verbal cues for the visually impaired pupil.

Caution should be exercised to prevent blind pupils from losing the ability to control the environment. Dependency relationships between blind and sighted individuals can be formed insidiously. A blind individual may feel unsure in a particular situation and seek assistance and reassurance from a sighted person. The sighted person assumes a paternalistic and overprotective manner. Over a period of time, this relationship can result in poor social and emotional development and can impede learning in all areas. Psychologically, this can be very debilitating. The practical implication is that you must guard against overprotective, oversolicitous behavior so that blind pupils can develop as independently as possible. You must avoid giving too much physical and psychological assistance so that self-confidence can be developed.

SELECTING MATERIALS

Adapted and specialized materials and equipment are available to facilitate the education and development of visually impaired pupils. Addresses for materials and equipment have been presented elsewhere in this chapter.

Obtaining Large-Print Materials

Pupils who have visual impairments should be encouraged to maximize their residual vision. Emphasis on sight saving has been discarded, and pupils are now trained to make the most of their remaining vision.

Most visually impaired pupils do use regular print and regular teaching materials. Many educators believe more attention should be directed to appliances and aids such as magnification devices and environmental factors such as favorable seating position and lighting. However, some pupils will benefit from using large print.

A primary typewriter can produce satisfactory teaching materials. The major advantages of a primary typewriter are:

1. It is readily available.
2. It is convenient and requires no unusual training.

3. Materials that are individualized to the teacher's lessons can be prepared.

Of course, textbooks are available in large print. There are specialized materials such as enlarged charts, graphs, and cookbooks that are written with the specificity of language helpful to the visually impaired.

In addition to the sources listed earlier, the following addresses can be used to obtain publication lists and catalogs for large-print materials as well as other aids and devices:

American Foundation for the Blind
15 West 16th Street
New York, New York 10011

Association for the Education of the Visually
  Handicapped
919 Walnut Street
Philadelphia, Pennsylvania 19107

National Association for the Visually
  Handicapped
3201 Balboa Street
San Francisco, California 94121

Using Tactile Materials

Tactile materials are used extensively to teach pupils with visual impairment. This is a natural learning modality for all young children. Braille, a tactile format, has been discussed earlier in this chapter. If the pupil is using a Braille textbook, you should be aware that it may not contain all of the maps and pictures of the regular version. The following is a representative list of the types of tactile materials that are available:

- Abacus
- Cooking aids
- Embossed and relief maps
- Three-dimensional models (heart, machine, etc.)
- Embossed graph paper
- Adapted mathematical equipment (rulers, protractors, etc.)
- Raised line drawings

Sometimes we tend to focus on specific materials for the visually impaired and fail to remember that we have readily available realia to use in teaching. For instance, real pulleys, weights, measuring cups, and counting blocks are just as effective as teaching aids for visually impaired pupils as for sighted pupils. You can save time, effort, and resources by focusing on tactile teaching aids that you already have.

Using Auditory Materials

A variety of auditory materials and aids to enhance learning can be secured. Some of these materials and aids are not specifically designed for visually impaired pupils. Examples of these auditory materials include recorded tapes and disks, audio cassettes, recorded foreign language lessons, and radios.

Talking calculators, talking computers, physical education equipment implanted with audio devices, and talking books are among the materials and aids designed especially for pupils with visual impairment. Information regarding talking books can be secured from:

Recording for the Blind
215 East 58th Street
New York, New York 10022

Occasionally, the teacher, parents, or a local group record stories or textbooks for a particular school. For instance, as a major service project one Woman's Club has assumed responsibility for recording materials for a local high school.

If you anticipate preparing audio tapes or records, consideration should be given to the format, which will improve the usefulness of the materials. Record short segments of materials, not to exceed one chapter per tape or cassette. Pupils often waste time waiting for others to finish so that they can use the particular part of the material they need. Short segments filed in a well-organized system result in a more efficient use of pupil and teacher time.

Another reason for recording in short segments is the ease with which pupils can locate the material on which they need to work. Again, pupils waste enormous amounts of time running the tape on a reel-to-reel machine backward and forward, trying to locate the appropriate section of material.

While learning materials that emphasize the auditory modality are appropriate for visually impaired pupils, they are also helpful for other pupils in the typical classroom. There are usually pupils who have not developed reading skill on the level at which content textbooks are written. Auditory materials can help to solve this common problem. Be sure that pupils visually follow the print material while listening to the auditory production. While research data are lacking, this practice appears to improve reading skills.

Using Multisensory Materials

The previous sections have focused on materials that emphasize learning through one modality to compensate for the impaired visual modality. Multisensory educational materials should not be overlooked in regard to visually impaired pupils. Many commercial multimedia kits are available. The Language Master and System 80 are examples of machines with learning materials that utilize more than one modality. Television provides another source for multisensory learning. The use of computers as an educational tool is discussed elsewhere in this book.

USING ANCILLARY SERVICES

Ancillary services are available for visually impaired pupils. Resource or itinerant teachers can provide the following services:

1. Information and suggestions for the regular classroom teacher
2. Worksheets and tests in Braille for those pupils who read Braille instead of print materials
3. Orientation and mobility training, if necessary
4. Adapted and special equipment
5. Tutoring on a one-to-one basis

The school nurse should be involved in monitoring progress if the vision problem is degenerative in nature. Speech therapy may be indicated. Readers may be provided, particularly at the secondary level.

PREPARING THE CLASS TO RECEIVE
VISUALLY IMPAIRED PUPILS

Your attitude toward receiving impaired pupils in the classroom sets the tone of acceptance. Integration into the classroom will be facilitated if the pupil is treated as "special" only in regard to accommodations for the visual impairment.

Several simulations will help pupils understand what it is like to have a visual impairment. A class discussion of what happens to pupils when the electrical source fails is one such activity. Bring out the difference between having this happen in an unfamiliar environment and in a place that is well known. Carrying out commands while blindfolded can be used. It is important to note that relatively few individuals are totally blind; therefore, the blindfold may serve as a partial screen with the commands related to seeing details such as copying work from the board, eating, or recognizing facial expressions. Do not use simulations as a game; the atmosphere during simulations should develop understanding.

Children's literature and films may be used to help pupils understand the effects of visual impairment. *Mary Lou and Johnny: An Adventure in Seeing* (Hart and McQueen, 1963) portrays the mutual benefits of friendship between sighted and visually impaired peers. *Connie's New Eyes* (Wolf, 1976) shows how a Seeing Eye puppy is raised and trained. Biographies and autobiographies such as *If You Could See What I Hear* (Sullivan and Gill, 1975) are interesting to pupils.

Class presentations by visually impaired individuals, parents of visually impaired pupils, or the vision specialist can improve knowledge of the effects of visual impairment. These presentations should conclude with a summary of ways to assist the pupil with the visual impairment and an emphasis on all the normal aspects of the pupil's functioning.

A science unit on the eye and sight might be introduced. This can be beneficial to the pupil with the visual impairment as well as the sighted pupils.

This section has stressed the importance of accepting the pupil with the visual impairment as you would any pupil with the exception of trying to foster understanding of the disability. Young children exhibit this attitude more naturally than older children and adults. We could benefit from their model.

SUMMING UP

Astute observation of physical and behavioral characteristics of pupils can lead to the identification of pupils with visual impairment. Observation should occur in a variety of settings because of the diversity of visual problems. Performance on tasks that require near-point and distance vision and width of vision field must be considered.

Unusual appearance of the eye, peculiar body postures, avoidance of visual tasks, or poor spatial orientation may be symptomatic of visual differences.

Environmental considerations are of extreme importance. Favorable seating and lighting are essential for an optimum learning environment. Numerous aids and appliances are available to facilitate learning by visually impaired pupils.

Teaching techniques should incorporate the use of other modalities such as hearing and touch. The abundance of modified and adapted educational materials for visually impaired pupils has been discussed.

The mainstreamed pupil with visual impairment may require little modification of the regular curriculum. Learning environment and materials modifications will generally accommodate the needs of the mainstreamed pupil. Some emphasis may be placed on spatial orientation, typewriting, and social skills.

In teaching pupils with visual impairment, remember that each pupil is unique. Each pupil has strengths and weaknesses. Be cautious about letting the handicap interfere with your knowledge of teaching.

Any special preparations you make for visually impaired pupils usually are appropriate for other pupils in a typical classroom. Teachers are seldom required to devote unusual amounts of time to the education of mainstreamed pupils with visual impairment.

REFERENCES AND SELECTED READINGS

Alonso, L. "What the Teacher Can Do for the Child with Impaired Vision." *NEA Journal* 56 (November 1967): 42–43.

Bateman, B. "Visually Handicapped Children." In N. G. Haring and R. L. Schiefelbush (eds.), *Methods in Special Education.* New York: McGraw-Hill, 1967.

Bruce, R. E. "Using the Overhead Projector with Visually Impaired Students." *Education of the Visually Handicapped* 5 (May 1973): 43–46.

Buell, C. E. "How to Include Blind and Partially Seeing Children in Public Secondary School Vigorous Physical Education." *Physical Education* 29 (March 1972): 6–8.

Corn, A. L. *Monocular Mac.* New York: National Association for the Visually Handicapped, 1977.

Cratty, B. J. *Movement and Spatial Awareness in Blind Children and Youth.* Springfield, Ill.: Charles C. Thomas, 1971.

Crist, L. M. "One Who Has Learned to 'See' and 'Hear' Guides Others." *The Christian Science Monitor* 21 (1975): 23.

Davidson, M. E. *The Abacus Made Easy: A Simplified Manual for Teaching Cramner Abacus.* Philadelphia: Overbrook School for the Blind, 1966.

Deahl, L. and M. Deahl. "Integrating Partially Sighted Children in the Classroom." *Instructor* 83 (October 1973): 142–143.

Dunn, L. M. (ed.). *Exceptional Children in the Schools.* New York: Holt, Rinehart, and Winston, 1973.

French, C. "Teaching Art to the Blind Child Integrated with Sighted Children." *New Outlook for the Blind* 63 (1969): 205–210.

Gibbons, H. "Low-Vision Aids: The Educator's Responsibility." *International Journal for the Education of the Blind* 12 (1963): 107–109.

Gill, D. L. T. *Tom Sullivan's Adventure in Darkness.* New York: David McKay, 1976.

Hart, M., and N. McQueen. *Mary Lou and Johnny: An Adventure in Seeing.* New York: Franklin Watts, 1963.

Hoffman, H. W. "Exceptional Child: 10 Ways to Help the Partially Sighted." *Teacher* 90 (September 1972): 140–141.

Huff, R., and F. Franks. "Educational Materials Development in Primary Mathematics: Fractional Parts of Wholes." *Education of the Visually Handicapped* 5 (May 1973): 46–54.

Johansen, G. "Integrating Visually Handicapped Children into a Public Elementary School Physical Education Program." *Journal of Health, Physical Education, Recreation* 42 (April 1971): 63–64.

Johnson, Y. *A Blind Child Becomes a Member of Your Class.* New York: American Foundation for the Blind, 1961.

Kephart, J., C. Kephart, and G. Schwartz. "A Journey into the World of the Blind Child." *Exceptional Children* 39 (September 1972): 37–43.

Kirk, S. A., and J. J. Gallagher. *Educating Exceptional Children.* Boston: Houghton-Mifflin, 1979.

L'Abate, L., and L. T. Curtis. *Teaching the Exceptional Child.* Philadelphia: Saunders, 1975.

Lowenfeld, B. *The Visually Handicapped Child in School.* New York: John Day, 1973.

Lowenfeld, B., G. L. Abel, and P. H. Hatten. *Blind Children Learn to Read.* Springfield, Ill.: Charles C. Thomas, 1969.

Napier, G., D. L. Kappan, D. W. Tuttle, W. C. Schrotberger, and A. L. Dennison. *Handbook for Teachers of the Visually Handicapped.* Louisville: American Printing House for the Blind, 1975.

National Society for the Prevention of Blindness Fact Book. New York: National Society for the Prevention of Blindness, 1966.

Schatz, D., H. Overman, and S. Luttrell. *Marine Science Activities for Visually Impaired.* Seattle: Pacific Science Center, 1979.

Simon, E. P., and A. E. Gillman. "Mainstreaming Visually Handicapped Preschoolers." *Exceptional Children* 45 (1979): 463–464.

Sullivan, T., and D. Gill. *If You Could See What I Hear.* New York: Harper and Row, 1975.

Tait, P. E. "Believing without Seeing: Teaching the Blind Child in a Regular Kindergarten." *Childhood Education* 50 (March 1974): 285–291.

Wolf, B. *Connie's New Eyes.* Philadelphia: J. B. Lippincott, 1976.

CHAPTER EIGHT

Health Impaired and Physically Handicapped

Pupils in the health impaired and physically handicapped category comprise the most heterogeneous group of exceptional individuals. The common cold, rheumatic fever, cerebral palsy, and arthritis are among conditions of those collectively called the health impaired and physically handicapped. A pupil with chronic respiratory infection may be more educationally handicapped than one who is confined to a wheelchair.

Some of these pupils will need modification in the school environment that includes schedules for medication and rest. Other pupils may require adaptive devices such as special writing equipment. Still other pupils in this category will need only modification in physical arrangement, such as doors wide enough for a wheelchair.

Variability among health impaired and physically handicapped pupils is compounded in some cases by mental retardation or giftedness, speech or language problems, learning or behavior problems, or sensory difficulties. All of these ancillary conditions must be considered in developing an appropriate educational program for each pupil.

Interdisciplinary cooperation with medical personnel, physical and occupational therapists, other related professionals, and parents is often required. You should rely on knowledgeable sources for information regarding specific needs.

This chapter will present descriptions of short-term and chronic health impairments, blood disorders, convulsive disorders, respiratory/cardiac disorders, neuromuscular conditions, orthopedic impairments, educational implications of health and physical impairments, communication with others, and preparation for mainstreaming.

HEALTH IMPAIRMENTS

Some types of health impairments can be considered *short-term* in effect. These diseases respond positively to medication. Measles, mumps, and other childhood ailments are typical short-term health problems.

Common Cold

Drippy nose, stuffy ears, hacking cough—teachers have no doubt when "cold season" arrives. The term *common cold* indicates the extensiveness of this affliction. Because pupils share the miseries of the common cold with the general population, there are educational implications:

1. Pupils often experience a debilitated energy level.
2. There may be fluid in the middle ear that results in diminished hearing.
3. A drippy nose, constant cough, and similar symptoms that accompany a cold may cause considerable distraction from schoolwork.

While you can do little to relieve the physical problems, minor adjustments may facilitate a more effective recovery period. Physical activity may need to be curtailed to some extent. You might provide rest periods to prevent fatigue.

When pupils experience temporary diminished hearing caused by colds, they tend to "tune out" rather than concentrate more on listening. Be aware that what appears to be failure to listen may really be inability to hear as well as usual. Compensatory efforts such as moving the pupil closer may alleviate some of the difficulty.

What teacher has not felt "covered with germs" after wiping drippy noses and being sneezed and coughed upon? Teaching proper hygiene and social conventions in regard to nasal discharge and coughing may help to reduce tensions that frequently result from these distractions in the classroom.

Influenza

Influenza encompasses the symptoms described for the common cold. In addition, the patient usually experiences elevated temperature. The severity of influenza will result in absence from school. Upon return to school the pupil may require continuation of medication and may be enervated, with the additional complication of being behind in schoolwork. The suggestions in other sections of this chapter may help accommodate the physical problems.

Rheumatic Fever

Rheumatic fever is inflammation of connective tissue affecting the heart, joints, and blood vessels. Use of antibiotic drugs in recent years has greatly reduced the recurrence of rheumatic fever attacks. Permanent heart damage is less likely; most children recover with little or no heart damage.

If a pupil does have a resultant heart condition, a physician should provide guidelines for rest and physical activity. If a pupil has a lengthy absence from school, try the suggestions for catching up described later in this chapter.

Mononucleosis

Mononucleosis is an infectious disease which may be manifested by a sore throat, enlarged lymph nodes, headache, stomach pain, and fever. In addition, there is usually a greatly reduced energy level. Treatment focuses on rest and medication to relieve discomfort.

During the initial stages of mononucleosis, the physician may prescribe a period of bed rest which will necessitate absence from school. Upon return to school, the pupil's performance may not be up to par. Schoolwork may need to be somewhat limited. The pupil will also need to be caught up as soon as the condition permits.

Other Health-Related Conditions

Medical advances have reduced the incidence of several disorders that once were of major concern to educators. Other conditions for which no cure is available affect relatively few pupils.

Children with tuberculosis can now be treated effectively in most cases. Recovery time has been reduced; therefore, pupils are absent from school for a shorter time.

Infectious hepatitis affects a small portion of school-aged pupils. Diet and bed rest are usually prescribed. Absence from school and reduction of physical activity may require attention.

Although there may be acute episodes of the following disorders, often they are chronic, *long-term,* and in some cases terminal.

Allergic Conditions, Including Asthma

An allergy is an adverse reaction or intolerance to a substance. An allergy may be manifested in such reactions as itching, rash, sneezing, eye and nasal discharge, and difficulty in breathing. These reactions can be caused by particular substances including dust, pollen, drugs, fur, and certain foods.

Asthma is an allergic condition that may be influenced by physical exertion, climate or temperature changes, and possibly emotional stress. During an asthma attack, the individual has difficulty breathing, may wheeze, and may perspire profusely. Witnessing an attack can be frightening to pupils. The class should be prepared for what to expect during an asthma attack and reassured that an attack usually looks more serious than it is to the individual. Medication can usually relieve and/or control allergic reactions.

Major considerations for the classroom teacher in regard to pupils with allergic conditions include fatigue, physical activity, and effects of medication. Parents, the school nurse, and other medical professionals should supply guidelines to the teacher in regard to specific pupils. Provisions can be made to avoid fatigue. While excess physical exertion may precipitate an asthmatic attack, it appears that exercise may be beneficial in long-term treatment. Medication may cause some changes in the pupil's behavior. Since teachers lack expertise in these areas, they should rely on information from reliable sources in regard to providing for these youngsters.

Nephritis

Nephritis is a disturbance in kidney function characterized by considerable passage of protein into the urine. Swelling of the body, headaches, loss of appetite, and anemia are among the symptoms that are associated with nephritis. Boys are affected more frequently by this disorder than girls. Chronic nephritis can have a debilitating effect on a pupil. Loss of energy and absenteeism present two difficulties for the teacher. Suggestions for dealing with these problems are presented later in this chapter.

Diabetes

Diabetes is a metabolic disturbance in which the body is unable to utilize and store sugar satisfactorily. The hormone insulin is produced in insufficient amounts by the pancreas. Children comprise a small portion of the individuals affected by diabetes. Treatment may include insulin, diet, exercise, and rest. When a stable treatment regime is carried out, the pupil can participate in normal school activities.

Neglect of some factor in proper treatment may result in insulin shock. This reaction is usually rapid in onset. Irritability, inattention, hunger, dizziness, and perspiration are common symptoms. Candy, a sugar cube, or orange juice will usually provide relief.

Although diabetic coma is rare, it is usually more serious. Excessive thirst, nausea, flushed skin, and deep breathing are symptoms that may occur during gradual onset. Immediate medical attention should be provided.

The teacher should be well informed by a physician in regard to a diabetic pupil. Implications of insulin reaction and diabetic coma should be thoroughly explained.

Cancer, Including Leukemia

Cancer tends to progress more rapidly in children than in adults. Long-term prognosis for leukemia, one of the most common forms of cancer affecting children, is not encouraging at the present time. However, recent medical advances have been effective in increasing life expectancy of children with leukemia.

The pupil with cancer will have stressful times that will affect schoolwork. Side effects of medication and chemotherapy may need accommodation. During remission episodes, school progress should be normal.

Tumors

The occurrence of tumors in school children may cause no problem, or it may lead to death. Some tumors can be surgically removed and present no further difficulty. Some are inoperable. If the student is receiving chemotherapy treatment, he or she may have adverse reactions that will affect school performance.

BLOOD DISORDERS

Hemophilia

Hemophilia is characterized by poor blood coagulation. This is a low-incidence genetic disorder. Prevention of injury is the major concern in dealing with pupils who have hemophilia. Active episodes of bleeding result in absence from school.

Sickle Cell Disease

Sickle cell disease is a form of anemia associated with black individuals. It is an inherited condition that affects about ten percent of the black population in the United States.

As with all forms of anemia, the oxygen-carrying ability of red blood cells is impaired. Blood flow may be restricted because the red cells can become misshapen and rigid. This causes pain to the individual. Other symptoms include fatigue, pale appearance, and yellowish tint in the whites of the eyes.

The major limitation of pupils with sickle cell anemia is in the area of physical involvement. Since a predisposition for a depleted oxygen supply exists, vigorous exercise might bring on a crisis situation. All other aspects of participation in the school environment should be normal.

Lupus (erythematosis)

Lupus is a type of allergy characterized by pathological changes in the vascular system. Collagen, which acts as a binding agent for small blood vessels, is affected. There are many possible symptoms, the most common including generalized aching, fatigue, low-grade fever, and skin rash. The rash spreads across the bridge of the nose and cheeks in a butterfly pattern. Arthritislike joint swelling with pain may occur. Lupus is erratic, with symptoms that come and go. Although prognosis is good if the condition is detected and treated early, the disease is not cured. Some medications produce unpleasant side effects.

CONVULSIVE DISORDERS

Convulsive disorders are characterized by seizures and convulsions. While the terms *seizures* and *convulsions* are often used synonymously, a seizure is a sudden onset of a group of symptoms and a convulsion is an irregular spasm. Seizures and convulsions may be associated with mild cerebral palsy, accidents to the head, tumors, or lesions. Epilepsy is probably the most common convulsive disorder among school-age pupils.

Epilepsy

Epileptic seizures occur when there is spontaneous, uncontrolled firing of electrical energy in neurons. Temporary loss of muscle control and consciousness occur. A seizure can last from a few seconds to several minutes. There can be great variability in severity and amount of involvment during a seizure. Most seizures can be controlled with medication.

Petit mal and grand mal are the most common types of seizures affecting children. Petit mal seizures usually last only a few seconds. The individual may appear to be daydreaming or staring into space. Sometimes there is rhythmic blinking of the eyelids. The occurrence of petit mal seizures can be difficult to detect, because the pupil will continue with the activity that was going on after the seizure, although there was momentary interruption in knowing what was happening. Since these petit mal seizures can occur as frequently as 100 times a day, a pupil could miss a considerable amount of educational information.

Grand mal seizures are characterized by loss of consciousnness and stiffening of the muscles followed by a convulsive state where muscles contract and relax. A seizure may last several minutes. After a seizure the individual may be tired, sleepy, and dazed. A short period of rest may be needed.

The effect of convulsive disorders on academic performance varies a great deal. Remember that placement in a regular classroom is indicative that the pupil can be expected to function normally at the grade level. Indeed, some of these pupils will be gifted.

Teachers should have adequate information from parents and medical personnel concerning pupils who have convulsive disorders. Sluggishness and inability to concentrate may result from taking anticonvulsant medication.

How to Handle Seizures in the Classroom

Witnessing a grand mal seizure can be a frightening experience for pupils in a classroom. If there is a possibility of a seizure occurring in the classroom, prepare the pupils. A traumatic experience can be avoided with advance information and proper handling of the situation. The Epilepsy Foundation of America recommends the following procedure:

1. Remain calm. Students will assume the same emotional reactions as their teacher. The seizure is painless to the child.

2. Do not try to restrain the child. There is nothing you can do to stop a seizure once it has begun. It must run its course.

3. Clear the area around him so that he does not injure himself on hard or sharp objects. Try not to interfere with his movements in any way.

4. Don't force anything between his teeth. If his mouth is already open, you might place a soft object like a handkerchief between his side teeth.

5. It isn't necessary to call a doctor unless the attack is followed almost immediately by another major seizure, or if the seizure lasts more than about ten minutes.

6. When the seizure is over, let the child rest if he wants to.

7. The child's parents and physician should be informed of the seizure.

8. Turn the incident into a learning experience for the entire class. Explain what a seizure is, that it is not contagious, and that it is nothing to be afraid of. Teach understanding for the child—not pity—so that his classmates will continue to accept him as "one of the gang."

RESPIRATORY/CARDIAC DISORDERS

Cystic Fibrosis

Cystic fibrosis is a genetic disease that is manifested as chronic lung and respiratory dysfunction. There may be difficulty breathing and excessive coughing. Hospital confinement may be necessary from time to time. Improved medical treatment has prolonged life expectancy, yet most individuals do not survive beyond adolescence.

The pupil with cystic fibrosis in the regular classroom should require little modification in the curriculum. There are three considerations in the educational setting:

1. Participation in physical activities will usually need to be limited.

2. Catching up will be necessary because of absenteeism.

3. Counseling may be helpful because of the depressing outcome of this disease.

The teacher and pupils should realize that germs are not spread during coughing episodes. The disorder is not infectious.

Heart Disease

Congenital heart defects (present at birth) occur much more frequently than acquired heart disease in children. Although there are several types of congenital heart disease, manifestations are similar. Symptoms may include shortness of breath, chest pain, general tiredness, bluish coloring (especially lips and fingernails), or chest deformity. The most common treatment involves surgical procedures and the use of antibiotics to prevent bacterial infections.

It is difficult to make definitive statements about participation in physical activity by pupils with heart disease because of the degree of impairment. Most often physical activity is restricted. Guidelines should be provided by the doctor. Periods of rest may be indicated.

NEUROMUSCULAR CONDITIONS

Muscular Dystrophy

Muscular dystrophy is a disorder characterized by gradual degeneration of muscle tissue which is replaced by fatty tissue. There are several types.

One of the first symptoms may be weakening of the muscles in the feet. The child may begin walking on his or her toes. The back will become swayed, and the child may begin to fall. The child appears to be healthy as fatty tissues take the place of muscle tissue, although progressive weakness occurs. Braces may be used to prolong the ability to walk, but eventually a wheelchair will be needed for mobility.

Since intellect is unaffected by muscular dystrophy, the pupil can benefit from remaining in the regular classroom as long as possible. The pupil should be able to participate in the regular curriculum. As the condition progresses, the pupil may need some adapted equipment. Physical or occupational therapists or other specialists will assume responsibility for instructing the pupil and the teacher in the use of any devices that are required.

Because prognosis is not encouraging, counseling should be provided for the pupil with muscular dystrophy and for peers. Means of encouragement should be identified in order to keep the pupil achieving academically.

Cerebral Palsy

Cerebral palsy is a condition characterized by disturbance in voluntary muscle movement caused by brain injury. There are several types of cerebral palsy. A brief description of the most common types follows.

Spasticity is manifested in jerky, uncontrolled movements. Some muscles are too tense and some are too relaxed; therefore, muscle groups do not pull against each other evenly.

Constant, random motion is indicative of *athetosis*. Attempts at voluntary motor actions increase these purposeless movements, which are not rhythmical.

Ataxia results in uncoordinated movement, impaired balance, and difficulty with orientation in space.

Generally, children exhibit a mixed type of cerebral palsy. They have characteristics of spasticity, athetosis, and possibly ataxia.

While pupils with this type of motor dysfunction may be gifted and have no concomitant problems, many do. Hearing and visual impairment, speech and language disorders, perceptual dysfunction, and mental retardation are most common.

The educational program for pupils with cerebral palsy who are mainstreamed in regular classrooms will not require modification. However, there may be a need for adaptive equipment. A physical or occupational therapist will usually secure any necessary equipment and instruct the pupil in its use.

Book and page holders, page turners, and pencils with adaptive grips are representative of the types of adaptive equipment used. The teacher should receive information from a physical or occupational therapist regarding any modifications that need to be made in the classroom setting. For instance, the pupil may require additional time to complete assignments, or arrangements may need to be made so that the pupil can stand for part of the day.

Spina Bifida

Spina bifida is a term used for a variety of conditions in which there is incomplete development of the spine and spinal column. It may cause little or no problems in the mildest form and therefore go undetected. In a severe form, the spinal cord, membranes around the cord, and spinal fluid may protrude from the spinal column. Paralysis usually occurs from the protrusion downward. Bladder and bowel control may be affected. Surgical procedures and artificial devices are used to improve and accommodate these conditions. Hydrocephalus, an increase in cerebral spinal fluid, may cause pressure and enlargement of the size of the head. This is often relieved by a shunt that drains fluid from the brain. Mental retardation may be present although abilities range through giftedness.

The regular classroom is an appropriate placement for most pupils with spina bifida because the upper part of the body is unaffected. The pupil may need to spend a portion of the day with appropriate therapists in order to learn how to use certain appliances. Several special considerations may require attention in the regular classroom setting:

1. While pupils with bladder and bowel control problems should be able to manage their toileting needs independently, a flexible toileting schedule should be arranged.

2. Odor may indicate some problem with the toileting program or equipment. Prompt solutions for the problem should be provided by appropriate therapists to avoid ostracism by peers.

3. Some pupils may lack background experiences because of difficulty with mobility. Verbalization may surpass conceptualization; consequently, the teacher will need to help develop comprehension and conceptualization.

Paralysis

Paralysis is characterized by inability to move certain portions of the body. Sensation is usually affected as well. Injury, congenital defects, infections, and drugs are the most frequent causes. Paraplegia (paralysis of the lower part of the body) or quadriplegia (paralysis of upper and lower limbs) may occur.

Participation in academics should be satisfactory since intellectual functioning is usually within the normal range. Modifications will include accommodations for a wheelchair and/or adaptive equipment that may be necessary.

ORTHOPEDIC IMPAIRMENTS

Although arthritis occurs more frequently among adults than children, some children suffer from juvenile rheumatoid arthritis, characterized by pain and swelling in one or more joints of the body.

The knees are most frequently affected. The effects and complications are variable, with some children becoming progressively worse and some improving, particularly at puberty. Treatment may involve surgical procedures, special exercises, medication, and splints, braces, or casts.

The regular classroom curriculum should not require modification for pupils with arthritis. Nevertheless, there are other considerations:

1. Special writing materials may be needed if the hand, arm, or shoulder joints are affected.
2. More time for completion of assignments or travel may be necessary if movement is limited.
3. One complication that can accompany arthritis is eye disease. The teacher should watch for inflammation of the eyes or any changes in vision.
4. An adapted physical education program may be indicated.

Absence of upper or lower limbs may be present at birth or may result from accident or surgery. The entire limb may be missing, or a partial or underdeveloped appendage may be present.

Prosthetic devices such as artificial limbs are commonly used. A specialist will provide rehabilitative training in the use of these appliances. A wheelchair may be used at least part-time with lower limb absence.

Since intellectual functioning is usually within the normal range, participation in the average school program should be possible with the exception of physical education. An adapted physical education program may be required. The major consideration in the classroom will be any modification in the environment needed to accommodate a wheelchair or adaptive equipment the pupil may be using.

Legg-Perthes is a condition in which the hip socket and end of the upper leg bone degenerate. The condition generally occurs between the ages of four and eight years. The usual symptoms are pain in the knee or thigh accompanying a limp. Treatment may include extended bed rest, surgery, or the use of braces or casts. The bone regenerative process may require up to three years.

Brittle bone disease is an inherited condition characterized by frequent broken bones caused by weak bone structure. In addition to susceptibility to bone fractures, discoloration of the whites of the eyes is symptomatic. The whites of the eyes have a bluish tint or are opaque around the edges. Hearing and visual impairments and problems with the teeth may be associated with brittle bone disease.

Although results are not definitive, diet or chemical treatment is being tried to allieviate this condition. A surgical technique of implanting rods in the long bones is perhaps the most effective treatment. The use of a wheelchair may be indicated at least part of the time.

Pupils with brittle bones cannot engage in physical education activity but should be able to participate in all other aspects of a typical school program.

Arthrogryposis is a condition in which the child is born with nonflexible joints and weak muscles. Treatment may include surgery, braces, and casts. The deformities may recur, but the disease is not degenerative.

Academic performance should be within the normal range. The major limitations will occur for pupils who have restricted mobility in the hands. Handwriting may be slow.

Poliomyelitis used to be one of the most feared afflictions of school-aged children. Vaccines have been successful in virtually wiping out this crippling disease.

EDUCATIONAL IMPLICATIONS

There are several factors associated with health and physical impairments that may require consideration in the school setting. Among these factors are absenteeism, debilitation, effects of medication, use of adaptive equipment, and environmental adjustments.

Absenteeism

Pupils with short-term, long-term, or chronic disorders will be absent from school. Many physical conditions require surgery or other procedures that result in school absenteeism. Many of these pupils will also have to attend therapy sessions, which will necessitate further absence from the classroom.

Catching pupils up with schoolwork is always a difficult task for classroom teachers. A buddy system peer tutoring arrangement can be successful in solving this problem. When a pupil is absent, have a buddy keep a record of class activities and assignments and use carbon paper to make a duplicate of class notes. Most parents will express concern about academic progress and will want to help at home. When the absent pupil returns, arrange some time for the buddy to tutor.

Most pupils can be back on track within a week or two, depending on the length of time absent and the amount and complexity of material missed.

Debilitation

Health-related conditions usually leave the pupil with a lowered energy level temporarily. Fatigue must be considered when the pupil returns to school following illness and certain types of therapeutic procedures. Assignments may need to be modified to allow for brief rest periods. This can be frustrating when pupils are already behind their peers because of absence. However, remember that when the body is in a debilitated condition, mental processes are unlikely to be alert.

Effects of Medication

You will need information from health and medical professionals as well as parents concerning medication schedules and possible effects of medical treatment. It would be wise to be sure of school policy regarding dispensing medical treatment because of legal aspects. You may be asked to observe and report to the physician the pupil's reaction to prescribed treatment.

Use of Adaptive Equipment

Some physically impaired pupils will need adaptive equipment to participate in classroom activities. A special education teacher, therapist, or parent should assist you in understanding this equipment. Representative types of equipment are listed below:

- Page turner operated with a toggle switch
- Head wand to operate a typewriter
- Recorders to replace writing
- Calculator with printout tape
- Eating aids
- Tactile writing paper
- Pencil grips
- Lap trays
- Larger and/or weighted objects for manipulation

Some minor adaptations can assist these pupils in better performance and independence in the classroom. Taping paper to the desk top and attaching a pencil to the desk with string are examples of minor adaptations to assist a pupil with poor motor control such as might result from cerebral palsy.

Environmental Adjustments

Physically impaired pupils often require modification of the environment to meet their individual needs. One of the most common needs is extra time. It takes longer than average for some pupils to respond, particularly to activities that require motor movements, such as writing.

Another consideration centers on the use of a buddy. A buddy can help in many ways such as carrying books or opening doors. An especially critical service of the buddy concerns personal safety in emergency situations like a fire.

Other types of environmental adjustments may include the following:

- Adjustable tables to accommodate a wheelchair
- Wide doorways
- Lower coat hooks, water fountains, etc.
- Textured surface to prevent papers or books from slipping
- Storage for crutches

COMMUNICATION WITH OTHERS

Communication with various specialized professionals and parents will be very important for the teacher of health or physically impaired pupils. Professionals may include the special education teacher, occupational therapist, physical therapist, speech therapist, doctors and/or nurses, medical equipment suppliers, and associations devoted to health and physical impairments.

Special Education Teacher

The special education teacher can assist you by helping to set realistic goals and offering modifications for achieving the goals such as varying teaching strategies to accommodate the needs of particular pupils. If the pupil spends part of the school day with each of these teachers, curriculum and activities need to be coordinated to provide a sequential and consistent program for the pupil.

Occupational Therapist

The occupational therapist can provide information regarding positioning the pupil, use of adaptive aids, and suggestions for eye–hand coordination. Best practices for managing pupils' needs can be suggested by the occupational therapist.

Physical Therapist

The physical therapist is mainly concerned with mobility and physical strength and control. Help will be focused in these areas as well as use of adaptive equipment.

Speech Therapist

The speech therapist can provide an understanding of speech patterns and the use of other communication systems. Suggestions for reinforcement activities in the regular classroom can be supplied.

Doctors and Nurses

While providing information regarding appropriate care as well as medication schedules and possible effects, medical personnel may request information from you. You may be called on to complete observation checklists to determine the effectiveness of prescribed treatment. You are in a position to provide valuable assistance in this regard.

Medical Equipment Suppliers

Medical equipment suppliers often come to the school to service and adjust equipment. They can explain the use and care of the equipment.

Associations

Printed information and resource speakers are among the services of associations whose focus is the health and physically impaired. Several sources of information are provided below:

American Association for Health, Physical Education,
and Recreation
1201 16th Street, N.W.
Washington, D.C. 20036

American Heart Association
44 East 23rd Street
New York, New York 10010

American Physical Therapy Association
1740 Broadway
New York, New York 10019

The Council for Exceptional Children
Division on Physically Handicapped
1920 Association Drive
Reston, Virginia 22091

Easter Seal Society
2023 West Ogden Avenue
Chicago, Illinois 60612

Epilepsy Foundation of America
1828 L Street, N.W.
Washington, D.C. 20036

March of Dimes
800 Second Avenue
New York, New York 10017

Muscular Dystrophy Association
1790 Broadway
New York, New York 10019

National Cancer Care Institute
National Heart Institute
National Institute of Allergy and Infectious Diseases
National Institute of Arthritis and Metabolic Diseases
U.S. Public Health Service
HEW South Building, Room 5312
Washington, D.C. 20201

Spina Bifida Association
104 Festone Avenue
New Castle, Delaware 19801

United Cerebral Palsy
321 West 44th Street
New York, New York 10036

Parents

Pupils' parents should be able to provide information in all of the areas discussed in the preceding section. Parents acquire extensive knowledge in understanding their children's condition, treatment, and proper care. An exchange of information concerning the pupil will be invaluable for both you and the parents.

PREPARATION FOR MAINSTREAMING

Mainstreaming exceptional pupils means more than physical placement in classes with normal peers. Complete integration of these pupils requires preparation of the special education teacher, the regular classroom teacher, and regular classroom pupils. Special methods, techniques, and adaptations should be supplied by the special education teachers, therapists, and other ancillary personnel. Appendix A is offered as a model. While these suggestions apply to physically impaired pupils, the same format can be modified to prepare for mainstreaming all other exceptionalities.

Literature can be used to extend understanding of physically handicapping conditions. *The FDR Story* (Pearce, 1962) and *Let the Balloon Go* (Southall, 1968), whose main character is a boy with cerebral palsy, are representative of available books. *Howie Helps Himself* (Fassler, 1975) is a book that accompanies a filmstrip about a physically handicapped child and his accomplishments with a wheelchair.

Other suggestions to facilitate understanding of health and physically impaired pupils include guest speakers such as doctors, nurses, and association resource persons. Simulations can also be used. One simulation is to have students go into the restroom unassisted in a wheelchair. Another simulation involves using a splint on the preferred writing hand while completing a writing assignment.

SUMMING UP

Pupils with health impairments and physical handicaps comprise an extremely heterogeneous group. Various health and physical disabilities have been described. The diversity within this category makes it impossible to make definitive statements regarding the educational implications of these disorders.

The regular curriculum requires little change for these pupils, with the possible exception of physical education. Consideration of the effects of absenteeism, debilitation, and medication, as well as adaptive equipment and environmental adjustments have been discussed.

It is important to remember that the basic educational needs of these pupils is the same as for all others. Because of the visibility of the handicap in many cases, one tends to focus on modifications and adjustments necessary for these pupils instead of the total program. If you utilize the strengths and abilities of each pupil, necessary modifications and adjustments should be perceived as minimal.

REFERENCES AND SELECTED READINGS

Adams, R. C., A. N. Daniel, and L. Rullman. *Games, Sports, and Exercises for the Physically Handicapped.* Philadelphia: Lea and Febiger, 1972.

American Medical Association. "The Epileptic Child and Competitive School Athletics." *Pediatrics* 42 (1968): 100.

Arnhein, D. D., D. Auxter, and W. C. Crowe. *Principles and Methods of Adapted Physical Education.* St. Louis: C. V. Mosby, 1977.

Bleck, E. E., and D. A. Nagel. *Physically Handicapped Children: A Medical Atlas for Teachers.* New York: Grune and Stratton, 1975.

Calabro, J. J. "Management of Juvenile Rheumatoid Arthritis." *Journal of Pediatrics* 77 (1970): 355–365.

Calhoun, M. L., and M. Hawisher. *Teaching and Learning Strategies for Physically Handicapped Students.* Baltimore: University Park Press, 1979.

Chancey, C. M. and N. C. Kephart. *Motoric Aids to Perceptual Training.* Columbus, Ohio: Charles E. Merrill, 1968.

Connor, F. P. "Safety for the Crippled Child and Child with Special Health Problems." *Exceptional Children* 28 (1962): 237–244.

Deahl, T., and M. Deahl. "The Orthopedically Handicapped." *Instructor* 80 (1971): 34.

Eddy, C. "No Fingers to Play a Horn." In M. E. Besson (ed.), *Music in Special Education.* Washington, D.C.: Music Educators National Conference, 1972.

Fassler, J. *Howie Helps Himself.* Chicago: Albert Whitman, 1975.

Gearheart, B. R., and M. W. Weishahn. *The Handicapped Child in the Regular Classroom.* St. Louis: C. V. Mosby, 1976.

Graham, R. "Safety Features in School Housing for Handicapped Children." *Exceptional Children* 27 (1961): 361–364.

Guerin, G. R., "School Achievement and Behavior of Children with Mild or Moderate Health Conditions." *The Journal of Special Education* 13 (1979): 179–186.

Harlin, V. K. "Experiences with Epileptic Children in a Public School Program." *Journal of School Health.* 35 (1965): 20–24.

Livingston, S. "What the Teacher Can Do for the Student with Epilepsy." *NEA Journal* 65 (1966): 24–26.

Mullins, J. *A Teacher's Guide to Management of Physically Handicapped Students.* Springfield, Ill.: Charles C. Thomas, 1979.

Myers, B. A. "The Child with a Chronic Illness," in R. H. A. Haslam and P. J. Valletutti (eds.), *Medical Problems in the Classroom.* Baltimore: University Park Press, 1975.

National Cystic Fibrosis. *Guide to the Diagnosis and Management of Cystic Fibrosis.* Altanta: National Cystic Fibrosis Research Foundation, 1971.

National Epilepsy League. *Teacher Tips.* Washington, D. C.: National Epilepsy League, 1974.

Peare, C. O. *The FDR Story.* Scranton, Pa.: Thomas Y. Crowell, 1962.

Pieper, B. *The Teacher and the Child with Spina Bifida.* Argyle, N.Y.: Upstate Spina Bifida Association, 1975.

Puthoff, M. "Instructional Strategies for Mainstreaming." In *Mainstreaming Physical Education.* Washington, D.C.: National Association for Physical Education of College Women, 1976.

Sauer, L. W. "Heart Diseases in Children." *PTA Magazine* 66 (1967): 29–30.

Seligman, T., H. O. Randel, and J. J. Stevens. "Conditioning Program for Children with Asthma." *Physical Therapy Journal* 50 (1970): 641–647.

Southall, I. *Let the Balloon Go.* New York: St. Martin's Press, 1968.

CHAPTER NINE

Organizing the Classroom for Effective Mainstreaming

Teachers who know how to individualize instruction will have little difficulty integrating exceptional pupils into their classes. Many teachers devise ways to organize their classrooms to meet individual needs, and with slight modifications these already successful techniques will accommodate the exceptional learner. For example, the second grade teacher who has four reading groups functioning simultaneously is already individualizing. By developing a peer tutoring program and a systematic method of charting individual pupil progress in specific reading skills, this teacher can extend individualization to the highest and lowest achievers.

Seldom is it necessary to plan activities that will benefit just one exceptional child in a classroom. More often, there are other pupils who can also benefit from the same activities. By forgetting labels and looking at educational needs, we often find more similarities than differences in the individual learning of children requiring special help.

The second grade teacher who has a learning disabled or physically handicapped pupil with severe visual–motor problems will find the special techniques used to help the handicapped learner master handwriting useful for the four other children in the classroom who form their letters poorly and cannot write on the line.

On hearing the term *individualized instruction*, teachers may envision 30 pupils doing 30 different things at the same time. However, individualized instruction in a typical classroom can usually be accomplished by dividing pupils into three or four groups for part of their instruction. In fact, many activities can and should begin with whole group instruction followed by breakdown into small groups. It is in the small groups that the most pressing individual needs can usually be met.

Planning for individualized instruction requires you to view the teaching role in a less traditional manner than is typical; that is, teachers become more like managers of the learning environment than dispensers of information. Advance preparation is necessary, but once the organization for individualizing instruction is in place, the system tends to operate automatically, freeing you to circulate among various pupils or to work with a single group. The findings of researchers such as Gage (1977) support the value of actively circulating among pupils rather than remaining at the desk and having pupils report there for help. Pupil awareness of the teacher's presence appears to have a positive impact on pupil effort and learning as well as behavior.

You may find that once you decide on a system for individualizing instruction, prepare for the groups, and teach the pupils how the system works, teaching becomes much less tiring. While the preparation requires considerable initial work, the rest of the school year's load is lighter than it would have been. You have time to *teach*.

The previous chapters have suggested ways to recognize exceptional pupils and to make adjustments in instruction to meet the needs of these learners. How can this be accomplished in the mainstreamed classroom? This chapter contains suggestions for organizing the classroom for individualized instruction. Included are scheduling time, mastery learning, small groups, peer tutoring, resource units, learning centers, programmed instruction, and microcomputers.

SCHEDULING TIME

All teachers need time to work with individual pupils or groups of pupils. There always seem to be some who did not understand what was being taught or who could work on another project if teachers had a few minutes to spend with them. However, most school days are so filled with required activities that it is difficult to find this extra time.

If you study teachers who are successful at managing to have time for conferring with individuals and groups, you discover that they have *planned* for this important need. For example, if such teachers are in a self-contained room, they usually set aside catch-up time in the few minutes before recess, lunch, or school dismissal. This arrangement allows pupils who have not completed their work to catch up; it also allows teachers some time to spend with those pupils who need the extra instruction. The pupils who are already caught up use this time for free reading from the library, beginning their homework, or working on a long-term assignment or special project.

For teachers whose pupils change classes each period, the last few minutes of the class are often used in the manner described above. Some teachers build this time in not only for catch-up but also to insure that pupils get started on their homework. There is evidence that if students have begun their homework they are more likely to complete it than if it had not been begun at all.

Some teachers prefer a catch-up period once each week, perhaps on Friday. In any event, planning for teacher time during which individual and small group needs can be met is crucial. If you do not plan, this extra time is unlikely to be available.

Increasingly, teachers are being given some formally arranged planning time during the day. Sometimes these arrangements come about through the use of special teachers like those in art, music, and physical education. Other arrangements include doubling up pupils, using paraprofessionals, hiring a floating teacher, and, in very small schools, substituting by the principal. While teachers need and deserve these times away from children, if necessary, they can use part of such time to meet with individual pupils, with parents, or both.

PROVIDING FOR MASTERY LEARNING

In addition to planning daily blocks of time to provide individual help, mastery learning techniques offer a systematic way to give pupils longer periods of time to master skills and concepts without penalty. Over the long term, mastery learning can save teacher time by reducing the need for remediation as pupils are not locked into a preset time frame for learning. The child who learns faster may go on with other work while the slower child is still learning lower-level concepts or skills.

Mastery learning is a teaching strategy designed to bring almost all pupils to a high level of achievement while increasing motivation for further learning. It may also be the single best way to improve end-of-year test scores, as pupils are continually checked for mastery of essential skills before moving on to more complex objectives. It is especially important to ensure mastery in the primary grades where the seeds of failure germinate.

Reduced to its essence, mastery learning means that how much pupils learn will depend in large part on how much time they are allowed to spend compared with the time they need to spend to master an objective. Since the objectives are very clear, both to the teacher and to the pupils, and since achievement is not demanded in a certain time frame, when pupils attain mastery they can receive an A. Grades do not depend on how rapidly pupils reach mastery but whether they do so.

Pupils are pretested to establish objectives to be achieved. They are checked periodically for mastery of subskills prerequisite to mastery of more complex skills. Those pupils who do not achieve mastery do not proceed with new and different work until mastery is achieved; they recycle learning activities until they reach the objective previously established.

If mastery does not seem possible for a number of pupils, even with different teaching methods such as tutoring, it is conceivable that the objective is not appropriate for that age and grade level and should be postponed. For example, researchers have discovered that certain concepts, such as telling time to the minute, are in large part a function of maturation. Drilling on time telling too early is an expensive waste of teacher time. Given the appropriate learning conditions, there is significant evidence to support the claim by Bloom (1981) that most (more than 90 percent) pupils can master most of what we have to teach them.

Bloom has found that mastery learning hinges, assuming enough time, on appropriateness of the teacher's methodology, on pupil perseverance and aptitude, and on the clarity of the teacher's instructions. Further, he found that pupil perseverance tends to increase as pupils realize they are learning. As pupils discover they are learning, their aptitude for further learning rises. That is, the ease with which pupils are able to learn new material in a subject gradually increases as learning takes place.

How to Use Mastery Learning

The basic steps to follow are:

1. Confine mastery learning to the basic curriculum.
2. Pretest in the subject on the curriculum objectives.
3. Begin with the most essential basic skills.
4. Provide pupils with a short list of the three or four skills they need to learn.
5. Have each pupil study, practice, self-test, recycle, and retest, with final checking (testing) by the teacher until mastery is achieved.
6. Initially, allow about 10 to 15 percent more time. Paying teachers extra to accomplish this after normal school hours is one recommended procedure. Later on, the time needed becomes less.
7. Draw on any possible sources of assistance such as tutors from other grades or the same grade, teacher aides, parent volunteers, programmed instructional units, microcomputer drills, and so on.

A specific example, in some detail, follows:

Step 1. Choose an objective that is clearly defined and part of the planned curriculum. For example, "Each pupil can spell the 100 most common English nouns."

Step 2. Pretest the pupils on these 100 nouns.

Step 3. Pupils score their own papers and make a list of the noun words spelled incorrectly.

Step 4. Form four or five small groups with the best spellers on that test as tutors. Each day allow ten minutes or so for practice and help on these.

Step 5. Because learning to spell consists of much more than just correct spelling, challenge the tutors to use the words in sentences and have their tutees use these orally and in writing sentences.

Step 6. As soon as a pupil spells all correctly, that pupil becomes a tutor; this is a strong motivator. Note, too, that each day the tutoring groups become smaller until soon there are one or more tutors per pupil. This is an ideal situation. The teacher's role is one of observation and assistance.

Practical Examples of Mastery Learning

1. Almost all children learn to write their own names.
2. Almost all children learn to tell time.
3. Almost all children learn to make the letters of the alphabet.
4. Almost all children can learn to count to 100.
5. Almost all children can learn their multiplication tables.
6. Almost all children learn to speak their native language.

The aforementioned skills are mastered because teachers keep coming back to them. Teachers expect all pupils to learn these things, and the pupils do so. In the same vein, more abstract skills are learned as there is insistence on these basics.

Implementation of mastery learning in the mainstreamed classroom reflects the teacher's belief that *all* children *can* learn. The use of mastery learning exemplifies the essence of the philosophy of mainstreaming exceptional pupils because they are respected as equal members of the class and are not penalized because their rate of learning varies from the norm.

One very exciting experience with mastery learning was a three-day visit in the Johnson City, New York, public school system in the spring of 1982. They have it, and it works. The visitor was particularly interested in discovering how they solved the problem of what to do with the pupils who mastered the material early. The solution is as follows:

1. Only the basic curriculum objectives are on a mastery basis.
2. Pupils are tested for mastery on each objective.
3. Pupils who finish early can:
   a. Do elective work of interest to them.
   b. Become tutors of other children.
   c. Some combination.

To develop a system of mastery learning in a classroom, the teacher can use one or more of several instructional arrangements that will be presented in the following sections. Small group instruction, the development of resource units and learning centers, peer teachers, and the use of programmed instruction and microcomputers can be adapted to meet the needs of atypical learners in the most formal or the most informal classroom settings. Teachers do not have to change their teaching style drastically to use the concepts of mastery learning in their classrooms.

USING SMALL GROUP INSTRUCTION

Small group instruction typically takes place in the primary grades; it becomes less and less in evidence moving up through upper elementary, middle, and high school. This reduction in frequency of small group learning is ironic when it is recognized that differences in achievement levels of pupils become even more pronounced in the upper grades than in the lower grades than would be the case if small group techniques were more widely used. So few teachers use small groups because they do not know how to get started.

How to Get Started

Basic to the effective use of small groups is that teachers have sufficiently developed their classroom grouping skills to enable small pupil groups to function smoothly; this is crucial. Just to place pupils in groups without teaching them how to work in groups is virtually to guarantee failure and cause the teacher to vow never to try such a scheme again. If you are interested in using small group instruction, proceed in the following way:

1. Choose your two most reliable pupils.
2. Assign them a specific task to be completed outside class, such as preparing for a science demonstration.
3. Excuse the pupils from regular class work. Make the assignment a choice one.
4. Have the pupils put on their demonstration.
5. Compliment pupils for a job well done.
6. Do this several times using the same pupils.
7. Get ready for complaints from others for such choice assignments. Now the stage is set.
8. Select a reliable pupil and one of the less reliable ones.
9. Gradually extend this procedure over five or six weeks to more and more small groups.
10. Make sure that having a group assignment remains a privilege; this will encourage good behavior.

An advantage of the procedure described above is that it becomes more and more easy to make the transition between large and small group instruction later in the year once the pupils have acquired the skills of small group operation. A key point worth repeating is that the pupils must be taught how to behave appropriately in the groups. Such group skills are valuable in peer tutoring, mastery learning, science laboratory work, and many other areas.

The basic rationale underlying the above procedure is that the teacher:

1. Proceeds slowly.
2. Establishes powerful models of how pupils behave in the small group.
3. Assigns clear, discreet, short-term tasks.
4. Gives the assignment status.
5. Gradually extends to more and more pupils.
6. As pupils learn how to behave in groups, makes assignments more and more abstract and complex.

There is absolutely no doubt that almost any teacher, having acquired the skills of using carefully structured small groups, will want to use them from that point on. Students learn so much from one another. In effect, teachers have multiplied themselves manifold. To assume that pupils can only learn from the teacher is to deprive them of one of their most valuable opportunities for learning.

Some teachers who do not use small group work have had bad experiences and are extremely fearful of using it. They are afraid of losing control of the class. This fear is understandable. However, in view of the effectiveness of small group activity in facilitating pupil achievement, and rather than continuing to avoid it, such teachers might consider seeking out a trusted colleague who can use it and request the opportunity to observe and learn how to conduct small group sessions. Gage (1977) sets forth the steps to mastery in teacher training. These steps are:

1. Read about the skill.
2. Observe the skill in operation.
3. Try the skill.
4. Receive feedback.

5. If mastery not achieved, go to step 4.

6. Mastery is achieved.

It is important to realize that you must put your pupils through similar steps if they are to master the intricacies of small group behavior. If the pupils are very young, you will, of course, omit step 1. The pupils will learn how to behave in groups but won't have grasped the theory behind it.

Some teachers have observed bad behavior patterns in groups as (1) one person dominates the group, (2) a pupil just sits and does not participate, (3) a third pupil doesn't listen to what others say and interrupts when she wishes, (4) a fourth is a "cutup," (5) the work degenerates to a "bull session," and so on. These unpleasant incidents do occur but only underscore the fact that pupils must be taught how to behave effectively in groups. The modeling procedures set forth above can help with this. Monitoring of groups, helping them to clarify goals, speaking privately with those who are not doing their share or who are dominating the group, and so on, are all part of the process. The most important thing is for you to communicate to the pupils an attitude that you *expect* good behavior.

Practical Examples of Small Group Work

1. Groups of two or three conducting a science experiment

2. Pairs using flash cards in first grade

3. Groups of three or four practicing parts for a classroom play

4. Groups of three to five carrying on a discussion in a foreign language in middle school

5. Groups of two to five working through the social studies questions at the end of a chapter

6. Groups of three or four practicing a physical education skill on the playground

7. Groups of two or three working in the library to look up information for a class presentation

8. Temporary "buzz" groups to come up with ideas for a school picnic or other activity

A seldom mentioned value of small group work is that it is one of the most common of adult activities in both the social and work worlds. In the adult world—at work, attending PTA meetings, school committees, work committees, or church committees—the skills of effective committee behavior are important. In fact, there is evidence suggesting that those who have mastered the skills of effective group interaction have acquired one of the most important sets of skills possible for adult success.

In summary, small group instruction is an effective way to meet the varied needs of exceptional pupils in the mainstreamed classroom, provided adequate planning has been done and the pupils are taught to use the small group process appropriately. One of the better books on using groups is *Small-Group Teaching* (Sharan and Sharan 1976). In the following section, specific suggestions will be made for teaching pupils to teach one another.

USING PEER TUTORING

Training pupils to teach one another one-to-one or in small groups provides extensive opportunities for individualized instruction. Peer tutoring is defined here as two, three, and sometimes four or five pupils working together on the same task. Typically, one pupil is being taught by another. In some instances, peer teaching and learning are mutual and interactive, with two or three pupils working together on an assigned task such as a science experiment, or two students may alternate drilling each other with flash cards of arithmetic sums or reading vocabulary words and science terms.

The above situations contrast sharply with a very common scenario:

Teacher: "Johnny, spell *chief.*"
Johnny: "c-h-e-i-f."
Teacher: "No. Who will help Johnny?"

The teacher then calls on one of the many hands that are waving wildly.

Johnny does not interpret the above as help; actually, it is somewhat humiliating, for it makes him look dumb. Peer tutoring is not like this. In fact, the research shows that pupils working together on a common task come to like one another better than before they started.

Peer tutoring benefits the tutor as well as the tutee, and it accomplishes this without embarrassing anyone. One of the best ways to learn anything extremely well is to teach it to someone else. You can reassure parents that when a pupil is helping another pupil, the tutor is benefiting from the experience as much, if not more than, the tutee.

It is probably advisable to meet with parents in advance of instituting peer tutoring for the first time in order to explain the advantages for both tutor and tutee. These advantages include developing a sense of responsibility, improving one's own knowledge of the subject, recognizing the good feelings that come from helping a classmate, and acquiring some of the communication skills so important in successful human relationships.

How to Start Peer Tutoring

The following suggestions will help you put peer tutoring into practice:

1. Explain to the class that all of us, at times, can be a teacher of something. This idea is crucial if there is not to be a stigma attached to peer tutoring. It is very important for slower pupils to learn that they have much to offer, too, particularly to children in lower grades.
2. State that all of us, at times, need assistance.
3. Ask the pupils to make a short list of things they can teach others, at that grade or below. Give some examples: selected multiplication facts, short division by single digits, spelling words in science, catching a ball. Some pupils are pleasantly surprised to realize that they know so much. This is especially true of the lower-achieving pupils who have been led to believe for years that they know little or nothing.
4. Next, ask the pupils to list a few things with which they could use help. Have them be specific here, too. It is important for all to recognize that no one knows everything.
5. Start with a responsible pupil. It is important to establish a very good model for the others to follow.
6. Assign the tutor a specific choice job, one that is clearcut and for a definite task. Choose a task that is obviously important. For example, "Joe, why don't you come up here and hear Sam read to you while I am working with Susy?"
7. Set the task for a specific time, perhaps ten minutes. This way you won't have to "terminate" something if the pupil tires; the time will be so short that there is little to waste.

8. When the pupils are finished, make it a point to chat with them about how it went. Indicate that you will be calling on more and more of them, both in and out of class.

9. Gradually increase to two, three, even four or more pairs of pupils. Remember, peer tutoring is supposed to ease burdens, not make them more difficult.

10. As pupils become accustomed to the method, you can mention the tutoring program to teachers in a lower grade and ask if they want a tutor. Because the pupils will already know how to tutor, special training will not be necessary for the lower-ability pupils. To repeat, lower-ability pupils are especially in need of seeing that they have learned many things and that it is not only the faster pupils who have something to offer. Otherwise, you are dooming the program to an early death.

11. By beginning slowly, establishing clear objectives, working first with reliable pupils for others to imitate, recognizing the work as worthy, making it a privilege to be a helper, and avoiding the stigma that only the smart ones can be helpers, you will find yourself in six or eight weeks handling large numbers of tutors both in and out of the class with ease. When this time arrives, you will find that not only is more learning going on, but classroom management problems involving discipline have diminished.

Once in a while you will discover that the two pupils teaching each other can reverse roles. Perhaps the pupil who was taught long division by a "smart" pupil can be the one to show the "smart" pupil how to catch a ball, hold a saw, or hold and swing a hammer correctly. Activities of this type are important in fostering respect for the individual.

Organizing Recordkeeping

An efficient system for assigning and keeping records of the tutoring experience must be planned. A simple tutor assignment form is presented in Figure 9-1.

Pupils should keep logs of their tutoring activities. A suggested log is given in Figure 9-2. You can collect these from time to time and give recognition to parents and other teachers. Notes can also be used as an exercise in communication. Encouraging the pupils to compose their own notes gives them this practice in communication skills. You can add a brief note and signature. This will save much teacher time.

TUTOR ASSIGNMENT FORM				
Tutor	**Tutee**	**Room**	**Teacher**	**Time**
John Brown	Susy Smith	No. 8	Mr. Jones	Wed., 2:00 P.M.

Objective: Multiplication facts 6 and 7.
Signature (home teacher): _____

FIGURE 9-1

LOG OF TUTORING ACTIVITIES			
Name of tutor: _____			
Date	Worked with	Activity	What accomplished

FIGURE 9-2

It should be emphasized that not only can virtually all pupils benefit from tutoring experiences, but almost all pupils can be tutors of some skill that is important. Academically talented pupils benefit from the tutoring role by improving their own basic skills. Too often they have been bored with practice activities when they were introduced to them and as a consequence have not fully mastered these skills themselves. Becoming a tutor forces them to focus on their own basic skills. They will enthusiastically "bone up" on things they are getting ready to teach. These pupils frequently have an IEP (Individual Educational Program) objective of improving their personal interaction skills. Tutoring provides a natural opportunity to practice these skills.

Less academically talented pupils receive tremendous satisfaction from realizing that they know some things other pupils in the class or in lower grades do not know. Few of these pupils have ever realized that they know things others do not know; typically, they have experienced being seen as dumb or slow, inadequate. Such feelings of inadequacy tend to operate to the detriment of pupils all through their school years, even throughout life.

Student Teams Achievement Divisions (STAD) described by Slavin (1982) is one of the most powerful and effective approaches. Figure 9-3 shows a sample scorecard. Steps in STAD are as follows:

1. Pupils are placed in four- or five-member teams.
2. Teams are heterogeneous in achievement.
3. Teacher introduces new material.
4. Team members study the worksheets, work the problems out together, quiz one another.
5. A team is tested when *all* say they are ready.
6. During the quiz no member helps another.
7. Quizzes are scored.
8. Team scores are made up of contributions from each team player.
9. The amount each team player contributes to the team score is the amount he has exceeded his average score plus 5 points, up to a maximum of 10 points for a perfect player.
10. The team with the largest total number of points wins.

The remarkable thing about this game is that even the lowest achievers contribute 5 points, unless there is no improvement over that pupil's average score or even a drop. In this way even the lowest-achieving pupil becomes a welcome team addition. Pupils can make a maximum of 10 points. If a paper is perfect, it is an automatic 10.

Slavin's book also contains a number of other creative approaches such as TAI (Team-Assisted Instruction), Jigsaw, and TGT (Teams–Games–Tournaments).

Pupil	Average score	Quiz score	Improvement score
Sue	82%	85%	5 + 3 = 8 points
Mary	90	90 no improvement	0 points
Jim	95	100	10 points
Bill	57	77	5 + 5 = 10 points
Sarah	77	65	0

FIGURE 9-3

Lippitt (1975) points up some traps to watch for when using peer tutoring. Avoiding exploitation of pupils, ensuring rewards for the tutors, not just assigning the "dirty work," and keeping parents informed are among the areas that may cause problems.

Teachers who develop a system to use peer tutors often find this to be an effective organizational arrangement for all pupils in the class, not just the mainstreamed exceptional children. Theoretically, all 30 pupils can develop the ability to tutor another classmate in some area, freeing you from time-consuming, repetitive one-to-one or small group drill. You become the manager of the learning environment as children teach each other.

DEVELOPING RESOURCE UNITS

Developing resource units allows you to have multilevel activities and materials available in various subject areas. While preparation of resource units requires some expenditure of time, the rewards are great. Instructional units can be assembled quickly by selecting from the numerous ideas in the resource unit.

Steps for compiling a resource unit follow:

1. Determine the subject area for the resource unit.
2. Develop the curriculum by writing behavioral objectives for possible knowledge, skills, and concepts associated with the unit topic. Be sure to include levels from basic to complex.
3. Identify and list related study skills that might be developed while completing the unit. Letter writing, public speaking, library use, outlining, and map skills are examples.
4. Identify and describe ways to initiate the unit to create pupil interest. Bulletin boards, dramatizations, reading a poem or story, or a visit by a resource person are examples.
5. Compile an extensive list of activities for the unit. Study trips, completing a scrapbook, identifying possible resource persons, small group projects, debates, developing a game, and art projects are examples of the types of activities that might be appropriate for the unit.
6. Compile a teacher bibliography. This should include pamphlets, books, and any reference material that is available to you. Be sure to record complete bibliographic information and where the

material is located, such as the public library, foreign embassy, school system materials depository, and so on.

7. Compile a list of available publications for pupils. Be sure to include a wide range of reading levels and content levels. This will ensure appropriate material for individual pupils or groups in the class.

8. Compile a list of resources to include sites for study trips, records, films, filmstrips, tapes, songs and dances, charts, maps, and so on.

9. Identify and describe a variety of ways to evaluate the unit. Evaluation techniques might include debates, class discussions, art projects, cumulative folders of work on the unit, and writing an essay, as well as the traditional test.

A collection of teacher's editions of several grade levels of textbooks and textbooks on the same grade level from different publishing companies are of great assistance in preparing resource units. For example, to prepare a resource unit on cells for an eighth grade class, reviewing the unit on cells in textbooks from fourth through tenth grades would yield numerous activities and resources that would be suitable for a variety of pupil needs.

From this extensive compilation, you can select those objectives and activities that are especially suited to the needs of individual pupils. Examples follow:

1. Pupils with low learning aptitude could make a picture collection.

2. Films are available for those pupils who learn best through a visual mode.

3. Activities requiring artistic talent are provided.

4. There are many enrichment activities for gifted pupils.

5. Tactile items can be included for visually impaired pupils as well as other pupils who learn through this mode.

6. Opportunities to develop deficit skills are plentiful. For pupils who need practice in letter writing, ample opportunities are provided.

7. Social skills can be improved by preparing pupils to conduct interviews before actual interviews.

You can continue to expand the unit as new ideas and sources of materials are available. An excellent reference for preparing resource units can be found in *Social Studies for Children in a Democracy* by John U. Michaelis (1976).

Resource units can be used in both large and small group settings, as well as in independent activities. Resource units can also provide the basis for the development of learning centers, which will be described in the next section.

ORGANIZING LEARNING CENTERS

Classroom learning centers provide another way to organize instruction for individualization. Learning centers are collections of multilevel activities, materials, and equipment, so arranged that pupils can simultaneously work at different tasks whether individually or in small groups. The multilevel activities and materials provide for the needs of different functional levels and learning styles of pupils. Learning centers should include activities from concrete to abstract and from simple to complex.

Learning centers are usually organized around subjects such as Mathematics, Reading, Science, Language Arts, or Social Studies, although some teachers prefer to organize their learning centers around special interest topics, changing these from time to time during the year. Still others prefer to organize centers around types of activity, such as a media center for listening stations and viewing slides and films, a drill and practice station for basic skills, a discovery center for science activities, or a contruction center for finger painting, sculpting, or creative thinking. Many teachers prefer an eclectic approach; that is, they combine aspects of different centers into one.

Learning center activities do not have to be completed in a specified area. If space is limited, activity cards and materials can be stored on a bookshelf or in a cabinet, and pupils can complete the work at their desks. This arrangement is workable except when the use of machines is an integral part of the task.

How to Develop and Use Learning Centers

Let's assume that you want a basic skills learning center containing a mixture of reading, mathematics, social studies, and science skill activities. The purpose is to reinforce those skills being studied in the regular curriculum. Steps in creating a center follow:

1. On 3 by 5 cards, write down the behavioral objectives, giving each a number (1, 2, 3, 4, 5 ...).

Examples: 1. Pupils understand and can explain in writing the food chain concept.
2. Pupils can connect batteries and light in series and/or in parallel.
3. Given the latitude and longitude, pupils can go to the globe and locate a position.
4. Pupils can measure, record, and graph their weekly weight and height in English and metric.

2. Under each objective, on each card, list the equipment needed to accomplish the objective. (See Figures 9-4 and 9-5.)

Objective 1: The pupil can hook batteries and a light bulb in series and in parallel. The pupil can draw each wiring diagram and explain the advantages and disadvantages of each.

Equipment and materials needed:

1. Cassette recorder with tape describing experiment
2. Spool of copper wire
3. Three dry cell batteries
4. Pliers
5. Small flashlight bulb
6. Switch

(turn card over for directions)

FIGURE 9-4

WIRING IN SERIES AND IN PARALLEL

Directions: Read all of the directions before going on.

Directions to pupil:

Step 1. Listen to tape on recorder.
Step 2. Hook up batteries and lights in series. Then draw a diagram of this showing wires connected.
Step 3. Hook up batteries and bulb in parallel.
Step 4. Review pages 59–63 in your science book.
Step 5. Write out the answers to the questions on page 63.
Step 6. Put the material away.
Step 7. Turn your paper in to the teacher.

FIGURE 9-5

It is important for both pupil and teacher to know which objectives have been mastered. One way to facilitate this is by means of a record sheet. (See Figure 9-6.)

PUPIL NAMES						
Tasks	Joe	Sue	Tom			
1						
2						
3						

Pupil's check in pencil indicates task completed. Teacher's initial in ink indicates task checked. Teacher erasure of pupil mark with replacement by question mark indicates pupil should see the teacher.

FIGURE 9-6

In summary, in using learning centers you should:

1. Establish objectives of the learning center. Be sure objectives are specific and clear.
2. Decide on room arrangement.
3. Prepare the learning activities.
4. Develop the pupil recordkeeping system.
5. Teach pupils how to behave in the center.
6. Change objectives and materials of center to relate to class text assignments.

Flexible scheduling of pupils to use centers is advantageous for exceptional pupils in the class. Because pupils work at the learning centers at different times and on different activities, they are not singled out as being slower or more advanced than other pupils in the classroom. One of the best references is *Classroom Learning Centers* (Morlan, 1974), a fine little book full of practical ideas.

Once you complete the steps described above, the learning center is self-instructional. Another self-instructional technique is the use of programmed instruction, which will be presented in the next section.

USING PROGRAMMED INSTRUCTION

Programmed instruction is the presentation of a stimulus to pupils, requirement of pupils' response, and provision for immediate feedback to pupils of whether or not they are correct. Usually the stimulus is in the form of a question; pupils answer the question and then turn to the correct answer for confirmation. For example:

The words of a language are combinations of sounds. When you speak English, you use English sounds. When you speak Spanish, you will use Spanish _____.

sounds

Spanish and English are related languages. Thus, they have some similar sounds. But they also have many different _____.

sounds

Each of the above is a frame. The answer is hidden from the pupils' sight but appears when a slider on the teaching machine containing the paper is moved downward. In this way pupils are able to check answers and immediately confirm whether they are right or wrong. This immediate feedback has been found to be very effective with numbers of pupils.

Programmed instruction can be done with materials in a book or monograph, a teaching machine, a large centrally connected computer, or, more recently, a microcomputer. Programmed instruction combines material; that is, the material is organized to teach without teacher intervention except to get the pupils started. Usually some other pupil will have used programmed instruction and can instruct a new pupil in how to use it.

Programmed materials are designed in various formats. In some instances, the answers are covered and the pupils remove the cover to check the response. Sometimes the answer is visible when pupils turn the page. Some machines give the answer verbally, and some flash the answer on a viewing screen.

All types of programmed instruction materials have four basic characteristics:

1. Pupils are able to go at their own pace.
2. Pupils have their attention focused on a limited amount of information, often called a frame.
3. Pupils cannot be passive as in television, but must make a response.
4. Pupils receive immediate feedback on the correctness of their response.

Programmed instruction is especially well suited for individualized instruction and for mastery learning because well-designed materials must have their objectives clearly specified. It also has the advantage of being prepared in advance. The busy teacher does not have to adapt the material.

Programmed instruction can be effective in meeting the needs of several types of exceptional pupils:

1. Because the material content has been thoroughly task-analyzed, slower-learning pupils experience success. Teachers frequently do not break the task into such small hierarchical steps.
2. Visually impaired pupils can benefit from those programmed materials that have verbal responses.
3. Hearing impaired pupils can benefit from visual response formats.
4. Pupils with superior abilities can often experience an enriched curriculum by using programmed material. This is especially true when curriculum offerings do not contain subjects that are of particular interest to the pupils.
5. Programmed materials also help pupils who have health problems to catch up on content when they have been absent for a period of time.
6. Physically handicapped pupils whose upper extremities are involved can benefit from programmed materials that do not require written responses, especially if the machine is easily advanced to the next frame.

Rarely is programmed instruction appropriate for entire courses. The exceptions to this rule seem to be those pupils who are far behind or far ahead of most of the class. For example, one very advanced, highly motivated pupil in an algebra class was saved an entire year's work in second year algebra by means of programmed instruction. Without programmed instruction, the teacher would not have had the time.

In summary, programmed materials can provide regular classroom teachers with another method of meeting the individual needs of a variety of pupils. The ultimate format for presenting programmed instruction is the microcomputer, which will be discussed in the next section.

USING MICROCOMPUTERS

The virtual explosion of microcomputers in the classroom is reassuring because here is another very powerful tool for the mainstreaming teacher. Unlike many other education innovations:

1. The computer is here to stay.
2. The computer is probably the most powerful tool ever developed for helping pupils of widely varying needs, achievement levels, learning problems, or interests.
3. The computer promises to bring teachers extra pairs of quality hands.
4. The computer seems highly motivating to most pupils.

One would think that the microcomputer has been designed especially for mainstreaming. The assistance that can be rendered to the visually impaired, the hearing impaired, the physically impaired, and the intellectually superior, as well as other types of exceptional pupils, is astonishing. Here are just a few of the things it can do right now.

For pupils:

1. Writes extremely large words on a screen for the visually impaired pupil.
2. Provides auditory accompaniment to visual symbols on the screen. What is typed on the computer is read back immediately by the microcomputer.
3. Allows 30 pupils to work at 30 different skill levels in spelling, arithmetic, or other subject areas.
4. Provides practice in typing.
5. Provides eye–motor coordination skill drills.
6. Teaches children how to read music.
7. Increases reading speed and comprehension.
8. Provides opportunities for creative art work using the screen and a "brush" with many colors.
9. Provides opportunities for creative thinking.
10. Enables the physically handicapped or vocally handicapped to enter words with a pressure board and talk to others with ease.
11. Presents visual simulations of difficult concepts in animated form, slow or fast, repeatedly.

12. Furnishes endless drill and practice on virtually any skill or concept to be mastered.
13. Provides simulations of hard-to-view, dangerous, or expensive processes (such as an internal combustion engine in operation).
14. Provides practice in problem solving.

For teachers:

1. Facilitates data-based management such as storage and retrieval of individual and class pupil records with the data analyzed, summarized, and in consumable form for easy interpretation.
2. Provides information retrieval such as finding specific references to go with special pupil needs, such as, Project PLAN (Programmed Learning in Accordance with Need) by Westinghouse.
3. Develops daily pupil schedules. An example is LRDC (Learning Research and Development Center) at the University of Pittsburgh, which has developed a system that enables pupils to come in and sign up at the computer terminal for various activities in various sequences throughout the day. Pupils type in their names and then see the options open to them from teacher planning.
4. Observes demonstration teaching. There is a large screen that blows up everything on the microcomputer so an entire class can see what is happening. Using this, you can show and explain very abstract ideas, repeating them as often as necessary.

Why the Microcomputer Works

The major reason why microcomputers really work as educational tools are as follows:

1. The machine is interactive; it is not passive as television.
2. The machine can be infinitely patient, unlike a human being.
3. The pupil—in a tutorial setting, for example—tends to become more relaxed, less tense and uptight than around a human being.
4. The drill and practice programs are similar to programmed instructional materials and work for the same reasons of immediate feedback, reinforcement, and pacing.
5. Many of the learning activities resemble arcade games; there is a fascination about these arcade games which we have yet to be able to define precisely.

6. Micros are different in kind, not just in degree, from any learning system yet devised.

7. Sound programs have been field-tested, revised, and rerevised until they do work, until pupils do learn.

8. Microcomputers are incredibly fast and incredibly accurate.

9. Microcomputers enable both competency-based mastery learning of skills and open-ended, divergent-type thinking.

How do you use the microcomputer? You will need some training in the use of microcomputers. After that, all you have to do is introduce it to your class. If properly introduced, the microcomputer will be so appealing and so motivating that pupils will not only want to use it but will also want to take good care of it.

Begin introducing a microcomputer into the classroom by permitting each pupil about ten minutes per day on the machine. This need not take much time because you only need to teach the first two pupils how to carefully handle the diskette, insert it, close the door (or load the cassette tape), turn on the machine, and so on. It is recommended that pupils work in pairs, taking turns at the console. The exception to these suggestions is the student who needs a specially designed microcomputer. These dedicated machines should probably be reserved for the mainstreamed student, although at times there will be opportunities for these pupils to peer-teach others about the specialized capabilities of their microcomputers.

When you introduce the machine to two pupils, those two pupils can teach two others, and so on. You will also find all eyes on those who are using it, at least initially. Much teacher time can be saved in this way.

Begin with simple arithmetic or reading drills of varying levels of complexity—there are many—or with a simple but appealing game such as "Lemonade," which teaches elementary economics, or "Darts," which teaches the concept of estimation in arithmetic. (These games are available from *Elementary, My Dear Apple*, Education Series No. A2D0015, Apple Computers, Inc., Cupertino, California 91980.)

Practical Examples

One program written for first grade children presents a simple single-digit addition, subtraction, or multiplication problems as follows:

1	5	8
+ 2	− 3	x 5

The problem is presented. The child enters an answer. The child is told both verbally and with a smiling or frowning face if she is correct or not. A record of the incorrect problems is kept; these are represented. If missed a second time, a hint is given, as follows:

$$7 = 1+1+1+1+1+1+1 \quad \text{Here is a hint.}$$
$$- 3 = 1+1+1$$
$$\text{Try again.}$$

If missed a third time, the correct answer is given. The problems are presented in groups of ten, and the pupil's score is presented.

In effect, ten minutes a day per child enables each child to receive needed practice on problems *at his or her level,* have them immediately scored, be given some help, and have the final score calculated. This kind of individual attention is impossible for a teacher with 30 pupils and many different subject areas.

Today, there are programs that furnish choices of difficulty level from 1 to 100, give choices of subject material (whether spelling, arithmetic, social studies, English, or science) and can and do help pupils to learn. The big problem here is to become sufficiently knowledgeable about educational software that you can critique it and select only the best.

Sources of Information

Two sources of information that are designed especially for the classroom teacher are:

Classroom Computer News
Box 266
Cambridge, Massachusetts 02138

The Computing Teacher
Department of Computer and
Information Science
University of Oregon
Eugene, Oregon 97403

There is a regular section entitled "Input/Output Ideas for the Classroom" in *Classroom Computer News.* In *The Computing Teacher,* **a**

March 1983 article was entitled "To Meet All Children's Needs." Both journals evaluate some computer software, review textbooks on computers, report developments in schools across the country, and solicit information and practical tips from classroom teachers for educational function of the microcomputer.

The Classroom Directory, published by Classroom Computer News, is extremely comprehensive. It is periodically updated, which is an important feature in this rapidly expanding field.

Many book companies now carry computer programs intended to be educational. For example, SRA has an extensive listing of educational software for elementary schools. Many cities and even small towns are getting their own microcomputer stores.

One way to begin to become computer-literate is to go to a bookstore, buy several computer magazines such as *Byte, Interface Age, Popular Computing, Creative Computing, Recreational Computing, Microcomputing, Classroom Computer News, The Computing Teacher, Apple Orchard, Nibble, Peelings II,* and so on. Tear the mailout cards from several of these, check off interesting products by circling the appropriate numbers, and your mailbox will shortly be overflowing with ads.

To help you judge software, there are now journals that review it. For example, there is *Peelings II,* published at P.O. Box 188, Las Cruces, New Mexico 88004, which grades software from F through AAA and pulls no punches.

In summary, the microcomputer should be brought into *every* mainstreamed classroom as soon as possible. There is an almost infinite variety of tasks that these little gems can perform for the busy teacher.

SUMMING UP

Mainstreamed classrooms require organization of instruction that provides for the various educational needs of pupils. Regular classroom teachers often do not have to make drastic changes in their instruction to accomplish mainstreaming. Teachers who successfully individualize instruction have little difficulty teaching exceptional pupils in regular classrooms. Remember that individualizing instruction does not usually mean teaching each pupil separately.

A representative sample of ways to organize classrooms for individualizing instruction has been provided. A discussion of scheduling time has been presented. Other methods to facilitate individualizing instruction include mastery learning, small groups, peer tutoring, resource units, learning centers, and programmed instruction. The expanding use of microcomputers in classrooms may be the ultimate answer to the need for individualizing instruction. Microcomputers are adaptable to meet the educational needs of most exceptional pupils.

Organizational arrangements for individualizing instruction can provide multimedia materials for pupils who learn best by seeing, doing, listening, and talking. Manipulative materials can be available for pupils who learn best through tactile and kinesthetic learning aids. It is usually easy to integrate the use of adaptive aids for exceptional pupils into classroom instruction when pupils in the class are accustomed to seeing different groups of pupils using a variety of learning aids. Arrangements of this type also allow those pupils who learn at different rates to be successful. Strengths and preferences for pupils with superior abilities can be taken into consideration.

Teachers who provide individualized instruction for the unique learning characteristics of exceptional pupils recognize that these pupils *can* achieve successfully in the regular classroom. They are also better teachers of *all* pupils in their classes.

REFERENCES AND SELECTED READINGS

Ames, L. B., C. Gillespie, and J. W. Streff. *Stop School Failure.* New York: Harper and Row, 1972.

Baker, J. *Computers in the Curriculum.* Bloomington, Ind.: Phi Delta Kappa, 1976.

Beach, D. M. *Reaching Teenagers: Learning Centers for the Secondary Classroom.* Santa Monica, Calif.: Goodyear, 1977.

Blackburn, J. E., and W. C. Powell. *One at a Time All at Once: The Creative Teacher's Guide to Individualized Instruction Without Anarchy.* Pacific Palisades, Calif.: Goodyear, 1976.

Block, J. H. (ed.). *Mastery Learning: Theory and Practice.* New York: Holt, Rinehart, and Winston, 1976.

Bloom, B. S. *All Our Children Learning.* New York: McGraw-Hill, 1981.

Borich, G. D. "Implications for Developing Teacher Competencies from Process–Product Research." *Journal of Teacher Education* XXX (1979): 1.

Davidson, L., P. Fountain, R. Grogan, V. Short, and J. Steely. *The Learning Center Book: An Integrated Approach.* Santa Monica, Calif.: Goodyear, 1976.

Dunn, R., and K. Dunn. *Practical Approaches to Individualizing Instruction: Contracts and Other Effective Teaching Strategies.* West Nyack, N.Y.: Parker, 1972.

Ehly, S. W., and S. C. Larsen. *Individualized Instruction.* Allyn and Bacon, 1980.

Fisk, L., and H. C. Lindgren. *Learning Centers.* Glen Ridge, N.J.: Exceptional Press, 1974.

Folio, M. R., and A. Norman. "Toward More Success in Mainstreaming: A Peer Teacher Approach to Physical Education." *Teaching Exceptional Children* 13 (1981): 110–114.

Gage, N. L. *The Scientific Basis of the Art of Teaching.* New York: Teachers College Press 1977.

Hedges, W. D. *At What Age Should a Child Enter First Grade: A Comprehensive Review of the Research.* Ann Arbor, Michigan: University Microfilms, 1977.

Johnson, S., and R. B. Johnson. *Developing Individualized Instructional Materials.* Palo Alto, Calif.: Westinghouse Learning Press, 1970.

Lippitt, P. *Students Teach Students.* Bloomington, Ind.: Phi Delta Kappa, 1975.

Michaelis, J. U. *Social Studies for Children in a Democracy.* Englewood Cliffs, N.J.: Prentice-Hall, 1976.

Morlan, John E. *Classroom Learning Centers.* Belmont, Calif.: Fearon Publishers, 1974.

Neuyohr, J. L. *The Individualized Instruction Game.* New York: Teachers College Press, 1976.

Piechoweah, A. B., and M. B. Cook. *Complete Guide to the Elementary Learning Center.* West Nyack, N.Y.: Parker, 1976.

Rosenbaum, P. S. *Peer-Mediated Instruction.* New York: Teachers College Press, 1973.

Sharan, S, and Y. Sharan. *Small-Group Teaching.* Englewood Cliffs, N.J.: Educational Technology Publications, 1976.

Slavin, R. E. *Cooperative Learning: Student Teams.* Washington, D.C.: National Education Association, 1982.

APPENDIX A

Preparation for Successful Mainstreaming*

The following suggestions for preparing for mainstreaming were developed for physically handicapped pupils. The basic model can be adapted to fit the needs of any group of exceptional pupils.

PREPARATION FOR SUCCESSFUL MAINSTREAMING

I. Preparation of the Special Education Teacher

A. Determine that the student has the skills to function in the classroom.

B. Identify the physical or academic adaptations needed for the student to function in the regular class.

*Developed by Kitty Doyle, Consultant for the Physically Handicapped, Jacksonville, Florida

C. Identify the student's strengths and weaknesses.

D. Select class or time to begin initial mainstreaming. (It is important to select a class that would provide maximum opportunity for success—usually one to two periods in areas of student's strengths, where schoolwork is on the student's academic skill level.)

E. Provide the handicapped student an opportunity to visit the regular education class and meet the teacher before assignment is made.

F. Determine adapted equipment or special services needed by student to function in the regular class.

II. Preparation of the Regular Education Teacher

A. Learn about the student's handicapping condition. What are common characteristics? What can be expected in the way of performance? What are common difficulties the student will experience? Resource: E. E. Bleck, and A. D. Nagel, *Physically Handicapped Children—A Medical Atlas for Teachers*, New York: Grune & Stratton, 1975.

B. Learn about the appliances and special materials the student uses. How do you push a wheelchair up or down stairs correctly? How do you store wheelchairs?

C. Determine if any special methods, techniques, or adaptations are needed for this student to function more independently and more successfully.

D. Meet with the special education teacher to determine specific strengths, weaknesses, and needs of the handicapped student.

E. Prepare the classroom. Remove obstacles, make necessary adaptations to furniture, rearrange furniture, and so on.

III. Preparation of Regular Education Students

A. Invite a special education teacher to speak to the class about the physically handicapped program, what the common medical problems are, what the classes are like in the program, and so on.

B. Provide the class with a set of crutches or a wheelchair, and let them experience how it feels to be in a wheelchair or on crutches.

C. Let a student spend a day in the special education class, simulating the handicap for the entire day, and then report the experiences to the regular education class.

    D. Have the students role play positive and negative ways to help or not help people with handicaps.

    E. Provide the students with reading materials about handicaps.

IV. Preparation of Special Education Students

    A. Provide students with activities that may be different in the regular classroom, such as copying from the board, completing assignments with little assistance, and so on.

    B. Invite one or more pupils from the regular class to become acquainted with students before mainstreaming. This is best accomplished through cooperative involvement in a task. The students will have buddies in the regular classroom.

    C. Give the handicapped student an opportunity to meet the regular classroom teacher before placement.

An information sheet similar to the following, which contains hints for methods, techniques, and adaptations, should be prepared for the teacher:

1. Appoint a buddy to bring teacher handouts to the student's desk, carry books, open doors, assist in a fire drill, and so on.

2. Be sure that handicapped students know the class rules. They are not to be exempted from safety rules or classroom behaviors simply because they are handicapped.

3. Make sure your room is free of obstructions and that there is enough room between furniture groupings to avoid collisions.

4. Keep crutches, wheelchairs, and so on, where the student needs them, not in everyone's way.

5. Tape the student's paper to the desk with a piece of masking tape applied to the top and bottom of the paper.

6. If there are accompanying perceptual problems, pages or assignments should be simple with only a few problems per page, and often a larger print is helpful.

7. Attach one end of a string to a pencil and the other end to the desk with a thumbtack or masking tape so that a student can easily retrieve a dropped pencil.

8. A typewriter or a tape recorder may be helpful for an involved student.

9. If the child is unable to get a good grasp on pencils, crayons, or paint brushes, make them fatter by wrapping them in tape.

10. Triangular rubber holders can be put on pencils, crayons, and paint brushes to prevent rolling.

11. Cork may be glued to the bottoms of rulers to prevent slipping.

12. Dismiss handicapped students a few minutes earlier for recess, lunchroom, or gym so that they have enough time to reach their destination. A buddy can be sent along as a safety precaution.

13. Allow students to answer test questions orally, or have them record answers for later evaluation.

14. Use a chair equipped with wheels for children who need crutches, so that they can move easily from group to group, or add a platform with wheels to a regular chair.

15. Make a copy of your lecture notes for a handicapped student who writes slowly or with difficulty. It would also be simple for classmates to insert a sheet of carbon paper under their paper so that a duplicate set of notes can be given to handicapped students.

16. Obtain a small rubber suction mat to anchor a student's dish on the cafeteria table.

17. Provide a plastic or wooden ruler to use as a bookmark. They are easier to manipulate than a paper marker.

18. In uncarpeted rooms, it is sometimes difficult for a young student with crutches to get up from the floor. A regular classmate can be appointed to place a foot on the floor so that the handicapped student may brace a crutch against it for leverage, thus permitting more independence.

19. The handicapped student may use a shoulder bag to carry books and supplies to class.

20. Students who are required to drink a certain amount of water every day can be reminded with a pocket chart, which can eliminate teacher nagging.

21. Regular students can help push the wheelchair for a child who cannot push.

22. Overprotecting a child is harmful. Ask yourself, "Is this really impossible for this child? Could he do it alone if I gave him more time?"

23. Be extra patient and give extra encouragement to the child who is trying to be independent.
24. In learning centers with manipulatives, the student may require an extra pair of hands.
25. The student may require assistance in holding a ruler, cutting with scissors, opening doors, turning pages, picking up books, copying materials, and fastening clothing.

APPENDIX B

Questions Teachers Most Frequently Ask

The Education for All Handicapped Children Act, PL94-142, specifies the requirements for educating handicapped pupils. What does the law say about mainstreaming? The term *mainstreaming* is not used in the law. Although the term is not used, many people have interpreted the requirement to place a pupil in the least restrictive environment to be synonymous with mainstreaming. It is not the intent of the law to place all handicapped pupils in regular classrooms.

How is the least restrictive environment determined? A placement committee determines the most appropriate placement on an individual basis. The law stipulates that (1) to the extent possible, handicapped children will be educated with nonhandicapped children, and (2) special placement occurs only when education in regular classes with supplementary aids and service cannot be achieved satisfactorily.

What is an IEP? PL 94-142 requires an individualized education program (IEP) for each handicapped pupil. An IEP specifies the special education and related services that a particular child will receive.

Who develops an IEP? The placement committee, which is composed of a representative of the education agency who is qualified to provide or supervise the provision of special education, the teachers of the pupil, the parents or guardian, and, when appropriate, the pupil.

What information is included in an IEP?

1. The pupil's present level of educational achievement
2. A statement of annual goals
3. Short-term instructional objectives
4. Special education and related services to meet the unique needs of the pupil
5. The dates for initiation and termination of services
6. Evaluation procedures and schedules (at least annually) to determine attainment of short-term objectives
7. The extent to which the pupil will participate in regular education

A recommended source for guidance in developing an IEP is *How to Write an IEP* by John Arena, published by Academic Therapy Publications, 28 Commercial Boulevard, Novato, California 94947.

What about lack of training for educating handicapped pupils? Each state receiving federal funds is required to develop a comprehensive plan for personnel development. Teachers are encouraged to participate in planning inservice training programs. Inservice training programs should be readily available for teachers who work with handicapped children.

What about specialized materials and equipment? PL-94-142 and Section 504 of the Rehabilitation Act of 1973, subpart B, "Preschool, Elementary, and Secondary Edcuation," have provisions for appropriate materials and equipment.

What about class size? There is no stipulation regarding class size. Authorization for the use of supplementary aids and services to assist teachers with handicapped pupils who need individual attention is provided.

How will I have time to plan for an exceptional pupil when I have all the other children in the class? If the exceptional pupil cannot succeed with slight modification and/or support services, regular class placement would be inappropriate. Usually the modifications required for the exceptional pupil are also appropriate for other pupils in the class; therefore, extra planning time is not necessary.

What about coordination between the regular class program and the special class program? Many pupils are receiving part of their education in a regular class and part in a special class. One major problem area is the unclear guidelines for each part of the pupil's educational program. It is grossly unfair to the pupil who is having difficulties for all personnel involved not to plan and carry out a consistent educational program. Close monitoring of this program requires regular communication and cooperation among all participants.

What about acceptance of exceptional pupils by the regular pupils? For the most part, exceptional pupils tend to be less well accepted in the class. Provisions for changing attitudes must be made and carried out. The teacher's model will be a powerful influence in improving the atmosphere in the classroom. Numerous suggestions have been made in each chapter in this book. In addition, there is a special appendix that provides a guide for preparation for mainstreaming.

Index